Women in the Language and Society of Japan

Women in the Language and Society of Japan

The Linguistic Roots of Bias

NAOKO TAKEMARU

McFarland & Company, Inc., Publishers
Jefferson, North Carolina, and London

LIBRARY OF CONGRESS CATALOGUING-IN-PUBLICATION DATA

Takemaru, Naoko, 1964–
  Women in the language and society of Japan : the linguistic roots of bias / Naoko Takemaru.
      p.   cm.
  Includes bibliographical references and index.

  ISBN 978-0-7864-4003-0
  softcover : 50# alkaline paper ∞

  1. Japanese language — Social aspects.   2. Japanese language — Sex differences.   3. Sexism in language — Japan.   4. Sociolinguistics — Japan.   5. Women — Japan — Social conditions.   6. Social surveys — Japan.   7. Sexism — Japan.   8. Sex role — Japan.   9. Japan — Social conditions.   10. Japan — Surveys.   I. Title.
  PL524.75.T35   2010
  306.44'089956 — dc22   2010002125

British Library cataloguing data are available

©2010 Naoko Takemaru. All rights reserved

No part of this book may be reproduced or transmitted in any form or by any means, electronic or mechanical, including photocopying or recording, or by any information storage and retrieval system, without permission in writing from the publisher.

Cover images ©2010 Shutterstock

Manufactured in the United States of America

McFarland & Company, Inc., Publishers
  Box 611, Jefferson, North Carolina 28640
    www.mcfarlandpub.com

For my mother, Mitsue Takemaru,
my father, Tsuneo Takemaru,
and my brother, Hisashi Takemaru.
With my heartfelt gratitude.

Contents

List of Tables	viii
Acknowledgments	ix
Preface	1
Introduction	3

Part I: Representation of Women in Japanese Society

1 — Status and Roles of Women in Japan	9
2 — Family and Marriage in Japan	27
3 — Women and Education in Japan	44
4 — Women in the Japanese Workplace	56
5 — Feminism in Japan	72

Part II: Representation of Women in the Japanese Language

6 — Survey: Voices from Japanese Women	87
7 — Women and the Japanese Language: The Present and the Future	145

Appendix A: Demographic Information about the Survey Participants	203
Appendix B: Japanese Words and Phrases Listed by the Survey Participants	205
Bibliography	211
Index	223

List of Tables

1. Demographic Information on the Survey Participants — 89
2. Distribution of Listed Words and Phrases by Category — 90
3. Words and Phrases Frequently Listed by the Survey Participants — 91
4. Distribution of Words and Phrases Listed by Age Groups — 129
5. Words and Phrases Listed by All Age Groups — 130
6. Words and Phrases Listed Exclusively by Each Age Group — 130
7. Distribution of Words and Phrases Listed by Education Levels — 133
8. Words and Phrases Listed by All Education Levels — 134
9. Words and Phrases Listed Exclusively by Each Education Level — 134
10. Distribution of Words and Phrases Listed by Occupation Groups — 135
11. Words and Phrases Listed by All Occupation Groups — 136
12. Words and Phrases Listed Exclusively by Each Occupation Group — 136

Acknowledgments

A series of unexpected events took place in my life while preparing this book. It has made me realize how truly blessed I am to have family, friends, colleagues, and mentors willing to go out of their way to offer me support. I wish I could adequately express my gratitude to all of them, and return their favors someday.

This project would not have been possible without the input of a group of women who took the time to take part in the survey, and shared with me their candid thoughts on the Japanese language. My sincere gratitude goes to these women as well as to my colleagues who helped me with collecting data for the book.

I am also indebted to many people who helped me at various stages of this project. Kawaguchi Aiko sensei gave me guidance, and always believed in me. Professor Widigen Michiko inspired me to strive to become better. Professor Lynne Miyake kindly shared her expertise with me. Professor Joanne Goodwin helped me during the early stages of this project with her invaluable advice and encouragement. Annette Amdal spent many hours reading the drafts of this manuscript, and cheered me on with her kind words. Laura Padilla, Kashihara Sachiyo, Carol Mason, and Mitsuno Kazuko offered me comfort when I needed it the most. My colleagues and mentors at the University of Nevada gave me generous support and guidance. Secchan, Ho-kun, Kuro-chan, and Eri-chan kept me company, and made me smile.

Finally, I would like to express my heartfelt gratitude to my mother, Mitsue Takemaru, whose ongoing brave fight against serious illnesses has given me courage and strength to take many challenges in life in stride; to my father, Tsuneo Takemaru, whose footsteps I am proud to follow, and whose advice I always keep close to my heart; and to my brother, Hisashi Takemaru, whose insight has given me a new perspective on life.

Preface

When I was a child, I always looked forward to the bedtime stories that my parents took turns reading to me every night. Among evil characters in Japanese folk tales, there is an ogre called *oni baba* who is disguised as an old woman. I often wondered why there was no ogre disguised as an old man. In the real world, *oni baba* is defined as "a malicious and merciless old woman," and is used when making derogatory remarks about elderly women. Just as in the folk tales, there is no equivalent expression in the Japanese language for "a malicious and merciless old man."

In junior high school, I learned a term for a widow, *miboojin*, which is commonly used among Japanese people both in informal and formal settings. Without knowing its exact meaning or origin, I used the term, *miboojin*, and also heard some widows referring to themselves as such. It came as a shock to learn in high school that *miboojin* actually means "a person who is not yet dead," and is originated from the notion in ancient China that a wife should follow her husband upon his passing.

After graduating from college, I became an instructor at a language school in Tokyo. One day during a class discussion, a student who was a medical doctor mentioned that he had a difficult time dealing with his female patients. He concluded that women tended to be irrational and hysterical because "*onna wa shikyuu de mono o kangaeru* (women think with their uteruses)." The phrase he quoted is now mostly archaic, but was often used by Japanese men of the older generation.

Several years later, I decided to pursue my graduate studies in the United States, and informed the school principal about my intention to resign. Rather than wishing me well, he made a reference to my being a "*kurisumasu keeki* (Christmas cake)." In the 1980s, single Japanese women were likened to cakes that people in Japan consume on or before Christmas day: They are both much in demand for a limited time, the cake

Preface

until the 25th day of December, the woman until the 25th year of her life, and undesirable thereafter.

When I was a novice language professional in Japan, my women friends and I often talked about the numerous expressions in Japanese that are disrespectful to women, which triggered my interest in gender bias in language. I now have a rewarding career teaching Japanese in the United States, and take pride in introducing simply beautiful expressions in my native language. At the same time, as a woman, I continue to find a number of Japanese expressions hurtful and degrading.

This study was made possible by a group of Japanese women who candidly shared with me their thoughts about the representation of women in the Japanese language. I was amazed how vocal they were in their discontent and concern with many Japanese expressions about women, as well as with various issues surrounding women in the society that are represented by these expressions. It was also a very gratifying experience for me to find commonality in our thoughts.

In *Manyoshu* (*The Collection of Ten Thousand Leaves*), the oldest anthology of Japanese poetry compiled in the 8th century, Japan is described as *kotodama no sakiwau kuni*, a country where happiness is brought by the mystical power of *kotodama*, the spirits that inhabit words. Words are powerful mediums to transmit happiness and joy as well as hatred and contempt. My long-time dream and aspiration as a language professional is to help eliminate instances in which words are used as weapons to wound people. I would be delighted if this book serves to that end.

Introduction

Several years ago, a friend of my family sent me a copy of the small booklet that her colleagues had compiled. It was a 23-page-long collection of 1,145 Japanese words and phrases describing women. My heart sank as I browsed through page after page of mostly derogatory expressions based on gender bias and stereotypes. I recalled having the same feeling not long before receiving the booklet, when I looked up the entries related to the term "*onna* (woman)" in many highly regarded Japanese language dictionaries in order to collect data for this book.

The following are some of the phrases found in the booklet as well as in the dictionaries: "*Onna no ichinen iwa omo toosu* (Women's determination even penetrates rocks; Although women appear to be weak and helpless, they are obsessive and vindictive)"; "*Onna wa bakemono* (Women are monsters; Women are capable of changing their appearances with make-up and clothes)"; "*Onna no chie wa ushiro e mawaru* (Women's wits turn backward; Women are slow and cannot think quickly)"; "*Otoko wa matsu, onna wa fuji* (A man is a pine tree, a woman is a wisteria; a woman depends on a man just like a wisteria, a climbing plant with white or purple flowers that winds around a pine tree)"; and "*Otoko wa dokyoo, onna wa aikyoo* (Men should be daring, women should be charming)."

Many Japanese expressions for women and men including those listed above reflect prevalent gender stereotypes and bias in society. Likewise, a large number of gender-related expressions in the Japanese language not only define acceptable and unacceptable traits and demeanors of women and men, but also designate their roles and status in society.

The Japanese language has a wide variety of terms that denote females and males depending on the formality and the age. *Onna* (woman) and *otoko* (man) are the most commonly used informal terms referring to an adult woman and an adult man. Furthermore, *onna* has

Introduction

inherently more negative and sexual undertones than *otoko*. These gender-based connotative differences have been closely studied by a number of feminist scholars and researchers, particularly since the second wave of feminism that began in the 1970s (Endo, 1995; Hio, 2000; Hiraga, 1991; Nakamura, 1990; Takahashi, 1991).

The negativity associated with the term *onna* can be found in many expressions including "*Onna san nin yoreba kashimashii* (When three women get together, they make too much noise)"; "*onna no asajie* (woman's shallow intelligence)"; "*Onna sakashuu shite ushi urisokonau* (A smart woman fails to sell a cow; women may appear to be smart, but they fail to succeed, because they do not see the forest for the trees)," to name but a few.

Similarly, the following are some examples of a large number of expressions describing women as sex objects: *onna guse* (ways with women; men's inclination to seduce any women that they encounter), *onna asobi / onna dooraku* (pleasures with women / indulgence in women; having affairs with many women), and *onna tarashi* (women seducer; man who seduces and takes advantage of many women), among others.

In addition to negativity and sexual undertones associated with terms used for women, there are other distinct connotative differences between the terms denoting females and males. In general, femaleness is associated with being small, quiet, passive, while maleness is associated with being large, loud, active, and positive, as can be seen in the following examples: *onna zaka* (female slope — gentle slope) versus *otoko zaka* (male slope — steep slope), *medaki* (female waterfall — quiet and small waterfall) versus *odaki* (male waterfall — loud and big waterfall), *menami* (female wave — short and weak wave) versus *onami* (male wave — tall and strong wave), *medoki* (female time — unlucky time) versus *odoki* (male time — lucky time), and *memeshii* (effeminate, unmanly) versus *ooshii* (brave, manly). Incidentally, *memeshii* (effeminate, unmanly) is commonly used to criticize the demeanor of a man being "like a woman." There is a similar, yet more derogatory expression, *onna no kusatta yoona* (like a rotten woman) that is also frequently used to criticize a man being cowardly and indecisive. Both of these expressions use women and femaleness as a point of reference to describe the traits and demeanors of a man that are considered undesirable.

Introduction

Furthermore, gender asymmetry is found among the vast majority of expressions for women. For instance, the following words and phrases do not have reciprocal expressions describing males: *jonan* (trouble with women, sufferings of men in the relationships with women); *makeinu* (loser, underdog, single woman in her 30s without children); *akujo* (bad woman, woman who has many flaws in her character and behavior); *rooba* (old woman); *gusai* (stupid wife, humble term for one's wife); and *jukujo* (ripe woman, sexually attractive middle-aged woman).

In my early childhood, when I first came across *oni baba*, an ogre disguised as an old woman in Japanese folk tales, I wondered why there was no male equivalent. Since then, my interest in how women are represented in language has continued to grow, and many years later, has resulted in this publication. This book makes an inquiry into the representation of women in Japanese language and society. Central to this work are the voices of a group of Japanese women who took part in the survey as actual language users and expressed their candid thoughts, concerns, and experiences resulting from living with the traditionally biased representation of women that manifests itself in the Japanese language.

Part I presents various social and cultural contexts that have shaped the representation of women in the Japanese language. Chapter 1 describes the status and roles of women in historical context by focusing on the influence of Shinto, Buddhism, and Confucianism in shaping the image of women in Japan. It is followed by a discussion on the status and roles of homemakers and mothers, one of the frequently studied topics concerning Japanese women. Chapter 2 explains the historical evolution of family and marriage in Japan by making a reference to the *ie* (family, household) system which supported the pre–World War II patriarchal society. Its residual effects are observed in many spheres of life today. Various issues regarding family and marriage in present-day Japan, including the rising divorce rate since the 1980s, are also discussed in this chapter. Chapter 3 begins by presenting an overview on the development of women's education from the Edo period (1603–1867) through the end of World War II, which is followed by the recent trends and ongoing changes in women's education in Japan. Chapter 4 explains the prevailing working patterns of women in the Japanese labor force, many

Introduction

issues surrounding today's working women, and a climate of positive changes for women in the Japanese workplace. Chapter 5 presents a historical overview of feminism in Japan starting in the late 19th century, when the first wave of feminism began. It is followed by a discussion on some current and unresolved issues, as well as the new directions of Japanese feminism.

Part II of this book discusses in detail the representation of women in the Japanese language based on the survey of women, which is followed by a critique of the Japanese language. Furthermore, explanations are provided regarding the progress of nonsexist language reform that began in the 1970s, and the ongoing changes in the Japanese language that have resulted from the reform. Chapter 6 presents the detailed results and analysis of the survey on Japanese women's perceptions of gender bias in language. A group of women who took part in the survey provided a list of gender-related Japanese words and phrases that they considered degrading to women, along with their own personal interpretations of these expressions. The vast majority of these women also shared with me their thoughts, concerns, and experiences in regard to unfair representation of women in the Japanese language. Some of their thoughts and concerns are presented in various sections of Chapter 7 as well. Chapter 7 begins with instances of ongoing changes in prevailing gender bias in the Japanese language, and the recent coinages of expressions free of gender bias and stereotypes. It is followed by a discussion on the history of nonsexist language reform since the 1970s, and the progress that has been taking place in the media and in some dictionaries, as well as by the government. Various views on nonsexist language reform, and the future prospects of the Japanese language are presented to conclude the chapter.

An earlier version of Chapter 6 appeared in "Japanese Women's Perceptions of Sexism in Language," *Women and Language 28*(1), 39–48. In this book, the Hepburn system is used for the romanization of the Japanese language. Except for proper nouns, long vowels are marked with additional vowels. Translations from Japanese are my own, unless noted otherwise. The exchange rate of 100 yen per U.S. dollar was used for the conversion of currency. Japanese names are listed with surnames preceding given names, according to the Japanese convention.

Part I

Representation of Women in Japanese Society

1

Status and Roles of Women in Japan

In the beginning, woman was the sun.
She was an authentic person.
Now woman is the moon.
She depends on others for her life,
And reflects the light of others.
She is sickly as a wane, blue-white moon
[Hiratsuka, 1911, pp. 1–2].

Historical and Religious Context

Women in ancient Japan are believed to have been quite powerful and influential as Hiratsuka (1886–1971), a feminist pioneer in Japan, described in this poem which appeared in the first issue of *Seito* (*Bluestocking*), the feminist literary journal she founded in 1911. What Hiratsuka alluded at the beginning of this poem is the Sun Goddess named Amaterasu Omikami. According to the Japanese creation myths, Amaterasu Omikami was the first ancestral goddess from whom all creations derived. Tales about Amaterasu Omikami are found in *Kojiki* (*The Record of Ancient Matters*), the oldest historical and literary record in Japan, compiled in 712, as well as in *Nihon Shoki* (*The Chronicles of Japan*), the oldest historical record in Japan completed by the order of the Imperial Court in 720. Similarly, in ancient Japanese legends women often appeared as sovereigns, shamans, and chieftains who were believed to be closer to the divine than men, and performed sacred rituals. For instance, *Gishi Wajinden*, the document on prehistoric Japan compiled in the late 3rd century in China, says that a charismatic shaman called Himiko was recognized as the sovereign of Japan in 239 when she established diplomatic relations with the Wei dynasty, the most powerful of the three dynasties in China during the period of 220 to 265 (Hane, 1991; Sugimoto, 1999).

Part I: Representation of Women in Japanese Society

From the Nara period (710–794) through the early Heian period (794–1185), there was a marriage institution called *tsumadoikon* or *kayoikon*, in which a couple maintained separate residences, and a husband made visits to his wife. In this marriage institution, family estate and property were inherited by matrilineal lines (Obayashi, 2005). This custom was described in love poems in *Manyoshu* (*The Collection of Ten Thousand Leaves*), the oldest anthology of poetry in Japan, completed in the 8th century, as well as in *Kokin Wakashu* (*The Collection of Past and Present Poetry*), the first anthology of poetry, compiled by the Japanese Imperial Court in the 10th century (P. Smith, 1997).

Women made a significant contribution to Japanese literary history when a writing system was established. It is believed that ideographic characters called *kanji* were first introduced to Japan from China in the 3rd to 4th centuries, and were used mostly by educated men. During the Heian period (794–1185), phonetic letters called *hiragana* were created from ideographic characters in order to transcribe the Japanese language. *Kanji*, angular ideographic characters, were called *otoko de* (male hand), while *hiragana*, rounded phonetic letters derived from ideographic characters, were called *onna de* (female hand), and were used predominantly by women (Ide & McGloin, 1990). The Heian period (794–1185), known for its aristocratic culture, witnessed court women flourishing in literary circles. A number of classic masterpieces were created by Ono no Komachi, Izumi Shikibu, Seisho Nagon, and Murasaki Shikibu, to name but a few. Their works are widely read and studied to this day, among which the most legendary is *Genji Monogatari* (*The Tale of Genji*) by Murasaki Shikibu.

In the late Heian period (794–1185), Buddhist and Shinto beliefs that associated women with impurity and sinfulness became widespread. During the Kamakura period (1185–1333) when the samurai took over the aristocrats, the notion of "men superior, women inferior (*danson johi*)" that was based on these religious beliefs had developed, particularly in the privileged samurai class. This notion to hold women in subjugation to men prevailed mainly among the upper and ruling samurai class in the Edo period (1603–1867). In contrast to women of the samurai class whose roles were mostly limited to producing male heirs, women of the middle and lower working class of farmers, artisans, and merchants, still enjoyed autonomy to some extent (Kaneko, 1995; Okano, 1995).

However, the notion of "men superior, women inferior (*danson johi*)" permeated all social classes during the Meiji period (1868–1912), when the Civil Code of 1898 legitimized the *ie* (family, household) system that was based on the family system of the samurai class between the Kamakura period (1185–1333) and the Edo period (1603–1867). Under the *ie* system, the eldest son typically became the head of the family, and not only inherited the property to maintain the lineage, but also exercised absolute authority over family members. There was extreme gender inequality under this patriarchal family system, which became an indispensable element to support the hierarchical structure of pre–World War II patriarchal Japanese society (Kinjo, 1995; Meguro, 1990; Sodei, 1990; Uno, 1991).

Industrialization and the emergence of *sarariiman* (salary men, male white-collar workers) in the Taisho period (1912–1926) further promoted gender-based role division, and the idea of "men at work, women at home (*otoko wa shigoto, onna wa katei*)" was widely adopted in the postwar urbanized Japanese society. Although the patriarchal family system was officially abolished shortly after World War II, and gender equality is guaranteed by the 14th article of the Constitution of Japan that was proclaimed in 1946, the residual effects of the notion, "men superior, women inferior (*danson johi*)" are still observed today in many spheres of life (Y. Tanaka, 1995; Yoshizumi, 1995).

Various factors had caused the inferior status of women in Japan, among which Shinto, Confucianism, and Buddhism played a decisive role in shaping the image of women and establishing the gender-based role division in society (Okano, 1995). Shinto originated in Japan as a folk religion that was based on nature and ancestor worship. Shinto was first documented in *Nihon Shoki* (*The Chronicles of Japan*), the oldest Japanese historical record, compiled by the Imperial Court in 720. Since then, Shinto was further conceptualized under the influence of Buddhism and Confucianism. From the Meiji period (1868–1912) until the end of World War II, when the emperor was considered the head of state

Part I: Representation of Women in Japanese Society

with divine power, Shinto became the state religion of Japan in order to promote a nationalistic ideology. Since 1946, when the emperor officially renounced his divinity, Shinto has been disassociated from the state (Buckley, 2002).

Objects of worship in Shinto, such as trees, springs, and rocks are often found in nature. They are usually marked by *shimenawa* (sacred Shinto ropes) as well as by *torii* (gates). Traditionally made of wood or stone, a *torii* (gate) is built where *kami* (God) is believed to reside. *Torii* (gates) are also located at the entrance of Shinto shrines that are built on the sacred sites (Buckley, 2002; Sugiura & Gillespie, 1993). In Shinto there is a notion of *kegare* (defilement) caused by death as well as by blood. This notion was interpreted against women by associating them with impurity, which became a decisive factor in promoting the inferior status of women (Minamoto, 2005).

Confucianism was founded by Kong-zi (551–479 B.C.), a Chinese scholar and theorist. It is not a religion per se, but a set of moral principles and political ethics emphasizing filial piety, diligence, loyalty, education, meritocracy, and observance of rigid social hierarchy, among other things. Confucianism was brought to Japan through Korea in the 5th century, and had considerable influence on the formation of Japanese legal and political systems throughout the 7th century. Although the prevalence of Buddhism prevented Confucianism from gaining popularity, neo-Confucianism, founded by Zhu-zi (1130–1200), a Chinese philosopher in the 12th century, was received favorably by the shoguns in the Edo period (1603–1867) who desired to strengthen their reign. Neo-Confucianism's emphasis on the importance of Chinese classical studies contributed to a high literacy rate in Japan (Hane, 1991).

However, neo-Confucianism had an adverse effect on women's status due to its unfavorable views on women and its perspectives on gender relations, which advocated total submission of women to men. These views and perspectives were reflected in a number of old maxims based on Confucian ethics which served as moral principles for women. For instance, these maxims were incorporated in *Onna Daigaku* (*Maxims for Women*), which typified moral books for women in the early 18th century, preaching women's complete submission and obedience to men.

1—Status and Roles of Women in Japan

Onna Daigaku was based on the writing of a neo-Confucian scholar, Kaibara Ekiken, and consisted of 20 maxims. One maxim states that disobedience, discontentment, slander, jealousy, and stupidity are the five worst disorders that torment women and make them inferior to men. Another maxim preaches that married women should unconditionally worship, obey, and serve their husbands, as well as their in-laws, with utmost reverence, humbleness, and courtesy. *Onna Daigaku* not only embodied the Confucian doctrine, but also the patriarchal ideology of "men superior, women inferior (*danson johi*)," which subjected women to a subordinate position in society (Buckley, 2002; Endo, 2006).

Buddhism was introduced to Japan from Korea in the 6th century as a means of solidifying a political alliance between the two countries. Those who were in power accepted Buddhism despite its foreign origin, and supported its development as the state religion in the Nara period (710–794). Various Buddhist sects have developed since then, including meditation-based Zen Buddhism introduced in the Kamakura period (1185–1333) by Japanese Buddhist monks who studied Zen in China. In principle, Buddhism aims to attain enlightenment and reach the state of nirvana by overcoming suffering and worldly desires. In present-day Japan, Shinto and Buddhism co-exist, and it is estimated that over two thirds of the population practice both religions (Sugiura & Gillespie, 1993; Tanabe, 2002).

At the time of its arrival in Japan in the 6th century, Buddhism emphasized the importance of asceticism for monks, and strictly forbade their sexual relations with women, who were considered hindrances to ascetic monks. Unfavorable views on women in Buddhism are reflected in a number of its sutras. One Buddhist sutra, for instance, defines "five hindrances (*goshoo*)" of women and "three obediences (*sanjuu*)" for women. Five hindrances of women prevent them from attaining salvation by becoming four Indian Gods (Brahma, Shakra, Mara, and Cakravartin) and the Buddha. This has created the concept of a "metamorphosed male," through which women attain salvation by turning into men. Three obediences (*sanjuu*) for women states, "As a daughter, obey your father; once married, obey your husband; when widowed, obey your son." Similarly, another Buddhist sutra states, "*Onna san-*

gai ni ie nashi (Women have no home in the three realms of existence: the past, present, and future)" (Minamoto, 1990, 1997; Ogoshi, 1990; Okano, 1995).

The notion of blood impurity originated in Buddhism as well as in Shinto created the image of women being sinful and impure. For instance, *Kepponkyo*, the Buddhist sutra established in China in the 10th century, claimed that women had fallen to hell due to profuse blood defilement caused by childbirth and menstruation (Minamoto, 2005; Okano, 1995). In Shinto, the notion of blood impurity by childbirth and menstruation developed in the Imperial Court in the 9th century. In her classical work, *Genji Monogatari* (*The Tale of Genji*), Murasaki Shikibu wrote about a custom called *miyasagari* (withdrawal from the court) which made women leave the court when they became pregnant (Minamoto, 2005).

This association of women and blood impurity caused the exclusion of women from various spheres of life, and created the tradition of "no females allowed (*nyonin kinsei*)" which prevailed by the 12th century. Women were forbidden from taking part in rituals and festivals of Shinto and Buddhism as well as from setting foot in "holy" places such as Shinto shrines, Buddhist temples, and mountains called *reizan* that were revered in Shinto and Buddhism. Incidentally, Mt. Fuji, the tallest mountain in Japan, was designated as *reizan* (holy mountain), and was off limits to women until the late 19th century. Women were also banned in many secular places including fishing boats, construction sites, sake breweries, sumo rings, and behind the sushi counter, to name but a few (Cherry, 1987; Minamoto, 2005; Okano, 1995).

In 1872, the Japanese government issued a decree to abolish the tradition of "no females allowed (*nyonin kinsei*)." It was intended to improve the image of the country as a modern state, and was also targeted at the overseas visitors to Japan's first industrial exposition held in Kyoto in 1876. Subsequently, the equality between women and men was written into the new Constitution of Japan, which was enacted in 1947, shortly after World War II. Nevertheless, the tradition of excluding women lingers on in present-day Japan. For instance, women are prohibited from taking part in *kabuki*, a traditional performing art. While *kabuki* was originally started in the early 17th century with women and gained popularity as an all-female stage entertainment, it was outlawed in 1629 on the grounds of causing corruption of public morals. Since then, *kabuki* has been performed exclusively by men, some of whom play the roles of women. Women are also banned from participating in a number of Shinto and Buddhist ceremonies and festivals, despite the record that religious events were mostly organized by women until around the 8th century, as described in *Kojiki* (*The Record of Ancient Matters*), compiled in 712 (Minamoto, 2005).

Furthermore, some mountains, construction sites, and Shinto shrines are among the places that remain off limits to women. Mt. Omine in Nara, south of Kyoto, is one of the well-known *reizan* (holy mountains) where women are banned from climbing to the top. At the foot of Mt. Omine, there is a stone pillar with an inscription that reads, "No women are allowed beyond this point." Stone pillars with similar inscriptions are called *kekkaiseki* (no trespassing stones), and used to be placed at the entrance of "sacred" places such as Buddhist temples and Shinto shrines to forbid women from entering (Minamoto, 2005). Women are also told to stay away from tunnels under construction, so as not to anger the goddess of mountains who is believed to cause accidents in a fit of jealousy over the presence of other women. The Seikan Tunnel between the mainland and the northern island of Hokkaido was completed in 1988 without any presence of women on site during its 16-year construction period. Requests by female government officials for inspection tours of this longest underwater tunnel in the world were all turned down due to the superstition (Asano, 2005; Okano, 1995).

Similarly, based on the Shinto belief that considers women "unclean" for a month after childbirth, some Shinto shrines forbid women to enter the precincts by passing under *torii* (gates) for a month to 72 days after childbirth. In Shinto, women are also considered "unclean" for 7 days during menstruation. There are some reports that *miko*, unmarried young female staff members at Shinto shrines who perform rituals and assist Shinto priests in ceremonies, are required to take hormone medication and control their menstrual cycles in order not to "defile" sacred rituals and ceremonies (Okano, 1995). Moreover, women are not allowed on a "holy" island called Okinoshima, located in the southern part of Japan. Currently, a male Shinto priest is the only resident of the island, where a number of Shinto rites were performed between the 4th and 10th centuries. Over 80,000 items used in these rites were excavated, and were designated national treasures by the Japanese government in 2006. Despite protests from concerned citizens' groups against the violation of women's rights, some local residents and historians have since then launched a campaign to register this island as a site to be protected by the World Heritage Treaty adopted by UNESCO in 1972. As of 2007, a total of 851 sites worldwide were protected by this treaty, including the Pyramids in Egypt, the Great Wall of China, and the Galapagos Islands (Kaji, 2007).

In recent years, an increasing number of women as well as human rights groups have been making various attempts to challenge and break with the tradition of "no females allowed (*nyonin kinsei*)." In 1990, the first woman Chief Cabinet Secretary, Moriyama Mayumi, requested access to the ring from the Japan Sumo Association in order to present a championship trophy to a wrestler. Similarly, in 2000, Ota Fusae, the first elected woman governor of Osaka, the largest metropolitan area next to Tokyo, expressed her intention to step up to the sumo ring and hand a trophy to a champion. Although the presentation of trophies to sumo wrestlers is a long-standing custom carried out by their male predecessors, both Moriyama and Ota were denied access to the ring. The Japan Sumo Association insisted that the tradition of "*nyonin kinsei*" must be maintained in order to keep the purity of the ring as well as the sacredness of sumo, which developed as a Shinto ritual (Hata, 2005).

These incidents got extensive public and media attention, particularly Governor Ota's case, which was covered widely by the Japanese media who declared in 1990 that *onna no jidai*, the era of women, had dawned. What the media referred to was a landslide victory of the Socialist Party led by its first female leader, Doi Takako, in the national elections in the summer of 1989. Doi was not only the first female leader of the Socialist Party in its over 40-year history, but also the very first female party leader in the history of Japanese politics. The Socialist Party's vic-

1—Status and Roles of Women in Japan

tory was epoch-making, since it ended the monopoly of the Liberal Democratic Party for over 30 years.

In contrast to Doi's popularity, Governor Ota received little public support. A number of polls taken on the governor's challenge to the tradition indicated that public sentiment was mostly in favor of the Japan Sumo Association's decision and was critical of the governor. Shortly after turning down the governor's last appeal, the Japan Sumo Association broke the male-only tradition of its most prestigious Sumo Championship Council, and selected to its board the first female member, Uchidate Makiko, who is an avid sumo fan, essayist, and scriptwriter. Uchidate not only supported the Japan Sumo Association's decision to maintain the tradition of *"nyonin kinsei,"* but also criticized the governor by commenting that unless the tradition is observed, women would end up setting foot in the sacred ring with high heels (Uchidate, 2006).

In 2005, a group of people opposing the *"nyonin kinsei"* tradition of Mt. Omine, one of the well-known *reizan* (holy mountains), visited the Omine Temple to negotiate the abolishment of the tradition. When the negotiation ended in failure, both sides agreed to further discuss the issue at a later date; however, three female members climbed to the top of Mt. Omine following the negotiation in protest of the tradition. While the action taken by the female members got some support, the Omine Temple, the local residents opposing the abolishment of the tradition, and several media networks criticized it on the grounds that *"nyonin kinsei"* is a deeply ingrained tradition in Japanese culture, and must be maintained. Incidentally, in 2004, Mt. Omine and its surrounding areas became the 12th site in Japan to be protected by the World Heritage Treaty despite repeated protests from women's and citizens' groups against the tradition of *"nyonin kinsei"* (Minamoto, 2005).

A few years later, in 2007, a group of women donated 4.3 million yen ($43,000) to build a float hoping to take part in the Gion festival in the foreseeable future. The Gion festival is held at Yasaka Shrine in Kyoto for the entire month of July. It is designated as an intangible cultural asset by the Japanese government, and its origin dates back to the mid–9th century. The festival is famous for its elaborate two-story floats with live bands performing on the second floor. Floats are put on display to the public, and they march in procession to downtown Kyoto on July 17. Although the "*nyonin kinsei*" with regard to the Gion festival was officially abolished in 2001, as a general rule women are still prohibited from playing in the band with men, and taking part in the procession. Furthermore, women are not allowed to view some of the floats on display (R. Inoue, 2005). The women's group had a float built which went on display by itself with an all-woman band in March of 2007. However, the festival organizers prohibited it from taking part in the official procession in July of that year. It was the second attempt by the group of women since the fall of 2002, and they expressed their determination to continue to negotiate with the festival organizers until they are able to fully participate in the festival ("Yamahoko Junkoo," 2007).

Status and Roles of Homemakers and Mothers

Homemakers in general are called *shufu* (main women) in Japanese and they are further divided into two categories. Those who devote themselves full-time to housework are called *sengyoo shufu* (full-time professional homemakers), and those who juggle housework with either part-time or full-time employment are called *kengyoo shufu* (part-time adjunct homemakers). As these words suggest, homemaking is regarded in Japan as a profession which consists of all aspects of housework, child-rearing, management of family finances, and care of elderly parents and parents-in-law, among other responsibilities (Y. Sato, 1995).

Gender-based role division symbolized by the phrase "men at work, women at home (*otoko wa shigoto, onna wa katei*)," was widely promoted in the early 20th century when Japan underwent industrialization and the emergence of *sarariiman* (salary men, male white-collar workers) took place (Mackie, 2003; Uno, 1991). Gender-based role division continued to be adopted in the postwar urbanized Japanese society, and became a contributing factor in Japan's unprecedented economic growth from the 1960s to the early 1970s (K. Tanaka, 1995b). During this period, a phrase denoting envy of the life of a full-time homemaker, *sanshoku hirune tsuki* (three meals a day accompanied by a nap), was frequently used by men spending long hours at work.

Homemakers in Japan enable their husbands not only to devote themselves to work, but also to participate in frequent business-related outings expected by their employers. Fundamental to Japanese business practice, these mandatory outings are called *tsukiai* (socializing with co-workers, subordinates, and supervisors) and *settai* (entertaining business clients). Gatherings at karaoke bars, restaurants, and clubs after hours as well as rounds of golf on weekends are typical examples of such outings. Japanese wives often complain about the lack of communication with their husbands who come home from work late at night, too exhausted to say anything but "*meshi, furo, neru* (supper, bath, sleep)" (Rosenberger, 2001).

The majority of Japanese homemakers are solely responsible for child-rearing due to the absence of husbands who spend long hours at work. Despite a steady increase in the number of *kengyoo shufu* (part-time adjunct homemakers) with part-time or full-time employment since the 1970s, it is still a common practice among married women in Japan to leave the work force either temporarily or permanently for child care, and become *sengyoo shufu* (full-time professional homemakers). When their children reach school age, many of these women re-enter the work force for part-time employment or engage in contractual work at home in order to earn supplementary income for the family (Kawashima, 1995; Morley, 1999; Saso, 1990).

The status and roles of Japanese homemakers, particularly those of *sengyoo shufu* (full-time professional homemakers), has been a frequent topic of debate among feminists and scholars both in Japan and overseas. Some maintain that Japanese *sengyoo shufu* wield considerable power within the domain of household by having control over family finances, child-rearing, and household management. They also claim that women's status in Japan is typically based on their autonomy in the household, and therefore, the status and roles of *sengyoo shufu* should be viewed in a positive light (Ide, 1997; Iwao, 1993; Martinez, 1987; Reischauer & Jansen, 1995). Others point out that the power of Japanese *sengyoo shufu* is not inherent in them, but rather is delegated to them by their husbands, and that their lack of financial independence as well as experience outside the domain of the household severely limits the options of Japanese *sengyoo shufu* (Aoki, 1997; Morley, 1999; Y. Tanaka, 1995).

Incidentally, Japanese homemakers are traditionally known for their custom to stash away money, called *hesokuri*, for their own use, a practice which is believed to have originated in the Edo period (1603–1867) among married women without means of earning money by themselves (Sugiura & Gillespie, 1993). This age-old custom is still widespread in present-day Japan. According to a survey conducted in 2007 by Japan DIY Life Insurance Company, 45 percent of 500 homemakers responded that they had secret savings in an average amount of 2.7 million yen ($27,000). These stashes gave them funds for a rainy day, spending money, and retirement, and provided them with a sense of security. The average amount of money saved by respondents was 2.3 million yen ($23,000) for full-time homemakers, 2.5 million yen ($25,000) for homemakers with part-time employment, and 4.8 million yen ($48,000) for homemakers with full-time employment.

One of the popular options among homemakers to expand their responsibilities beyond their households is to join consumer groups and community-based organizations. The Shufu Rengo Kai (the Federation of Homemakers), known as Shufuren for short, is the largest women's organization in Japan, founded in 1948 in the midst of postwar rationing and soaring inflation. Shufuren aims to protect consumer safety as well as interests from the perspective of homemakers. In its early days, Shufuren received media attention when its members demonstrated showing their pride as homemakers by wearing Japanese-style aprons called *kappogi*, and carrying placards in the shape of *shamoji* (rice-serving spatula), a traditional symbol of the status of homemakers (Mackie, 2002, 2003).

Over the years Shufuren has become one of the most powerful consumer advocate groups, and continues to exert its influence on various consumer-related issues with its extensive membership and mobility. Similarly, a large number of homemakers who are active leaders of consumer groups in their local communities belong to the nationwide membership of Seikyo (Consumer's Co-op). Since its inception in 1948 with the aim of protecting consumer rights and interests, Seikyo has developed its own brand, which is known for its reasonable price and strict safety standards approved by homemakers. Homemakers are also actively engaged in the research and development of a wide range of Seikyo brand products such as organic produce and ecosystem-friendly detergent, among others.

Gender-based role division in Japanese society can be partly ascribed to the notion of "good wives and wise mothers (*ryoosai kenbo*)" originating in the late 19th century. Based on the common belief that the primary role of women was to take care of household chores, bear and raise children, "*ryoosai kenbo*" represented ideal womanhood in the pre–World War II patriarchal society (Fujieda, 1995). As discussed in Chapter 5, there are various theories regarding the origin of the notion "*ryoosai kenbo*." Regardless of its origin, this notion played a major role in keeping women in separate and subordinate roles in the family as well as in society (Ishimoto, 1999). From the late 19th century until the end of World War II, the objective of women's education in Japan was characterized by *ryoosai kenbo kyooiku* (education for good wives and wise mothers), which systematically trained young women in skills, manners, and morals to be "good wives and wise mothers" (K. Hara, 1995; Kaneko, 1995). Nowadays the phrase *ryoosai kenbo* is quoted only occasionally by those who are critical about lifestyles of single women and *kengyoo shufu* (part-time adjunct homemakers) with either part- or full-time employment. However, the remnant of the *ryoosai kenbo* (good wives and wise mothers) mentality can still be observed in various spheres of life in Japan.

One of the marked differences between the pre– and post–World War II Japanese household is its size, particularly the number of children. A woman typically gave birth to four to five children in her lifetime before and during World War II, when bearing children was considered one of the war efforts of women under the national slogan, "*Umeyo, Fuyaseyo* (Bear children! Multiply!)" (Fujieda, 1995). After the war, the birth rate continued to decline steadily except for the period of

Part I: Representation of Women in Japanese Society

the second baby boom in the early 1970s. According to the dynamic statistics of population released by the Ministry of Health, Labor, and Welfare, the average number of children that women gave birth to was 3.65 in 1950, in contrast to 2005, when it hit a new low of 1.26. The declining birth rate has become a frequent topic in the news media, which created the term, *shooshika* (trend toward fewer children). Several factors that account for this current trend include the increase in the number of late marriages as well as married women in the work force, the rising cost of education, the lack of male participation in housework and child-rearing, and insufficient public support for child care.

In 1994, the Japanese government adopted countermeasures against *shooshika* for the first time, and has continued to introduce a series of policies and financial incentives to reverse the trend. However, these measures are perceived as unrealistic and not feasible by the public, particularly by women who feel that their needs are not adequately met. It is ironic that in recent years, some of the influential male politicians who have been responsible for introducing these countermeasures made a series of controversial remarks on women as well as on Japan's declining birth rate. In 2007, the Minister of Health, Labor, and Welfare, Yanagisawa Hakuo, called women between the ages of 15 and 50 "childbearing machines (*kodomo o umu kikai*)" in his speech at a local assembly. He further stated that because the numbers of these "childbearing machines" are limited, each one of them should make an earnest effort to bear more children, so that there will be enough population to support the social security system in the future. Despite a number of protests from lawmakers, assemblywomen, and women's groups calling for his resignation, Yanagisawa continued to hold his post. After being reprimanded by the Prime Minister for making such inappropriate remarks, Yanagisawa, in his statement of apology, insisted that he had no intention of insulting women, but figuratively used the expression of women being "childbearing machines (*kodomo o umu kikai*)" to interest the audience in his talk ("Josei Wa," 2007).

Earlier in 2003, a former Prime Minister, Mori Yoshiro, commented that women with no children who took many liberties in their youth without the responsibility for child-rearing should not be entitled to

1—Status and Roles of Women in Japan

expect the government to look after them in their old age. Mori further argued that social security ought to be acknowledged as a token of appreciation from the government to women who have given birth to children and raised them (Faiola, 2004). Mori's remark is not an isolated case in the Japanese society, where childless women are often considered odd or pitiful based on the prevailing belief that motherhood completes women.

Motherhood in Japan involves multiple responsibilities, particularly for children. The absence of fathers who spend long hours at work makes mothers responsible for the behavior and academic achievement of children. Since children are typically judged as reflections of their mothers, it is common for expectant mothers to make a head start by engaging in prenatal education called *taikyoo*. Maintaining emotional stability and being cultured are thought to be the two most important goals for expectant mothers, and their behaviors as well as lifestyles are frequently scrutinized by their family members and society. In order to promote the well-being of their unborn babies, expectant mothers are encouraged to listen to soothing classical music, read literary masterpieces, appreciate fine works of art, and practice yoga and meditation, among other activities (White, 1986). Extensive selections of how-to books, periodicals, CDs, and DVDs, as well as prenatal education classes are available by popular demand. One such best-selling publication entitled *"IQ 200 Tensaiji wa hahaoya shidai! Anata no kodomo mo dondon nobiru (Mother holds the key to a child prodigy with an IQ of 200! Your child can also make great progress)"* sold over 1.2 million copies in 2007. It was published by Katei Hoikuen (Preschool at Home), the largest private organization in Japan focused on prenatal and infant education with over 100,000 members nationwide.

Japan is characterized by its "academic background-oriented society (*gakureki shakai*)," where education and academic credentials are highly valued. One of the objectives of the education system in Japan is to prepare children for highly competitive "entrance exams (*nyuugaku shiken*)" for junior high school through college. In addition to regular classes, children usually attend private preparatory schools called *juku* and *yobikoo*, or study at home with private tutors after school, on weekends, and during school recess for additional preparation for entrance exams. In order to avoid so-called "examination ordeal (*juken sensoo*)" later on, it is not uncommon for children to take entrance exams for highly selective private kindergartens and elementary schools that offer continuous education through colleges within their school systems.

A mother who is committed to the education of her children by providing an optimal learning environment for them is called an "education-conscious mother (*kyooiku mama*)." She monitors the study habits and academic progress of her children, consults with their teachers for advice, and finds them qualified private tutors as well as appropriate preparatory schools. Being in charge of the physical and emotional well-being of her children, a *kyooiku mama* not only prepares nutritious meals for her children, but also stays up late to serve them midnight snacks. She often curtails her social activities so that she has more time for her children who are preparing for entrance exams. The enrollment of her children in prestigious schools is a status symbol of a dedicated *kyooiku mama* who is willing to go to any lengths to help her children succeed (J. Gordon, 2002).

While the contribution and dedication of a *kyooiku mama* can be an asset to her children's education, her close involvement in her children's lives can also cause some tension between them (Allison, 1996b). For instance, an expression, "monster-like mother (*mamagon*)," was created in the 1970s among young children who found their mothers controlling and obsessed with their education. In recent years, there has been a steady increase in "dropout (*ochikobore*)," "refusal to go to school (*tookoo kyohi*)," "withdrawal (*hikikomori*)," and "domestic violence (*kateinai booryoku*)" among children who are under constant stress and pressure to succeed. Some critics argue that the highly competitive Japanese education system and preoccupation of *kyooiku mama* with the academic achievement of their children are to be blamed for these problems.

Being primarily responsible for child-rearing due to the absence of fathers who spend long hours at work, mothers are typically assigned the blame in Japan when things go wrong with children. This is evidenced by the expression, "illnesses caused by mothers (*bogenbyoo*)," which was coined by a pediatrician, Kyutoku Shigemori. In his 1979 best-selling book, aptly titled *Bogenbyo* (*Illnesses Caused by Mothers*), Kyutoku claims that mothers who do not properly guide their children's development are the fundamental cause of their various physical and psychological illnesses such as loss of appetite, serious asthma, bed-wetting, chronic abdominal pains, diarrhea, speech impediments, refusal to go to school, and domestic violence. Those who dispute with Kyutoku's claims have coined the word "illnesses caused by fathers (*fugenbyoo*)," asserting that the absence of fathers in child-rearing has serious consequences in child development as well. They further criticize that Kyutoku wrongly accuses mothers of being negligent and incompetent based on the gender biased perspective that women rather than men should be responsible for child-rearing.

Japanese mothers who assume full responsibilities for child-rearing often continue to look after their children well into adulthood. It is not unusual for mothers to do laundry for their adult children, clean their rooms or apartments, help them find spouses, and take care of their children. Due to the traditional practice of very little involvement of fathers in child-rearing, Japanese children, particularly sons, tend to develop strong lifelong bonds with their mothers (Allison, 1996b). An equivalent of "mother's boy" in the Japanese language is *mazakon otoko*, a man with *mazakon* (mother complex), many of whom can be found in all age and socioeconomic groups, and are the source of frequent complaints among women.

Japanese men often use a term of endearment for their mother, *ofukuro*, in an informal setting. Although *ofukuro* literally means "honorable bag," the etymology of which is unclear, mothers are flattered to be addressed as such. There are a number of Japanese songs about mothers. Those that are popular among middle-aged and elderly men typically include the term, *ofukuro* or *ofukuro-san* with a title, *-san*. While the term, *ofukuro*, is used exclusively by men, the phrase, "taste of *ofukuro* (*ofukuro no aji*)" is widely used by both women and men to describe meals that taste similar to what their mothers used to make. Some restaurants also use this phrase in their advertisements in order to attract customers who long for home-cooked meals (Cherry, 1987).

Part I: Representation of Women in Japanese Society

People often associate "taste of *ofukuro* (*ofukuro no aji*)," not only with meals their mothers used to make, but also with "box lunches (*obentoo*)" that their mothers prepared for them in their preschool through high school days, when school lunches were not usually provided. Preparing nutritious and visually aesthetic *obentoo* for her children is considered one of the most important tasks of a mother to show her commitment and dedication to child care. Cookbooks and magazines specializing in *obentoo* as well as a wide variety of paraphernalia ranging from colorful toothpicks to various shapes and sizes of vegetable cutters are on the market to help mothers with the daily chore of making special *obentoo* (Allison, 1996a).

Motherhood in Japan symbolizes a number of values such as unconditional love, affection, selflessness, devotion, and self-sacrifice. There are many who point out that Japanese mothers are perceived not only as caretakers of children, but also as the symbol of socio-cultural values (Ohinata, 1995). Yamamura (1971) further asserts that the devotion by the Japanese people to the concept of motherhood is similar to that of a religious faith. At the same time, more women, particularly among the younger generation, have begun to question the prevailing notion that motherhood completes women, and have started to seek other options for a sense of fulfillment (Lebra, 1984). With the decreasing birth rate and the increasing number of women in the labor force, the traditional status and roles of Japanese women may well be in a period of transition.

2

Family and Marriage in Japan

In pre–World War II Japanese society, little attention or respect was accorded to the dignity, personal autonomy, independence, and freedom of choice of women. Instead, the family and the nation were always given priority and exercised dominance over women [K. Hara, 1995, p. 104].

The Ie *(Family, Household) System in Pre–World War II Japan*

Pre–World War II Japanese society was characterized by the *ie* (family, household) system, which was based on the Confucian ethics prevalent in the upper and ruling samurai class in the Edo period (1603–1867). The primary aims of the *ie* system were the protection and maintenance of its assets, business, name, and reputation, as well as its continuity from generation to generation. In the *ie* system, achieving these goals customarily preceded the well-being of its members. The Confucian ethics were reflected in a number of distinctive characteristics of the *ie* system, which include absolute authority of *kachoo* (head of the household), extreme gender inequality, filial piety, and ancestor worship, among others (Meguro, 1990; Uno, 1991).

Under the *ie* system, a position of *kachoo* (head of the household) was traditionally inherited by the firstborn son. If there was no son in the family, a male heir such as a son-in-law succeeded the position. *Kachoo* was responsible for the management of the family property as well as the continuation of the lineage and family business. Moreover, *kachoo* had absolute authority over his family members, who pledged unconditional allegiance to him in exchange for protection and financial support. The *ie* system was legitimized by the Civil Code of 1898. It is often pointed out that the patriarchal *ie* system bears some similarity to the patriarchal social order based on the emperor system, under which Japan became a militaristic regime (Sodei, 1990).

The Civil Code of 1898 also made it mandatory for Japanese citizens to be listed in their family registers called *koseki*. *Koseki* played a vital role in the *ie* system by recording detailed personal information of each family member such as date and place of birth, marriage, divorce, adoption, and death. *Koshu* (head of the family) was the center of the family register, and members of the family were listed in relation to *koshu*. Similar to the position of *kachoo*, the position of *koshu* was typically inherited by the eldest son of the family or a male heir (Kinjo, 1995; Y. Tanaka, 1995).

Under the *ie* system, marriage served as a means of maintaining lineage; therefore, the interests of the family preceded personal preference in selecting a spouse. *Kachoo* usually played an active role in selecting suitable spouses for his family members. For family members who selected their prospective spouses by themselves, it was mandatory for men up to the age of 30, and women up to the age of 25, to obtain permission to marry from *kachoo* (Mackie, 2003). Upon marriage, a wife was registered in her husband's family register, and assumed the lowest position in his family as *yome* (daughter-in-law, bride). The Civil Code of 1898 granted a husband total control over his wife as well as over her property, if any. Parental rights and the custody of children were also granted exclusively to the father unless he became disabled, deceased, or deserted his wife and children (Yoshizumi, 1995). Under the Code, a wife was not only a legally unrecognized person without any rights, but also was considered an incompetent (Mackie, 2003; Sievers, 1983).

A wife was expected to serve her husband as well as her in-laws, and to bear children, particularly male heirs, due to the provision that illegitimate sons who were acknowledged by her husband had priority over legitimate daughters to inherit the family estate (Kaneko, 1995). Although monogamy was adopted by the Civil Code of 1898, it was publicly acceptable for a husband to have one or multiple mistresses in order to maintain lineage and to show off his wealth and masculinity. Incidentally, this sentiment, symbolized by a phrase, "*Uwaki wa otoko no kaishoo* (Affairs are proof of manliness)," remains prevalent in present-

2—Family and Marriage in Japan

day Japan to justify a husband's extramarital affairs. The Civil Code of 1898 also granted preferential treatment to men who committed adultery. While a husband would be divorced only if he committed adultery with a married woman, and was sued by her husband, a wife would not only be divorced, but also given a 2-year prison sentence for adultery (Mackie, 2003; Y. Tanaka, 1995).

As in the case of marriage, divorce was handled according to the interests of the family. For instance, a wife was divorced if she was unable to bear children, or did not get along with the in-laws (Kinjo, 1995; Yoshizumi, 1995). The following were so-called *shichikyo*, the seven legitimate reasons to divorce a wife, which were widely used to justify a unilateral decision on divorce: disobedience to parents-in-law, infertility, sexual promiscuity, chattering, stealing, jealousy, and serious illnesses such as Hansen's disease. *Shichikyo* were included in *Onna Daigaku* (*Maxims for Women*), based on the writings of a neo-Confucian scholar, Kaibara Ekiken (1630–1714). *Onna Daigaku* was one of the most widely read moral books for women in the Edo period (1603–1867), and preached to women unconditional obedience and submission to men (Endo, 2006).

During the Edo period (1603–1867), all that was required by law for a husband to finalize a divorce was to serve his wife with short notes. These notes were called *mikudari han* (three lines and a half), in which the reason for divorce was tersely stated in three and a half lines. Under the patriarchal *ie* system that was characterized by extreme gender inequality, a wife was not entitled to initiate a divorce. The only option for a wife seeking a divorce was to literally run away to find refuge in convents called *kakekomi dera* (runaway temples) or *enkiri dera* (divorce temples), where she stayed for 3 years as an ascetic before a divorce was granted. In the early Edo period (1603–1867), a number of convents were established to accommodate the needs of such women. While all convents were allowed to provide shelters for women during this period, the number was later reduced to merely two in the entire country (Kaneko, 1995).

In the pre–World War II Japanese society based on the patriarchal *ie* system, priority was always given to the interests of the nation and the family, rather than the well-being of individuals. Women, in particular, were granted little respect, freedom, or autonomy, and their status was secondary to men (K. Hara, 1995). This continued until the end of World War II when drastic measures were taken against the patriarchal *ie* system. In 1947, the Constitution was amended to abolish the prewar *ie* system and to guarantee gender equality. It was followed by the revised Civil Code issued in 1948, which rescinded the subordination of women to men, and granted the wife legal rights for the first time in Japanese history (Fujimura-Fanselow, 1995b; Kaneko, 1995).

Family and Marriage in Contemporary Japan

Although the patriarchal *ie* system was officially abolished shortly after World War II, its residual effects can be observed today in many spheres of life. For instance, *koseki seido* (the family registration system) continues to exist with some amendments in present-day Japan. Submission of copies of *koseki* (family register) as an official document of identification, is mandatory on a number of occasions such as applying for a driver's license and a passport, entering a school, and upon being employed, to name but a few. It is frequently pointed out that illegitimacy recorded in *koseki*, and the subsequent social stigma and discrimination against single mothers and their children, is the main reason behind Japan having the lowest birth rate outside marriage among the industrialized nations (Y. Tanaka, 1995; Yoshizumi, 1995). This family registration system has been widely criticized as a violation of privacy due to the possibility that detailed personal information regarding a family and its members recorded in *koseki* can be obtained and misused by third parties. Consequently, tighter restrictions are now placed on public access to copies of *koseki*, which used to be available to anyone upon request with nominal fees.

When registering a marriage in *koseki*, a couple is required to designate a head of the household, called *koseki hittoosha*. It is customarily a male, since it has to be the one who does not change their surname by marriage. In addition, the 750th article of the current Civil Code makes it mandatory for a couple to choose the same surname. The name of *koseki hittoosha* (head of the household) is registered in full in *koseki*, in contrast to his wife and children, who are registered by given names only. In recent years, an increasing number of women have expressed their objections to this system, in which a wife and children are listed as mere "appendages" (Y. Tanaka, 1995, p. 27) to a male *koseki hittoosha*.

While nearly 98 percent of women currently change their surnames to those of their husbands, the results of various surveys taken since the 1990s consistently indicate that more than 30 percent of the adult population prefers the flexibility to choose either the same or separate surnames upon marriage. For instance, according to the public opinion poll conducted by the Cabinet Office in 2006, 46 percent of people felt inconvenienced by the present system of changing the surname by marriage. This was an all-time record, up by 4 percent compared to the previous poll taken in 2001. Similarly, 62 percent of common-law husbands and wives did not submit their marriage registration because wives did not want to change their surnames (Yuzawa, 2008).

Furthermore, an increasing number of married women, particularly those in the work force, continue using their maiden names as aliases, and some even opt for filing for "paper divorce" in order to keep their maiden names (Yoshizumi, 1995). It should be noted that Japan is one of the few countries in the world where a wife is required by law to change her surname to that of her husband, if he does not agree to change his. Since the 1980s, there have been a number of attempts to amend the law, making it feasible for couples to choose either the same or separate surnames. For instance, in 1988, Sekiguchi Reiko, a university professor, filed a lawsuit in Tokyo District Court against the state and her new university employer for the right to continue using her maiden name at her workplace. In the following year, the Tokyo Lawyer's Association submitted a report supporting the optional use of separate surnames for married couples. Similarly, in 1996, a bill was introduced by the Legislation Council of the Ministry of Justice which requested the revision of the Civil Code. However, these attempts have not yet succeeded in producing tangible results (Mackie, 2003).

Incidentally, a small number of men in Japan also change their surnames upon marriage to become *muko yooshi* (adopted son-in-law). This is a long-standing Japanese custom which combines the adoption of a son, and his marriage to a daughter of his adopted parents. It was legitimized by the Civil Code of 1898 as the means to maintain lineage under the pre–World War II patriarchal *ie* system. Although the current Civil Code no longer includes this provision, it remains legal to make such an arrangement under the 734th article. This custom of adopting a son-in-law by marriage is commonly observed among well-to-do families without sons who would carry on lineage, estate, and family business. Usually the eldest daughter of the family is expected to undergo such an arrangement, and her husband is adopted by taking up her surname to become a male heir of the family. A man who has become *muko yooshi* (adopted son-in-law) is often referred to as *goyooshi-san* with a polite prefix, *go-* and a title, *-san*. The term typically connotes a sense of pity toward a man who loses his surname by marrying into his wife's family.

For the most part, Japanese people tend to consider marriage as the route to happiness, particularly for women, and as the means for men to stabilize their lives, and become respectable members of society. These sentiments are reflected by commonly used expressions in regard to marriage including *gooru in suru* (to reach the goal; to get married), which is used by and for both women and men, as well as *mi o katameru* (to consolidate oneself; to settle down, get married, and start a family), which is almost exclusively used by and for men.

Although not as prevalent as before, it should be noted that there remains a notion of *tekireiki* (the period of marriageable age) in Japanese society, ranging from the mid- to late 20s for women, and from the late 20s to early 30s for men. Throughout the 1970s, these age ranges were several years younger, and women more so than men were under strong pressure from society, family, and peer groups to marry before it is "too late." As a result, it was common for many women to rush into marriage by their mid–20s (Cherry, 1987; K. Tanaka, 1995b). This is no longer the case, and there have been a number of new trends and changes relating to marriage as well as family in Japan, particularly since the 1980s, which are discussed later in this chapter. However, many critics

2—Family and Marriage in Japan

claim that Japanese people remain largely marriage-oriented. For instance, Fujimura-Fanselow (1995a) asserts that "the notion that it is 'natural' and 'normal' to marry and have children is still quite prevailing in Japanese society" (p. 141). Similarly, Morley (1999) points out that "the compulsion to marry, and to marry before a certain age, remains an important factor in Japan's social and economic structures" (p. 38).

Generally speaking, people in Japan get married either by *miai kekkon* (arranged marriage) or *renai kekkon* (love marriage). In some instances, the combination of these two terms called *miai renai kekkon* (arranged love marriage) is used to refer to a couple who at first meet through a matchmaker in a formal setting, but later fall in love with each other and get married.

In the case of *miai kekkon*, matchmakers called *nakoodo* (go-between) are in charge of making arrangements to introduce singles. As the word *miai* denotes to be matched and to be in balance, compatibility in family backgrounds, socioeconomic status, age, and education levels are the major criteria that matchmakers use to select prospective couples. Matchmakers can be professionals as well as laypeople who are social and have many connections. In some cases, supervisors in the workplace play the role of matchmakers for their subordinates. Matchmakers keep a large stock of detailed resumes of singles with their family history called *tsurigaki* along with photographs of singles. For this reason, it is common, particularly among young single women in their 20s in Japan, to save their best photographs as *miai shashin* (photographs for arranged meeting for marriage).

Matchmakers routinely distribute these resumes and photographs among singles and their parents who show interest in choosing prospective spouses and in-laws through formal introduction. When there is a potential match, the parties concerned are contacted by a matchmaker, who arranges the first meeting. Typically, the first meeting is held in a public place such as a well-known restaurant or luxurious hotel lobby in the presence of a matchmaker and family members, who are mothers in most cases. Then, a couple meets by themselves several times before deciding whether to pursue the arrangement or not. Because a couple stays in contact through a matchmaker at the initial stage, they can avoid an awkward situation when a decision is made by either one or both of them not to pursue the arrangement.

While *miai kekkon* (arranged marriage) was the mainstream through the 1960s, since then it has been steadily replaced by *renai kekkon* (love marriage), mostly among the younger generation who view *miai kekkon* as old-fashioned and lacking in romance. As a matter of fact, by the 1990s, two in three marriages in Japan were *renai kekkon* (love marriage) (Morley, 1999; Y. Tanaka; 1995). At the same time, computerized matchmaking services and *omiai* (matching) parties which provide informal opportunities for singles to find their prospective mates, have gained huge popularity despite their costly membership fees. These options are well-received, particularly among those who are too busy with their careers to meet other singles, as well as by those who look for the convenience and practicality of *miai kekkon* without the formality associated with it.

There have been persistent arguments that the term, *renai kekkon* is misleading, since the criteria used in *renai kekkon* for selecting a prospective spouse are not necessarily based on romantic love, but rather on socioeconomic factors as well as personal compatibility, which are similar to those used by matchmakers for making arrangements to introduce singles in *miai kekkon* (Mura, 1991). These arguments can be substantiated by the results of a number of surveys taken among single women and men on the criteria for choosing their prospective spouses. Since the 1980s, there has been no change in the top three criteria: women choose men by their personality, occupation, and income, while men choose women by their personality, physical appearance, and age (Y. Tanaka, 1995). A similar standard is reflected by the coinage of the term called *sankoo* (three highs) that was frequently used among many single women during the 1980s and the 1990s. What *sankoo* refers to is a common criterion used by young women seeking ideal spouses, that is, those who are tall, highly-educated, and have a high income with respectable professions including medical doctors, business executives, and successful entrepreneurs, among others.

Furthermore, the following survey results also indicate that one of the criteria that women use to select their future spouses is the man's financial capability to support the household. The analysis of The 2002 Basic Survey on Employment Structure by Labor Policy Research and Induction Organization reveals an intriguing correlation between men's income level and their marital status. The survey was conducted on men in their late 20s at three different income levels. While only 15.3 percent of those whose annual income ranged between 1 and 2 million yen ($10,000 and $20,000) were married, the percentage went up to 22.8 percent among those who earned between 2 and 4 million yen ($20,000 and $40,000) a year. In contrast, the percentage of married men more than tripled at 72.5 percent among those whose annual income was between 10 and 15 million yen ($100,000 and $150,000). The survey concluded that men's income level could be a major factor in their prospects for marriage (Morinaga, 2008).

Despite the social conventions to marry by a certain age, the number of young single women and men in Japan has continued to increase at an unprecedented pace since the mid–1970s. It is noteworthy that the increase is far more significant among women than men. For instance, the percentage of single men in their mid– to late 20s rose from 25 percent in 1920 to 73 percent in 2005, while that of single women in the same age group increased dramatically by nearly eight times as much from a mere 8 percent to 60 percent during the same period. Moreover, between 1970 and 2000, the number of single women in their late 20s tripled from 18 percent to 54 percent, making the biggest increase in the 1990s (Yuzawa, 2008).

As a matter of fact, the 1990s were marked by a large number of publications on single women and their lifestyles, which were particularly popular with women in their 20s and 30s. Among them, the two best-sellers were *Kekkon Shinai Kamo Shirenai Shokogun* (*The "I may not marry" Syndrome*) published in 1990, and *Hikon Jidai: Onnatachi no Shinguru Raifu* (*The Era of Unmarried by Choice: Women's Single Life*) in 1993. The popularity of these books was reflected by the fact that the title of the first book, *Kekkon Shinai Kamo Shirenai Shokogun* (*The "I may not marry" Syndrome*) was selected among the top 10 buzzwords in 1991. Similarly, the terms, *hikon* (unmarried by choice) and *shinguru* (single) that appeared in the title of the second book became the coinages

Part I: Representation of Women in Japanese Society

of 1993 shortly after its publication. In addition, a number of gender inclusive terms referring to singles were coined in the 1990s such as *dokushin kizoku* (aristocratic singles) and *parasaito shinguru* (parasite singles), among others (Jiyukokuminsha, 2008). These terms are explained in detail in Chapter 7.

According to the 2005 and 2006 censuses, 49.4 percent of men in their early 30s were single in 2005, and the average age of the first marriage for men was 30 years in 2006, which reached the 30s for the first time (Yuzawa, 2008). As can be seen by the 2002 survey results presented earlier, one of the major reasons behind this increase in single men is the decrease in men's income as well as the instability of their employment status, due to the restructuring of the Japanese economy since the 1990s, following the collapse of the so-called "bubble economy" (Morinaga, 2008).

It is often pointed out that compared to men, more women tend to delay marriage or remain single, particularly since the 1980s (Iwao, 1988; Yoshizumi, 1995). For instance, the results of the 2006 census show that the average age of the first marriage for women has extended for 5 years since the 1930s from 23.2 years to 28.2 years in 2006, in contrast to 3 years for men during the same period. Furthermore, in 2006, 14 percent of women in their late 30s remained single, and over 50 percent of women in their 30s in the metropolitan Tokyo area were single. These single women tend to be well-educated as well as career-oriented, and are often characterized as being defiant against not only the prevailing concept of *tekireiki* (the period of marriageable age: for women from their mid– to late 20s), but also traditional gender-based role division among married couples (Borovoy, 2005).

Some critics claim that Japanese society is "same-sex-oriented," while Western societies are "couple-oriented" (Okonogi, 1983; Cherry, 1987). The notion of rigid gender segregation in society has become an integral part of the mentality of Japanese people since the Meiji period (1868–1912), when various Confucian values were propagated by the government (Yoshizumi, 1995). One such value emphasized the importance of gender segregation from a young age as stated in the Confucian doctrine, "*Danjo shichi sai ni shite, seki o onajuu sezu* (From the age of 7, boys and girls should not sit together on the same mat)." Those of the older generation in Japan are familiar with this doctrine, which says that from around the age of 7, children should recognize the gender differences, and avoid close contact with members of the opposite sex. Although Confucian values are no longer prevalent in post World War II Japan, their residual effects can be observed to this day. Since adolescence, many Japanese people tend to find more comfort being with members of the same sex, rather than those of the opposite sex. It is, therefore, not uncommon for a wife and a husband to compensate for the lack of emotional bonds between them with their bonds of friendship with members of the same sex (Yoshizumi, 1995).

Furthermore, gender-based role division that is widely practiced among married couples in Japan is reflected in the perception of a good marital relationship being based on the relative autonomy of wife and husband in their respective areas of responsibility. For instance, during the post–World War II economic hardship, the practice of a wife managing the household budget became widespread. Subsequently, the division of gender-specific roles became firmly established during the period of Japan's unprecedented rapid economic growth from the 1960s to 1980s (Y. Tanaka, 1995). As described by the phrase, "*Otoko wa shigoto, onna wa katei* (Men at work, women at home)," husbands worked longer hours, leaving the household chores and child-rearing to their wives. The perception of a good marriage based on gender-specific role division is reflected in a number of Japanese phrases, out of which one of the most well-known is "*Teishu genki de rusu ga ii* (It is good when a husband is healthy, and is away from home)." The phrase first appeared in a TV commercial for mothballs in the 1980s, and became an instant hit, particularly among middle-aged and elderly married women nationwide.

In Japan, a married couple with children is expected to give priority to their role as parents rather than as a couple. It is, therefore, a very common practice for a husband and a wife to call each other as *otoo-san* (father) or *papa*, and *okaa-san* (mother) or *mama*, rather than by their names, not only in the presence of their children, but also in their absence. Because of this prevalent societal expectation that the priority of a married couple is to play the role of parents, the lack of emotional bond between the couple has not been considered as a sufficient reason for divorce. Although the revised Civil Code and the Constitution introduced the principle of no-fault divorce to postwar Japanese society, divorce was not common before the 1980s, when claims of incompatibility were not allowed. These factors, along with the social stigma and financial troubles associated with divorce, which would adversely affect women in particular, contributed to the divorce rate in Japan being the lowest in the industrialized nations before the 1980s (K. Tanaka, 1995b; Yoshizumi, 1995).

However, there is a sharp increase in the number of divorces initiated by women since the 1980s, when claims of incompatibility were allowed for the first time. In addition to this new provision, the following factors have contributed to the steady increase in divorces: (1) the growing interest among women in pursuing a career outside the home, (2) the increase in the number of women with degrees in higher education, (3) the rise in women's earnings, (4) low birth rate: 1.26 children per woman in 2005, when it hit the record low, and (5) women's longer life expectancy; 85.99 years in 2007 (Fujiyama-Fanselow, 1995b; Christopher, 1983).

In 1983, the nation's first divorce hotline for women was set up in Tokyo. Its data listed the following three most common reasons for women to initiate a divorce: a husband's infidelity, his neglect of family, and financial problems. In 1984, Japan's first women's magazine on divorce titled *Sutato* (*Start*) was launched. According to the estimate by its editor-in-chief, in the 1980s, there were 10 times as many women who contemplated divorce as those who would actually undergo it (Y. Tanaka, 1995). This estimate was reflected by the term, *kateinai rikon* (domestic divorce) coined in the early 1980s, referring to a couple who remain legally married mostly for the sake of their children, despite the lack of a conjugal relationship. The steady increase in the number of such couples led to the coined term, *kateinai rikon* being selected among the top 10 buzzwords in 1986 (Jiyukokuminsha, 2008).

In addition to divorce hotlines and publications, various seminars, lectures, and workshops for women have been held on a regular basis since the 1980s. For example, the Niko Niko Rikon Koza (The Workshop on Happy Divorce) is one such workshop organized by a woman lawyer, providing women with practical legal advice and financial information on divorce. It has gained huge popularity, particularly among middle-aged and elderly homemakers without full-time employment, who have been reluctant to proceed due to the financial instability caused by divorce.

The dynamic statistics of population released by the Ministry of Health, Labor, and Welfare indicated that the total number of divorces more than doubled in the past 2 decades from 140,000 in 1980 to 290,000 in 2002, but it decreased for the following 4 years to about 260,000 in 2006. However, the actual divorce rate continues to rise because of the overall decrease in the number of marriages. As a result, the so-called "divorce probability," which is obtained by dividing the number of divorces by that of marriages, nearly doubled from 18.2 percent in 1980 to 35.2 percent in 2006.

Furthermore, in recent years, there is a steady increase in women who remarry. For instance, the percentage of remarriage out of all the marriages of women has continued to rise since the 1980s, from 9.5 percent in 1980 to 16.3 percent in 2006 (Morinaga, 2008). This is a new trend in Japan, where in the past, remarriage was a common option for divorced or widowed men, but not for women.

These new trends in divorce and remarriage have a positive outcome in the Japanese language. For instance, a commonly used derogatory term for a divorced woman, *demodori* (returnee to one's parents' place; divorced woman) has become mostly outdated. It is replaced by a newly coined unisex term, *batsu ichi* (one cross/mark against them; a person who is divorced once), which does not convey the stigma attached to divorce in the past, nor negativity toward those who are divorced. Similarly, the expression called *Narita rikon* (divorce at Narita, New Tokyo International Airport) was coined in 1990, and became the buzzword of that year (Jiyukokuminsha, 2008). It refers to the casual attitude toward divorce among young married couples who decide to go their separate ways at the airport on their way back from their honeymoon.

The increase in the number of divorces is not limited to the younger generation. Since the 1990s, the divorce rate among mature couples has also been steadily increasing. As a matter of fact, the term, *jukunen rikon* (divorce at the mature age) was coined to refer to this unprecedented phenomenon. In the vast majority of cases, a wife initiates a divorce at the time of her husband's retirement, claiming a part of his retirement allowance for spousal support as well as sacrifice. By the 2000s, *jukunen rikon* has become a buzzword that is widely used by the general public and by the media (Jiyukokuminsha, 2008). It is typically perceived as the ultimate rebellion by a wife who had to put up with her husband for a number of years mostly for the sake of her children and financial reasons. *Jukunen rikon* also has become a common theme of trendy TV dramas, in which a husband who is clueless about his wife's feelings is completely taken aback by her request for a divorce at the time of his retirement.

According to the dynamic statistics of population by the Ministry of Health, Labor, and Welfare, the number of divorces among couples who were married for more than 35 years hit the record high of 4,963 in 2003. While it remained steady from 2004 to 2006, ranging from 4,700 to 4,800, a record number of 5,507 couples filed for divorce in 2007, which was an increase of 16 percent compared to 2006. Because in 2007 there was a slight decrease of 1 percent in the total number of divorces in all age groups compared to 2006, the largest number of divorces actually took place among couples who were married for more than 35 years. The Ministry of Health, Labor, and Welfare speculated that a change in the pension distribution law which became effective in April, 2007, was one of the contributing factors for this drastic increase. The new system made it possible for a couple to make a prior arrangement to divide the husband's pension in half at the time of a divorce.

The results of *Kazoku Chosa 2008* (*Family Survey 2008*) by Hakuhodo Seikatsu Sogo Kenkyusho (Hakuhodo General Institute of Life) indicated that Japanese couples' perceptions of marital relationships have changed significantly since the late 1980s. A total of 600 married couples who were in their 20s to 50s and living in the Tokyo metropolitan area, took part in the survey in 2008. The results were compared with those of a similar survey conducted by Hakuhodo Seikatsu Sogo Kenkyusho in 1988. The following are some of the findings: the number of wives who were against divorce under any circumstances drastically decreased by 20 percent from 59.7 percent in 1988 to 39.7 percent in 2008, while the number of husbands who were against divorce under any circumstances decreased slightly over 4 percent from 68.4 percent in 1988 to 64.2 percent in 2008. These findings also make a clear contrast to the 1984 survey results by the government, which reported that two thirds of Japanese people did not believe that divorce was a solution for unhappy marriages (Cherry, 1987).

Moreover, wives who wanted to improve the quality of time spent with a spouse decreased by 9 percent from 35.2 percent in 1988 to 26.2 percent in 2008, while husbands who wanted to do the same increased by nearly 9 percent from 30.6 percent in 1988 to 39.3 percent in 2008. Based on these results, Hakuhodo Seikatsu Sogo Kenkyusho concluded that nowadays far more wives than husbands are in favor of divorce. In addition, since the late 1980s, husbands have become more inclined to spend time with their wives, while wives have not necessarily been responsive to their husbands' inclination.

Such differences in perceptions between wives and husbands are also found in the survey titled "*Otona no Fufu Chosa (Survey of Adult Married Couples)*," that was conducted on married couples in their 50s and 60s by Dentsu & Rikuruto (Recruit Corp.) in 2008. A total of 1,800 married women and men residing in the Tokyo metropolitan area took part in the survey on the internet. The following are the list of feelings that the survey participants had toward their spouses, and their corresponding percentages: love: 11 percent of wives and 23 percent of husbands; friendship: 42 percent of both wives and husbands; indifference: 32 percent of wives and 27 percent of husbands; and dislike/disgust: 15 percent of wives and 8 percent of husbands. In summary, among the middle-aged married couples surveyed, more than twice as many husbands had loving feelings toward their wives, while close to one third of wives were indifferent to their husbands. Furthermore, the number of wives who had negative feelings such as dislike and disgust toward their husbands was almost twice as many as husbands who had negative feelings toward their wives. According to Dentsu & Rikuruto (Recruit Corp.), these survey results indicated that there were noticeable discrepancies in feelings between wives and husbands despite the fact that mature married couples had more time to spend together.

Similar results were reported by the Hakuhodo Elder Business Promotion Office that conducted a survey in 2009 on 520 married couples in their 60s. Nearly 80 percent of wives responded that they were disappointed with their husbands, particularly for the lack of their help in household work as well as the lack of their overall appreciation; in contrast, 60 percent of husbands responded that they were disappointed in their wives. Furthermore, while more than half of wives no longer felt the same way toward their husbands since they first married, nearly 70 percent of husbands felt basically the same way toward their wives. The survey made a prediction that the differences in perceptions between wives and husbands would continue to widen, unless husbands were willing to make an effort to improve the relationship with their wives ("Dankai Zuma," 2009).

The family structure in post–World War II Japan has undergone a dramatic transformation from the prewar patriarchal and patrilineal *ie* (family, household) system, and has resulted in the emergence of some new variations, particularly since the 1980s. One such variation is *kateinai rikon* (domestic divorce), which was mentioned earlier. It is also called "latent-disorganization family" (Yoshizumi, 1995, p. 185), in which a couple continues to remain legally married mostly for the sake of their children, despite the lack of a conjugal relationship. However, because of the increase in the divorce rate, the number of such families is decreasing in recent years.

Another new variation in the family structure is called "pseudo-single-mother family" (Yoshizumi, 1995, p. 185), in which the father is mostly away from home due to the demanding nature of his work as can be seen in the following survey results. According to The 2008 Juvenile White Paper released by the Cabinet Office, the number of men who seldom have time to spend with their children is steadily increasing during the past several years due to longer working hours. The survey conducted on women and men with children ranging from 9 to 14 years old indicated that the number of men who seldom had time to spend with their children on weekdays increased by nearly 10 percent from 14.1

percent in 2000 to 23.3 percent in 2006. Moreover, while 65.1 percent, or nearly two thirds of women responded that they were fully aware of the causes of worries for their children, 31.4 percent, or less than one third of men did so. The white paper also reported that the working hours of men in their 30s and 40s increased by 5 hours per month between 2002 and 2007. As a result, while approximately 40 percent of men were able to get home from work by 7 in the evening in 2001, less than 30 percent of them were able to do so in 2007.

There also has been a steady increase in "single households" comprised of one person since the 1990s. The nuclear family is commonly thought to have been the mainstream of family structure in the post–World War II Japan; however since reaching its peak in 1975 by making up 63.5 percent of all the households in Japan, the number of nuclear families has been gradually decreasing to 58.9 percent in 2005. Instead, the number of "single households" has continued to rise since 1990 at 23.1 percent to 27.6 percent in 2005 (Yuzawa, 2008). The reason behind this trend is an increase in those of the older generation living by themselves, as well as those of the younger generation who are single and living alone, particularly past *tekireiki* (the period of marriageable age, from the mid– to late 20s for women, and from the late 20s to early 30s for men). While "single households" comprised of those of the older generation can be found in both rural and urban areas, those of the younger generation living alone are located predominantly in urban areas.

It is a welcome development that gender stereotypes and bias originating from the pre–World War II patriarchal *ie* (family, household) system are becoming less prevalent in present-day Japan, where family and marriage have continued to undergo transformation. Furthermore, this has resulted in a positive change in the Japanese language: a number of expressions for family and marriage that denote unfair representation of genders are becoming less commonly used, and are being replaced by coinages without embedded sexism.

3

Women and Education in Japan

The process of the development of women's education in Japan is none other than a long history of struggle against bondage toward the emancipation of women as individual human beings [K. Hara, 1995, p. 104].

Historical Context

Opportunities to receive education, especially at the post-secondary level, were not readily available to women in Japan prior to World War II, when there was prevailing gender inequality and discrimination against women in society. The government control of the education system which was established by the middle of the Meiji period (1868–1912) by *Kyoiku Chokugo* (the Imperial Rescript on Education) also had a negative effect on women's education. By placing particular emphasis on patriotism, loyalty to the emperor, and the Confucian morals, *Kyoiku Chokugo*, issued under the name of the Meiji emperor (1852–1912) in 1890, became the basis of the education system throughout the end of World War II (Mackie, 2003).

In the following section, a historical overview of women's education in Japan is presented, dating back to the Edo period (1603–1867) through the end of World War II, when Confucian philosophy had a significant influence on the education system. Women's education, in particular, was adversely affected by the Confucian notions of women, which intended to confine them to the roles of childbearing and childrearing, as well as to a subordinate status to men in the family and in society. Furthermore, public opinion supported the Confucian thinking that learning was not only unnecessary, but was also harmful for women. This sentiment is reflected by the following statement made by Matsudaira Sadanobu (1758–1829), a high-ranking official of the Tokugawa shogunate of the Edo Period (1603–1867), who was also well versed in neo–Confucianism: "Women should be illiterate. It is harmful for women to develop their abilities. There is no need for women to study" (K. Hara, 1995).

In addition to Confucian philosophy, the notion of *danson johi* (men superior, women inferior) prevailed mostly among the ruling samurai class in the Edo Period (1603–1867). Based on the Buddhist and Shinto beliefs that associated women with sinfulness and impurity, this notion to put women in subjugation to men also had an adverse effect on women's education. The primary objective of women's education in the Edo period (1603–1867) was to train girls and young women not only to be skilled in household work, but also to be submissive and obedient to their parents, particularly to fathers and other elder male family members as well as prospective husbands and in-laws. While the school curriculum for female students consisted of the three R's, the main emphasis was placed on instruction in housekeeping, manners, and moral education (K. Hara, 1995).

A large number of instructional books on morals and manners were written for women during the Edo period (1603–1867), out of which *Onna Daigaku* (*Maxims for Women*), published in the middle of this period, was one of the most prototypical and most widely read. It was based on the writings by a neo–Confucian scholar, Kaibara Ekiken (1630–1714), who made the following remarks regarding women: "The only qualities that befit women are gentle obedience, chastity, mercy, and quietness." *Onna Daigaku* consisted of 20 maxims preaching to women the absolute submission and obedience to men. Various instructional books on manners also emphasized the proper usage of "feminine" language, and girls and young women were told to speak in soft, gentle voices, as well as to refrain from using harsh, rough, and annoying "masculine" language (Endo, 1995, 2006).

Since the Meiji Restoration in 1868, Japan began to undergo a dramatic transformation from a feudalistic society into a modern state after the self-imposed seclusion of over 200 years under the Tokugawa shogunate during the Edo period (1603–1867). In order to facilitate the process of modernization by eliminating illiteracy, the government put a special emphasis on education in the early Meiji period (1868–1912). Following

Part I: Representation of Women in Japanese Society

the establishment of the Ministry of Education in 1871, the system of compulsory education was introduced by the Education Act of 1872, making a 4-year elementary education mandatory for both girls and boys (K. Hara, 1995).

Although equal opportunity for children to receive education materialized officially, in actuality, the attendance rate of boys (53.4 percent) was more than twice as high as that of girls (22.5 percent) in 1878, mainly because most parents preferred paying tuition for their sons rather than for their daughters. The abolishment of tuition in the late 1890s, however, resulted in the significant increase in the number of girls who received compulsory education; the attendance rate more than tripled from slightly over 30 percent in 1890 to 97.4 percent in 1910. During this period, the duration of compulsory education was also extended from 4 years to 6 years (Mackie, 2003).

Gender segregation was formally instituted in 1880, when the Education Act was issued to abolish coeducation beyond the third year of elementary school (K. Hara, 1995). It was based on the Confucian doctrine called "*Danjo shichi sai ni shite, seki o onajuu sezu* (From the age of 7, boys and girls should not sit together on the same mat)." As explained in Chapter 2, this doctrine urges children as young as the age of 7 to recognize gender differences, and avoid close contact with members of the opposite sex.

Furthermore, the term, *ryoosai kenbo kyooiku* (education to produce good wives and wise mothers) was adopted as the fundamental concept of women's education. In his following statement made in 1887, Mori Arinori (1847–1889), the first Minister of Education, elaborated on *ryoosai kenbo kyooiku* (education to produce good wives and wise mothers):

> If I summarize the point regarding the chief aim of female education, it is that the person will become a good wife (*ryoosai*) and a wise mother (*kenbo*); it is to nurture a disposition and train talents adequate for [the task] of rearing children and of managing a household [Mackie, 2003, p. 25].

Incidentally, in order for a woman to become *ryoosai kenbo* (good wife and wise mother), she was expected to cultivate the disposition including obedience, modesty, demureness, self-control, and self-sacrifice.

These qualities were also highly regarded as the "virtues" of Japanese women by male opinion makers and educators in the early 1900s (Endo, 2006).

From the 1880s throughout the outbreak of World War II, the fundamental objective of education for girls and young women was to prepare and train them to become *ryoosai kenbo*. To this end, government control on women's education was firmly established by the end of the Meiji period (1868–1912). The Girls' Higher School Act of 1899 mandated the increase in the number of public higher schools that offered post-elementary education for young women. As a result, the total number of schools and enrollment increased by 50 percent in the 2 years from 1898 to 1900—to 52 schools and 12,000 students (Mackie, 2003); however, the number of female students in higher schools remained less than half of male students until 1932 (Morley, 1999). Women's higher schools incorporated home economics, *shuushin* (moral education), and *sahoo* (manners) into the essential part of the curriculum, which was not designed to prepare female students to become academically competent to receive higher education. Furthermore, *ryoosai kenbo kyooiku* (education to produce good wives and wise mothers) also became the objective of the compulsory elementary education for girls by the end of the Meiji period (1868–1912) (Cherry, 1987; Nolte and Hastings, 1991).

It should be noted that there are different theories in regard to the origin of the notion of *ryoosai kenbo*, which represented the ideal of womanhood in pre–World War II Japan. Some assert that what underlay this notion was the Confucian thinking of *danson johi* (men superior, women inferior) prevalent during the Meiji period (1868–1912), which resulted in gender segregation and inequality in education (Fujimura-Fanselow, 1995a; Ishimoto, 1999; Kaneko, 1995). In contrast, others, including Smith, R. (1987), maintain that the notion of *ryoosai kenbo* was "the Japanese version of the 19th-century Western 'cult' of 'true womanhood'" (K. Tanaka, 1995b, p. 305). Moreover, there are some who claim that it was an imported notion from England during the Victorian Age (1837–1901) (Koyama, 1991; Uno, 1993).

Due to the prevailing Confucian thinking that learning was not only unnecessary for women, but also harmful to them, women were generally discouraged from receiving higher education, and there were very few opportunities available for them to do so, particularly if they lived in rural areas. For instance, in the late 1930s, the institutions that offered higher education for women consisted of approximately 40 private women's colleges, a number of which were established by Christian missionaries, and two national women's higher normal schools. However, none of these institutions were recognized with university accreditations, and they were mostly located in urban areas including Tokyo and Osaka. As a result, less than 0.5 percent of female students of the relevant age group received higher education during this period (Fujimura-Fanselow, 1995a; K. Hara, 1995).

Among those who made significant contributions to women's education in Japan, is Tsuda Umeko (1864–1929) a well-known pioneer, especially in English language education. In 1872, at the age of 8, Tsuda was among the first five female students sent abroad by the government, whose focus was on education under the policy of modernization in the early Meiji period (1868–1912). After studying in the United States for over a decade, Tsuda founded Joshi Eigaku Juku (Women's English School) in 1900, which later became a teacher's college, and is now known as Tsuda Juku Daigaku (Tsuda College). It was the first institution of higher education for women in Japan whose focus was on academic and professional training as well as character-building for women. These objectives were quite a departure from *ryoosai kenbo kyooiku* (education to produce good wives and wise mothers) that was prevalent in pre–World War II Japan (Mackie, 2003).

Women and Education in Contemporary Japan

The main aim of educational reforms which took place shortly after World War II was to bring about democratization and gender equality. Gender segregation in education was officially abolished, and gender equality in seeking education is guaranteed by the Constitution promulgated in 1946 as well as by the Basic Law of Education that was issued in the following year. The Law took the place of *Kyooiku*

Chokugo (the Imperial Rescript on Education) of 1890, which was based on the Confucian morals emphasizing unconditional loyalty to the emperor. Under the new educational system, the women's higher schools were transformed into 2-year junior colleges, and the national women's higher normal schools as well as most of the private women's colleges were accredited as 4-year universities. Moreover, women are eligible to attend national and private 4-year universities that closed the door to women prior to World War II (Fujimura-Fanselow, 1995a; K. Hara, 1995).

Despite these educational reforms, both the ideology of *ryoosai kenbo kyooiku* and the concept of gender segregation in education that were prevalent in pre–World War II have continued to surface periodically. For instance, when an increasing number of women began to attend 4-year universities in the 1960s, some male critics argued that the trend would have an adverse effect on the country because unlike men, women would not use their education for the good of society. These critics also insisted that the enrollment of women should be limited. This highly controversial argument was called *joshidaisei bookokuron* (a theory on the destruction of the nation by female college students), and triggered intense debate which received extensive media attention (K. Hara, 1995).

Furthermore, in 1969, when a measure was adopted to make home economics a required subject for female high school students, the chief of the Elementary and Secondary Education Bureau of the Ministry of Education (the Ministry of Education, Culture, Sports, Science and Technology since 2001) made the following comment: there should be no opposition to this measure, since its objective is to educate female students to be *ryoosai kenbo* (K. Hara, 1995).

It is noteworthy that a campaign against this measure was launched mostly by women's groups and associations organized in the 1970s as a result of the second wave of feminism, including the Kodo Suru Onnatachi no Kai (the Group of Women Who Take Action) whose members consisted of a large number of teachers. In addition, following the ratification of the United Nations Convention on the Elimination of All Forms of Discrimination against Women (CEDAW) by the Japanese government in 1985, it became necessary for the Ministry of Education to redesign an equal curriculum for female and male students, which was required by the 10th article of CEDAW. As a result, home economics became a required subject for both female and male students in junior high schools in 1993, and in high schools in 1994. Similar reform took place in physical education, which made it possible for students to choose either martial arts or dance as an elective (Kameda, 1995).

According to The 2005 Basic Survey of Schools conducted by the Ministry of Education, Culture, Sports, Science and Technology, 76.2 percent of female high school students entered institutions of higher education. The proportion of those entering colleges and universities rose over ninefold from 5.5 percent in 1960 to 49.8 percent in 2005. These statistics have continued to surpass males in the relevant age group since 1989. Moreover, the number of working women who continue their education in graduate schools has doubled between 2000 and 2005.

Despite these advances of women, gender imbalance remains in various spheres of education. For instance, the same survey indicated that among female students who went to institutions of higher education, less than half of them (36.8 percent) entered 4-year universities, while 26.4 percent went to vocational colleges called *senmon gakko*, and 13 percent chose 2-year junior colleges in 2005. It should be noted that 2-year junior colleges in Japan mostly offer majors in such disciplines as the humanities, nursing, home economics, and preschool education, and represent a separate educational track with little possibility of transferring to 4-year institutions (Fujimura-Fanselow, 1995a). In contrast, *senmon gakko* provide various practical training for students to acquire adequate skills in order to obtain professional licenses and certificates. Having been accredited in 1976, vocational colleges have continued to grow in number, and to gain popularity over junior colleges since the early 2000s.

The 2008 Basic Survey of Schools also indicated that females accounted for 40.2 percent of all 4-year university students compared to 88.9 percent of all 2-year junior college students. These percentages reflect a tendency among Japanese parents to seek out education at 4-year universities for their sons rather than for their daughters, as well as the residual effect of the notion that "too much education will make a woman unfit to be a good wife," which was prevalent in pre–World War II Japan (Fujimura-Fanselow, 1995a). For instance, at Tokyo University, the most prestigious institution in Japan, females accounted for 19 percent of the entire student population, which was nearly half the national average of 36 percent in 2007. In an attempt to increase the enrollment number of female students to a minimum of 30 percent, Tokyo University held a special meeting for prospective female high school students for the first time in its school history in December of that year, a few months prior to the start of the entrance exam season from February to March ("Todai Joshi," 2007).

Another pre–World War II notion that "the objective of women's education is to produce *ryoosai kenbo*" continues to have residual effects on societal perceptions of women's education as well. In fact, the phrase, "*ryoosai kenbo kyooiku* (education to produce good wives and wise mothers)" was included in the mission statements of some women's colleges throughout the 1970s. Some critics also point out that the mindset similar to the *ryoosai kenbo* mentality seems to discourage women from studying subjects that are considered masculine (Cherry, 1987; Y. Tanaka, 1995). For instance, since the 1970s there has been very little change in the number of women who major in medicine and dentistry (2 percent), and natural sciences (2 percent). However, as indicated by The 2005 Basic Survey of Schools, a new trend has been observed among female university students in terms of their field of study. The number of women majoring in law, political science, and economics increased by nearly 250 percent from 11.9 percent in 1970 to 29.2 percent in 2005. Although the numbers remain small, women majoring in engineering also showed a significant increase from 0.7 percent in 1970 to 4.5 percent in 2005.

Gender imbalance can also be found among faculty members of higher education and researchers. According to The 2000 Basic Survey of Schools, women comprised 7.35 percent of university presidents, 7.9 percent of full professors, 13.12 percent of assistant professors, 18.8 percent of lecturers, and 19.99 percent of teaching assistants (Gelb, 2003). In addition, The 2003 Basic Survey of Schools indicated that in terms of the percentage of women among faculty members at universities and graduate schools, Japan ranked the lowest at 14.1 percent among the member countries of the Organization for Economic Cooperation and Development (OECD), whose average was more than twice as high at 36.1 percent. Nevertheless, The 2005 Basic Survey of Schools reported that the number of women among full-time faculty members in Japan has continued to increase at a steady pace in recent years: in 2-year junior colleges, women accounted for 46.6 percent, which was an increase of over 150 percent since the 1950s, while in 4-year universities, the percentage of women tripled to 16.7 percent since the 1950s.

Furthermore, the total number of women researchers in Japan reached 102,900 in 2006, exceeding 100,000 for the first time since the first survey was conducted in 1953 by the Ministry of Public Management, Home Affairs, Posts and Telecommunications. The survey also reported that the number of women researchers in universities and colleges was 69,100, which accounted for 21.5 percent of all researchers. In humanities and social sciences, the percentage was higher at 28 percent, and in natural sciences, it was slightly lower at 18 percent. In contrast, the number of women researchers in the private sector was significantly less with a total of 33,800, representing 6.5 percent of all researchers. However, the ratio of women nearly quadrupled at 24.6 percent in the food industry, and more than tripled at 22.2 percent in the pharmaceutical industry ("Josei Kenkyuusha," 2007).

Despite the recent increase in the number of women researchers, Japan ranks the lowest among the industrialized countries in terms of the proportion of women among all researchers. The report by the Cabinet Office indicated that in 2008, women represented 12.4 percent of all researchers in Japan, compared to 34 percent in the United States, 28 percent in France, 26 percent in England, and 13 percent in South Korea. In order to increase the number of women researchers, the Ministry of Education, Culture, Sports, Science and Technology has adopted a policy to subsidize approximately 10 universities and research institutes nationwide that have specific plans to improve their facilities as well as their overall working environments to accommodate the needs of women researchers. The amount of the subsidy is 18 million yen ($180,000) per newly hired woman researcher, and the target disciplines are agriculture, natural sciences, and engineering, where the proportion of women researchers is particularly small: in 2006, women represented 16.3 percent of all the newly hired researchers in agriculture, 12.7 percent in science, and 5.9 percent in engineering. With this new policy, the Ministry plans to increase the number of women researchers by 100, and their proportion to 25 percent by 2010.

While the number of women who attend colleges and universities is steadily increasing, there has been a decline in the popularity of women's colleges and universities, particularly since the 1980s. This is due to the fact that these institutions offer degree programs mostly in so-called "traditionally female-dominated fields" such as the humanities, education, and home economics. However, a new and positive development in women's colleges and universities since the late 1980s has been the increasing presence of nontraditional female students who are of diverse age and occupational groups. Some of them are working women in their 40s or older, married with children, who wish to continue their education. Incidentally, nontraditional students, both female and male, account for less than 3 percent of the entire undergraduate student population in present-day Japan (Fujimura-Fanselow, 1995a).

There are a number of opportunities available for women in present-day Japan to receive education in addition to 4-year universities, vocational colleges, and 2-year junior colleges. For instance, a number of 4-year universities offer *tsuushin kyooiku* (education by correspondence) as degree-granting programs. Similarly, the government-sponsored Hoso Daigaku (the University of the Air) has granted a bachelor's degree in liberal arts through radio and TV broadcasting since 1985. Furthermore, *karuchaa sentaa* (culture centers) have gained popularity among homemakers by providing them with venues for continuing education as well as adult education since the mid–1970s. Private enterprises including newspaper and broadcasting companies, and major department stores operate "culture centers" that accommodate the needs of homemakers with convenient locations and reasonable fees. A wide variety of courses are offered such as classical Japanese literature and poetry, calligraphy, foreign languages, arts and crafts, tea ceremony, flower arrangement, cooking, social dance, yoga, swimming, and tennis, among others.

Part I: Representation of Women in Japanese Society

Although some feminist educators direct their criticism toward "culture centers," they continue to serve homemakers who seek opportunities to expand their social lives as well as their potential. In fact, there have been instances of homemakers becoming professional authors after taking courses in creative writing. For those who live in rural areas without access to "culture centers," *koominkan* (community centers) that are sponsored by local governments offer similar services.

As mentioned earlier, the second wave of feminism which began in Japan in the 1970s has made a significant contribution to women's education. One of the important developments was the creation of courses on women's studies called *joseigaku* during the late 1970s and early 1980s. The statistics by the National Women's Education Center (NWEC) indicated that a total of 512 courses related to women's studies were offered at 268 colleges and universities, which accounted for nearly 25 percent of institutions of higher education nationwide in 1992 (Fujieda & Fujimura-Fanselow, 1995). Since then, *joseigaku* (women's studies) has been frequently offered in combination with *jendaa ron* (gender theories), which has gained further popularity among female as well as male students. For instance, according to the NWEC database, as of 2008, a total of 4,221 courses on *joseigaku* and *jendaa ron* were offered at 614 institutions of higher education. This was an impressive increase of over eightfold (820 percent) in the number of course offerings, and of over twofold (220 percent) in the number of institutions in less than 2 decades.

It is noteworthy that among Japanese feminist scholars and researchers, there are two widely different views in regard to the nature and objectives of women's studies as an academic discipline. On the one hand, some scholars and researchers including Inoue, T. (1981, 1987) put emphasis on the political aspect of women's studies. They insist that women's studies should not only be an independent academic discipline on, by, and for women, but also be closely associated with the feminist movement. On the other hand, others, including Iwao and H. Hara (Iwao & H. Hara, 1979; H. Hara, 1987), place less emphasis on the political aspect, and instead claim that women's studies can make scholarly contributions to other academic disciplines by providing a feminist perspective. Consequently, they consider that the objective of women's studies is achieved once a feminist perspective is incorporated into other disciplines (Fujieda & Fujimura-Fanselow, 1995).

Many critics claim that "Japanese women are still on the periphery rather than in the mainstream of education" (K. Hara, 1995, p. 105), although there is a prevailing perception among the general public that equality for women to receive education has been guaranteed by the Constitution (Christopher, 1983; K. Hara, 1995; Kameda, 1995; Morley, 1999). While their claims are true to a certain extent, there are a number of encouraging developments in recent years, as mentioned throughout this section, which will certainly have positive effects on the prospect of women's education in Japan.

4

Women in the Japanese Workplace

Gradually, Japanese men are becoming aware that greater diversity in women's roles benefits themselves. Women's advance into the corporate world, for example, is changing working conditions for both sexes. In management studies and within companies, both men and women are urging that more consideration be paid to individuals and that more balanced work styles be adopted. Clearly pressure from women workers is fostering these trends [Morley, 1999, p. 186].

Various Issues Surrounding Women in the Japanese Workplace

According to the report, *Hataraku Josei no Jitsujo* (*The Actual State of Working Women*) *in 2007* released by the Ministry of Health, Labor and Welfare, the total number of women in the labor force tripled from 9.1 million in 1960 to 27.6 million in 2007, accounting for 41.6 percent of the entire Japanese work force. Similarly, the percentage of married women in the female work force increased over fivefold from 8.8 percent in 1960 to 48.5 percent in 2007. The traditional gender-based role division in Japanese society that is described by the phrase, "men at work, women at home (*otoko wa shigoto, onna wa katei*)" appears to be outdated statistically (Kawashima, 1995; Y. Tanaka, 1995). However, many critics claim that the economic growth of post–World War II Japan has been supported by the female labor force comprised predominantly of low-waged part-time workers (Gelb, 2003; Mackie, 2003; Morley, 1999; Saso, 1990; K. Tanaka, 1995b). For instance, the above report also indicated that the number of part-time workers nearly tripled since 1985, accounting for 41.7 percent of the entire female work force in 2007, while the percentage of full-time workers continued to decrease steadily from 67.9 percent to 46.5 percent during the same period.

Furthermore, The 2007 White Paper on Gender Equality released by the Cabinet Office reported that women earned 66.8 percent of men's wages. Although it was an increase by 8.8 percent from 58 percent in 1997, it was significantly lower compared to other advanced countries where women earned over 80 percent of men's wages. The white paper pointed out that the following two prevalent working patterns of Japanese women were the major reasons for their low wages: a significant number of married women in their mid–20s to mid–30s leave the work force for childbirth and child care, and the vast majority of married women in their late 30s to 40s take up low-waged part-time employment when they re-enter the labor force after their children have reached school age.

As indicated by these statistics, there is a strong correlation between the age and the type of work that women in Japan engage in: full-time workers are mostly young, part-time workers are typically middle-aged, contract workers as well as temporary workers dispatched by employment agencies are young to middle-aged, and most pieceworkers are elderly (Kawashima, 1995; Saso, 1990).

Most women in Japan work full-time until marriage, more than half of them as *OLs* (office ladies, female office workers) performing secondary and domestic functions in the workplace (Iwai, 1990; Nakano, 1984). Besides clerical work, they are responsible for housekeeping such as tidying up the office space and serving tea to visitors and clients as well as to their male colleagues and supervisors. Since young and single *OLs* in the Japanese workplace are traditionally considered ornamental and disposable "flowers in the workplace (*shokuba no hana*)," they are mostly expected to resign by the end of the so-called *tekireiki* (the period of marriageable age) that ranges from the mid– to late 20s for women. In fact, there is a prevailing custom called *kotobuki taishoku* (congratulatory resignations, resignations of female workers because of marriage) among young and single *OLs*. Those who do not opt to resign past *tekireiki* (the period of marriageable age; from mid– to late 20s) are often under pressure from their supervisors as well as colleagues to do so (Creighton, 1996; Lo, 1990). Incidentally, there is a term, *otsubone* (elderly court women, middle-aged female workers), that is commonly used to ridicule middle-aged female office workers behind their backs. It is noteworthy that before the mid–1980s when career opportunities available for women were limited, marriage was frequently referred to as *eikyuu shuushoku* (permanent employment) for young and single women who mostly became *sengyoo shufu* (full-time professional homemakers) upon marriage.

In Japan, where the number of daycare facilities are limited, and the idea of baby-sitting is virtually nonexistent, women are expected to raise their children by themselves with some help from their mothers or mothers-in-law (Morley, 1999). Because of the difficulty in balancing work and child care, approximately 70 percent of women leave the labor force at the birth of their first child ("Ikukyuho Kaisei," 2008). When their children reach school age, many of these women re-enter the labor force by taking up low-waged part-time employment, typically in manufacturing, sales, and service industries (Kawashima, 1995; Morley, 1999).

The taxation system is one of the main reasons for most married women in Japan to accept the low wages for part-time workers commonly called *paato* (part-timers). A wife's annual earned income of less than 1.03 million yen ($10,300) is tax-exempt, and her husband is also able to receive the tax deduction for a spouse. If a wife's income goes beyond this limit, she needs to earn substantially more to compensate for the increase in tax. Feminist critics argue that this taxation system plays a major role in keeping women tied to the home (Mackie, 2003; Morley, 1999; K. Tanaka, 1995b). Another reason why married women tend to accept low wages is because they often consider their earnings as supplementary to the household income. According to the 2006 survey by the Ministry of Health, Labor and Welfare, women gave the following reasons for re-entering the work force: to supplement the household income (62 percent), to improve the standard of living (22 percent), to enrich personal life (8 percent), and to use leisure time (8 percent).

As mentioned earlier, throughout the mid–1980s, women were customarily recruited to fill secondary clerical positions without any prospects for promotion. In order to improve women's career prospects, the Equal Employment Opportunity Law (EEOL) (Danjo Koyo Kikai Kinto Ho) was enacted in 1985. It was intended to provide support for women to enter managerial ranks, and to prohibit discrimination against women in the workplace. In order to comply with the EEOL, many companies introduced a two-track system consisting of the managerial track called *soogoo shoku,* and the clerical track called *ippan shoku.* The managerial track is characterized by the demanding nature of work, longer hours, frequent transfers, and promotions, while the clerical track consists of limited responsibility, shorter hours, and no transfers. Although both tracks are open for women and men, women are significantly underrepresented in the managerial track, while the clerical track consists predominantly of women (Mackie, 2003; K. Tanaka, 1995b).

The EEOL has been criticized by women workers and equal rights activists alike. They argue that it is not intended to make significant changes in the prevailing concept of gender-based role division in Japanese society. For instance, this was evidenced by the EEOL's undemanding nature of recommendations to employers in asking them to make efforts to treat women equally without assessing any penalties on violators (Kawashima, 1995; Kinjo, 1995; Creighton, 1996). In response to these criticisms, the EEOL was amended in 1997. As a result, penalties are assessed on violators who discriminate against women, and employers are also required to take necessary measures to prevent sexual harassment. Women labor lawyers in the advocacy of working women were the driving force behind this amendment to include the provision for the prevention of sexual harassment, which is commonly called *sekuhara* in the Japanese language (Mackie, 2003). Although there remain criticisms, the enactment of the EEOL was an important development in Japanese labor history by opening the door for women who hoped to play more active roles in the work force (Sodei, 2006).

The Child-Care Leave Law (Ikuji Kyugyo Ho) enacted in 1991 was another significant development that gave incentives for women to remain in the labor force after childbirth. The law was designed as a countermeasure against the steady decline in the birth rate in recent years. The dynamic statistics of population by the Ministry of Health, Labor and Welfare reported that the average number of children that a woman gives birth to in her lifetime hit a new low of 1.26 in 2005. This prompted the serious public concern that the resultant labor shortage would adversely affect the existing businesses as well as the Japanese economy (Gelb, 2003; Mackie, 2003; Sodei, 2006). The significance of the Child-Care Leave Law lies in the fact that it has made it possible for both women and men to take parenting leave for the first time in Japanese labor history.

The Child-Care Leave Law provides for either the mother or the father to take a child-care leave for up to a year and a half. If both the mother and the father take the leave, the duration is shortened to up to a year. During the leave, the government employment insurance system provides employees benefits equivalent to 50 percent of their wages prior to the leave. The Child-Care Leave Law was later integrated into the Child-Care Leave and Family-Care Leave Law (Ikuji Kaigo Kyugyo Ho) due to another public concern over the rapidly aging Japanese population.

The trend toward fewer children combined with the decline in the mortality rate because of the advancement in medical care and technology, makes Japan the fastest aging country in the world. The dynamic statistics of population released by the Ministry of Health, Labor and Welfare indicated that those over the age of 65 accounted for more than 20 percent of the entire population of Japan in 2006, and is expected to exceed 26 percent by the year 2015. Due to the tradition of rigid gender-based role division in Japanese society, it is customarily women who take up the role of caretakers of elderly parents as well as parents-in-law. This has resulted in additional responsibility for women who are in charge of household management and child-rearing, among others. Juggling multiple responsibilities has been an enormous challenge faced by women, particularly those with full-time employment. In order to accommodate the needs of these women, the Child-Care Leave and Family-Care Leave Law (Ikuji Kaigo Kyugyo Ho) was introduced in 1999. Under the law, employees are entitled to take a one-time up to 3-months paid leave per family member, including parents, parents-in-law, spouses, and children. While on the leave, the government employment insurance system provides employees benefits equivalent to 40 percent of their wages prior to the leave.

4—Women in the Japanese Workplace

The Child-Care and Family-Care Leave Law was amended in 2002 with the aim of providing a better environment for parents trying to balance work and child care. To that end, the law makes a recommendation to employers to introduce at least one of the following supportive measures for employees with children younger than 3 years of age: (1) shorter working hours, (2) exemption from overtime work, (3) flextime, (4) later starting time or earlier closing time, (5) creating and maintaining child-care facilities, and (6) assistance for child-care costs. While shorter hours for workers with small children have been gradually adopted by the private sector, a half day leave for child care is rarely granted for workers. For instance, based on its survey conducted in 2005 on 4,602 companies with approximately 100 employees, the National Personnel Authority reported that less than half (43.4 percent) of these companies adopted the system of shorter working hours. Out of the companies adopting the system, a mere 4.2 percent granted the reduction of less than 50 percent of full-time hours, while 24.6 percent granted the reduction ranging from 50 percent to 75 percent of full-time hours.

In 2007, when the Ministry of Health, Labor and Welfare conducted a survey of approximately 1,560 full-time workers younger than 40 years of age, the vast majority of them stressed the necessity of shorter working hours and the exemption from overtime work in order to raise children older than 18 months, for whom the child-care leave is not granted by the existing law. Despite these needs of workers with small children, another survey conducted during the same year by the Ministry indicated that among the major corporations, less than one third (31 percent) introduced the system of shorter working hours, and even fewer, 23 percent, provided the exemption from overtime work.

Furthermore, while the Child-Care and Family-Care Leave Law is progressive by providing for both women and men to take parenting leave, there is a discriminatory provision that excludes workers married to full-time homemakers from taking the leave, if there is a labor-management agreement. This provision has been adopted by 75 percent of businesses nationwide, which has resulted in an extremely small number of men taking the leave. According to the 2007 report by the Ministry of Health, Labor and Welfare, while 30 percent of full-time male

Part I: Representation of Women in Japanese Society

workers younger than 40 years of age were interested in taking a child-care leave, only 1.56 percent of them actually did so.

By taking these circumstances into consideration, the Ministry of Health, Labor and Welfare plans to amend the existing Child-Care and Family-Care Leave Law in 2009. By doing so, the Ministry and the government aim to raise the percentage of men taking a child-care leave by over sixfold to 10 percent by 2017, and to reduce the number of responsibilities of women who are traditionally in charge of child care and homemaking. The following are some of the new provisions to be included in the amended law. First, employers will be required to provide both the exemption from overtime work and shorter working hours of approximately 6 hours a day for all the employees with children younger than 3 years old. The names of the employers who violate the law will be announced publicly. The duration of a child-care leave taken by both the mother and the father will also be extended by 2 months, making it up to 14 months, rather than the 12 months which is provided by the existing law. In addition, employees who are married to full-time homemakers will be able to take a child-care leave.

It is often pointed out that the number of Japanese women who give up employment for homemaking and child care is significantly greater compared to other advanced countries. Based on its survey conducted in 2002, the Saitama-ken Center for Promotion of Gender Equality reported that the most significant factor for women to leave the work force was the pressure from their husbands and their parents-in-law who held traditional views on gender-based role division represented by the commonly used phrase, *otoko wa shigoto, onna wa katei* (men at work, women at home).

In 2007, the Cabinet Office released the results of the survey estimating that the Japanese labor force would increase by 440,000, and the economic growth of Japan would be fostered if women would not leave the labor force because of childbirth, child care, and other reasons. The survey was conducted by the Mitsubishi General Institute at the request of the government in order to estimate the effectiveness of shorter working hours and telecommuting that are commonly adopted by high-tech industries in the private sector. According to the survey, if women had continued to remain in the labor force, either by working shorter hours or telecommuting, the entire work force in Japan would have increased from 66.58 million to 67.02 million in 2006.

Furthermore, continued participation of women in the labor force would save their cumulative knowledge as well as their skills from being lost, and its overall effect on the economy would be significantly greater than replacing these skilled women with new workers who need substantial amounts of training due to their lack of such knowledge and skills. The survey estimated that the continuous participation of women in the labor force would contribute to the overall economic growth of the nation by 0.4 percent between 2006 and 2010. Based on these survey results, the Cabinet Office as well as the Ministry of Health, Labor and Welfare stresses the necessity of providing women with a variety of options in order to facilitate the re-entry process into the labor force following a child-care leave.

Prospect of Change for Women in the Japanese Workplace

Considering many urgent issues in Japanese society such as the rapidly aging population, falling birth rate, and declining supply of labor, critics have predicted that the government would find it necessary to take some drastic measures to encourage women to remain in the work force until retirement (Ozawa, 1994; Morley, 1999). As pointed out in the quote by Morley (1999) at the beginning of this chapter, a number of changes have been adopted and implemented by the government as well as by the private sector in recent years. These changes are aimed at not only giving incentives to women to remain in the work force and to advance their careers, but also creating a supportive environment for both women and men who want to balance work and family. This section presents a series of such positive developments that could certainly create a new climate in the Japanese workplace.

Since All Nippon Airways (ANA) opened its door to women pilots for the first time in 2003, eight women co-pilots have been hired. Similarly, nine women co-pilots have been hired in recent years by Japan Airlines (JAL). While JAL and ANA are the two major airline companies in Japan, women represent less than 1 percent of the entire number of pilots, and there has been much delay in accommodating the needs of women. For instance, both JAL and ANA have continued to supply women pilots with oversized uniforms made for their male colleagues, despite complaints from women who have to make necessary adjustments on their own, such as shortening the jacket and the tie. In the spring of 2008, 5 years after the first hire of women pilots in the company's history, ANA launched a project to design uniforms for women pilots based on their specific requests and needs. ANA officials anticipated that the new stylish uniforms would help to ease the overall shortage of pilots by giving an incentive for women to apply for the position ("Watashitachino," 2008).

Underrepresentation of Japanese women, particularly in the management-level positions, has been evidenced by a number of statistics. According to The 2006 Global Gender Gap Report released by the World Economic Forum, Japan ranked 79th among 115 countries surveyed in regard to the percentage of women holding influential positions in the workplace. Similarly, in The Report on Human Development released in 2006 by the United Nations Development Plan (UNDP), Japan ranked 42nd among 75 countries in terms of the advancement of women. The ranking was based on the gender empowerment index to measure the degree of advancement of women in the political arena and economic activity. The index was calculated by combining multiple factors including the percentages of women as assembly members and representatives, in corporate managerial positions, and medical and legal positions, as well as other professions. Incidentally, Norway, Sweden, Iceland, and Denmark were ranked as the top 4 among the top 10 countries on the list, followed by Canada and the United States. Furthermore, The 2007 White Paper on Gender Equality by the Cabinet Office indicated that regarding the percentage of women in managerial positions in the private sectors of Asian countries, Japan ranked the second from the lowest at 10.1 percent, followed by Korea at 7.8 percent, while the Philippines ranked the first at 57 percent, followed by Singapore at 25.9 percent.

4—Women in the Japanese Workplace

In order to increase the presence of women in management-level positions, the Japanese government and many companies in the private sector have continued to introduce various measures. For instance, a major conglomerate, Ito Chu Shoji, has revealed their new policy for increasing the number of women being hired on the managerial track. Compared to other industries, women are significantly underrepresented in industrial conglomerates called *soogoo shoosha*, commonly known for their elitist image of the *shoosha man* (businessman working for conglomerates) who travels globally.

Ito Chu Shoji set the target to increase the number of women being hired on the managerial track from 20 percent in the past to 30 percent in 2008, and to place the women hired on the managerial track in all its entire departments to a total of about 100. Furthermore, it plans to double the number of women in management-level positions by 2013; as of 2006, there were only 11 women section chiefs. Ito Chu Shoji also aims to promote women to department heads in its headquarters for the first time in its company history. In 2007, fewer than 5 percent of the total employees on the managerial track were women, who were assigned to 60 percent of the departments that were mostly dealing with textiles and foodstuffs. According to its public relations department, Ito Chu Shoji has decided to implement this major change in personnel matters based on the realization that its age-old practice of relying heavily on male employees would result in difficulty in securing necessary employees to maintain the work force in the future, due to the declining birth rate in recent years ("Ito Chu," 2007).

A number of non-profit organizations have also been established to support women who seek career advancement in the private sector. The Japan Women's Innovative Network (J-Win) is one such organization launched in 2007 by the joint effort of approximately 70 major corporations including Sony and Japan IBM. Its aim is to raise the awareness of male managers and executives of the member corporations about the importance and necessity of promoting women to managerial positions in order to increase Japan's industrial competitiveness in the global market. To that end, J-Win offers a number of workshops and seminars on a regular basis for male managers and executives to teach them the know-how as well as the strategies of the private sectors in the United States and in Europe, where an increasing number of women are promoted to managerial positions. Furthermore, J-Win actively assists women on the managerial track in networking with women executives in various industries. It also plans to set up an employment agency specifically for women executives. The first chief director of J-Win, Uchinaga Yukako, who was a member of the executive board at Japan IBM until her mandatory retirement at the age of 60, expects J-Win to play a pioneering role in changing the prevailing male-oriented structure and mentality of the private sector in Japan ("Nihon IBM," 2007).

Similarly, the Japanese government adopted measures to accelerate the rate of women's participation in society in 2008. One of the objectives is to increase the number of women at the management level by as much as 30 percent, both in the public and the private sectors, by the year 2020. As of 2007, women represented merely 1.7 percent of all the executive officers in public services, and the government measures have set the goal of tripling their numbers to 5 percent or more by the end of 2010. Furthermore, particular efforts are going to be made from 2008 to 2010 to increase the number of women in the occupations where women are traditionally underrepresented: in 2007, women accounted for 12.4 percent of researchers and 17.2 percent of medical doctors. In order to achieve these goals, the measures aim to shorten the working hours, implement more flextime systems, and expand the support system for women who re-enter the work force after taking maternity and child-care leaves. Some critics question the actual effectiveness of these measures by pointing out the fact that there is no specific numerical target set for the realization of these goals, except for the target number of women officers in public services. Nevertheless, it is a welcome development that such measures addressing the issue of underrepresentation of women in the Japanese workplace have been adopted by the government.

In order to cope with the declining birth rate by giving employees incentives to have more children, an increasing number of local governments and companies in the private sector have launched programs to offer a large sum of congratulatory money to employees at the birth of their third child. For instance, the headquarters of Yamato Shoken Group, one of the major stock brokerage firms, started a program in 2007 offering 2 million yen ($20,000) per employee. While the firm has been offering 550,000 yen ($5,500) to employees at the birth of their children, the sum has been raised in consideration of the additional financial burden on households with more than three children. Both female and male employees are eligible for the congratulatory money, and the firm expects that approximately 20 employees per year are going to receive the sum. According to the firm's personnel department, the program is specifically designed to aid a large number of female employees in the sales department who plan to take a maternity leave.

Similarly, Softbank, a conglomerate in multimedia, telecommunication, and finance, has also introduced a program that offers its employees 1 million yen ($10,000) for the third child, 3 million yen ($30,000) for the fourth, 5 million yen ($50,000) for the fifth, and each subsequent child thereafter. The 2006 survey conducted by the Institute of Labor Administration indicated that out of 213 companies in the private sector who responded to the survey, over 80 percent of them offered congratulatory money to their employees at the birth of their children; however, the average amount was around 20,000 yen ($200) per employee ("Kigyoo Ni," 2007).

Women who try to balance full-time employment with homemaking and child care face a number of obstacles in the workplace as well as at home. In order to assist women who are married with young children, and to accommodate their needs, an increasing number of policies and programs have been implemented by the government as well as by the private sector in recent years. For instance, the Ministry of Health, Labor and Welfare launched a program in 2008 offering grants to hospitals providing a supportive environment for women doctors who plan to return to their practices after taking a child-care leave. A total of 2.3 billion yen ($23 million) was initially allocated for this program and other measures to assist women doctors. It accounted for approximately 15 percent of the Ministry's 2008 fiscal year budget of 16 billion yen ($160 million) allocated for the plan to solve the nationwide shortage of medical doctors.

Part I: Representation of Women in Japanese Society

According to the Ministry, there has been a severe shortage of doctors in obstetrics/gynecology and pediatrics that are represented by a large number of women. In 2007, women in their 20s consisted of over 66 percent of obstetricians/gynecologists, and 50 percent of pediatricians. The main reason for the current shortage lies in the fact that a large number of women are unable to return to practice after childbirth and child care, due to their insufficient knowledge of up-to-date medicine and technology. Furthermore, long and irregular hours as well as an inadequate number of child-care facilities discourage women from continuing their practices. The grants are offered to hospitals to subsidize the cost of various re-entry orientations and workshops, and training programs for women doctors who plan to return to practice. Along with the grants, more child-care facilities are going to be provided inside the hospitals, and additional coordinators are going to be hired at "Women Doctors' Bank." The bank is delegated to the Japan Medical Society by the Ministry, aiming to offer various services and assistance to support women doctors who plan to resume their practices. Coordinators at the bank not only offer telephone consultations to those in need, but also act as agents for women doctors by searching for positions that meet their needs.

In the private sector, Kirin Beer Company introduced a new system in 2007 to rehire former female employees who voluntarily resigned because of such reasons as childbirth and transfer of their spouses. The company initially hires them back as contract workers with the possibility of offering them full-time positions at a later time, based on their performance. This system is also designed to increase the competitiveness of the company by securing a large pool of competent workers with extensive experience and expertise in sales and other areas. Those who wish to be rehired are required to register prior to voluntary resignation, and the company hires them back within 3 to 5 years. The salary is negotiable, and is based on the worker's experience prior to resignation as well as the worker's performance after being rehired.

The company has also adopted a system for women on the managerial track to spare them from being transferred for up to 10 years after marriage and childbirth. Kirin Beer Company has been making a specific effort to provide opportunities for continuous employment for approximately 1,200 women, who consist of roughly 20 percent of all employees. Typically, more than half of the women who have been with the company for over 5 years resign, mostly because of childbirth and transfer of their spouses ("Kekkon Shussan," 2007).

Furthermore, another major development took place in 2007, when Mitsui Bussan, one of the major conglomerates in Japan, revised its child-care leave policy by granting male employees an 8-week paid leave for the first time in the company history. This was an unprecedented child-care leave policy among major corporations in Japan, and a drastic departure from the average of 2-week paid leave granted to male workers at other companies supportive of such a system. In the past, female employees at Mitsui Bussan were granted a 16-week paid maternity leave, while male employees married to full-time homemakers were not granted any leave at all, and those who had spouses with employment were only granted an unpaid leave.

This policy change was implemented based on a survey of male employees at Mitsui Bussan in regard to a paid child-care leave. According to the survey, out of 60 percent of male employees who showed interest in taking a leave, 17 percent expressed a strong desire to do so. Moreover, the younger the employees, the more interest they showed in taking a leave: 82 percent in their 20s compared to 68 percent in their 30s. However, the remaining 43 percent of male employees who showed interest in a leave stated various reasons that could prevent them from doing so. Nearly 80 percent of the reasons pertained to the difficulty in obtaining an understanding from their colleagues and supervisors, 10 percent regarding the potential adverse effect on their promotions, and 10 percent on possible negative reactions from their clients. This change in the child-care leave policy was proposed by Mitsui Bussan's Office for Promoting Diversity that was launched to encourage employees to lead a well-balanced lifestyle between work and family. The personnel department of the company was hopeful that this new child-care leave policy would lead to a change in the Japanese corporate mentality, which customarily has given top priority to work over everything else ("Mitsui Bussan," 2007).

Part I: Representation of Women in Japanese Society

Another encouraging development was reported by the Institute of Labor Administration, a private research institute in Tokyo, which conducted a survey on child-care leave policies of 240 major corporations in 2007. While the Child-Care and Family-Care Leave Law provides for either the mother or the father to take a child-care leave for up to a year and a half, the number of corporations allowing their employees to take a longer leave than provided by the law more than doubled in 3 years from 11 percent in 2004 to 26.3 percent in 2007 ("Issai Han," 2007).

Although gender-based role division is a longstanding tradition in Japanese society, a survey by the Ministry of Health, Labor and Welfare indicates that the active participation by husbands in child-rearing not only increases the percentage of their wives' continued participation in the labor force after the birth of the first child, but also has a significant influence on the couple's decision to have more children. The survey was conducted annually between 2002 and 2008 using the sample of 18,000 married women and men who were between 20 and 34 years of age.

According to the survey results, among the couples with one child, the husband's participation in household work and child care on his day off was the decisive factor for the couple to have a second child. The percentages of couples who had a second child and the amount of the husband's participation in household work on his day off are shown in the following: 20.5 percent for no participation, 51.2 percent for 2 to 4 hours of participation, 56.3 percent for 4 to 6 hours of participation, and 63.8 percent for 6 to 8 hours of participation. It is noteworthy that the most active participation in household work by the husband more than tripled the birth rate of the second child, and even a few hours of the husband's participation more than doubled the rate. The survey also reported that the availability of a child-care leave at the wife's workplace was another contributing factor in the birth rate: the second child was born to 45.4 percent of women who were able to take a child-care leave, compared to 28 percent of women who were not.

Despite the enormous societal pressure to conform since childhood, an increasing number of women in Japan defy the prevalent work pattern for women to leave the labor force for child care and homemaking. For instance, those with higher education are more likely to continue their full-time employment not only after marriage and childbirth, but also until retirement. At the same time, support networks for women who intend to balance work with family have been expanding. Morley (1999) made a prediction that "Aided by national necessity, those women who wish to combine employment with homemaking may find it easier in years to come" (p. 88). It is fair to conclude that nearly a decade later, her prediction is on its way to becoming a reality.

5

Feminism in Japan

The day when the mountains move has come.
I say this, but no one would believe me.
The mountains have been asleep for so long.
But long ago they all moved fervently with fire.
You do not have to believe me,
As long as you believe this:
Women who have been asleep are awake and moving now
[Yosano, 1911, pp. 1–2].

Historical Overview

Two poems appeared in the first issue of *Seito* (*Bluestocking*), the feminist literary journal launched in 1911, which had immeasurable influence on feminism in Japan. One is this poem by Yosano Akiko (1878–1942), a feminist poet and author; another poem is by Hiratsuka Raicho (1886–1971), and was presented earlier at the beginning of Chapter 1. Hiratsuka was the founder of *Seito* and was one of the most wellknown feminist pioneers in Japan. Both the Seitosha (the Bluestocking Society), the feminist literary organization, and its journal, *Seito*, made significant contributions to the overall liberation of women as well as the emergence of the Japanese "New Women (*atarashii onna*)," who would defy old norms and expectations (Lowy, 2007). In this section, a historical overview on feminism in Japan is presented, dating back to the Meiji period (1868–1912) when the first wave of feminism began.

The national seclusion that lasted over 200 years under the ruling of Tokugawa shogunate in the Edo period (1603–1867) ended with the Meiji Restoration, which brought about major social, political, and economic changes. The new government was established in 1868, and Japan underwent a transformation from feudalism to capitalism as a modern state under the slogan called *fukoku kyoohei* (enriching the nation and strengthening the military). During the early Meiji period (1868–1912), the United States and Western Europe served as a model for Japan, and a number of political movements took place as a result. The Jiyu Minken Undo (The Liberal People's Rights Movement), which began in the mid–1870s and continued through the 1880s, was the most well-known such movement, calling for the establishment of the people's rights, the constitutional government, and Japan's national assembly called the Diet, among other things (Kaneko, 1995).

Kishida Toshiko (1863–1901), also known as Nakajima Shoen, and Kageyama (later Fukuda) Hideko (1865–1927) were among the several leading women who joined this nationwide political cause. In 1882, Kishida became the first woman to address the public on equal rights for women as well as on people's rights, and she inspired many women to join the movement. Similarly, Kishida's work in 1884 entitled, *Doho Shimai ni Tsugu* (*I Tell You, My Fellow Sisters*) that appeared in the Liberal Party's newspaper called *Jiyu no Tomoshibi* (*The Light of Freedom*), was the first series of articles on women's rights written by a woman. One of the women who followed Kishida as an advocate of people's rights and women's rights was Kageyama, who later became a socialist. Both Kishida and Kageyama are known as the pioneers of the women's movement in Japan. The Jiyu Minken Undo (The Liberal People's Rights Movement), however, was suppressed by the government by the 1890s, and subsequently, women's political rights, including their participation in political causes, were denied altogether (Fujieda, 1995; Kaneko, 1995).

During the Meiji period (1868–1912), the Christian women's groups in Japan were also very active in protesting against child prostitution. Girls in their early teens, mainly those of farmers, were often sold into prostitution by their parents who were in debt. Despite a series of protests, the Christian women's groups failed to attract the attention of politicians and gain influence on them because the right to vote was not granted to women. These protests against child prostitution that ended in failure were one of many incidents that led to a campaign for women's suffrage (Aoki, 1986).

In the Taisho period (1912–1926), a number of organizations were established and made concerted endeavors to call for women's suffrage.

Part I: Representation of Women in Japanese Society

The Shin Fujin Kyokai (The New Women's Association) was the first such organization in Japan that demanded political freedom for women. Launched in 1920 by Ichikawa Fusae (1893–1981) and Hiratsuka Raicho (1886–1971), its members consisted of over 400 women nationwide. Later, in 1924, Ichikawa, together with other suffragists, founded the Fujin Sanseiken Kakutoku Kisei Domeikai (the League for the Realization of Women's Suffrage) in Tokyo, whose members exceeded 1,700 in the early 1930s. In 1927, the League and the Zen Kansai Fujin Rengokai (the All-Kansai Federation of Women), located in the western part of Japan, sent the House of Representatives a total of 56,000 signatures they collected for a petition, and the government was ready to grant women suffrage at the local level. However, the increasing presence of militarism since the Manchurian Incident in 1931, and the subsequent government policy to suppress political movement prevented it from materializing (Kaneko, 1995).

During the early 1940s, the women's movement was mostly prohibited, except for patriotic campaigning in collaboration with the nation's war effort. Women's groups were consolidated into the Dai Nippon Fujinkai (the Great Japan Women's Organization) that was organized by the government and the military under the war slogan called *kokumin seishin sodoin taisei* (the system for a general mobilization of the national spirit). Leaders of women's groups had false expectations that their cooperation with the government and the military would raise the status of women in society, which had seen little progress since the beginning of the first wave of feminism in the Meiji period (1868–1912) (Fujieda, 1995; Kaneko, 1995).

Women's suffrage finally materialized shortly after World War II, when the Electoral Law was reformed in 1945. The first postwar national general election for the House of Representatives was held in the following year, and 67 percent of approximately 20 million women who were eligible cast their votes for the first time in Japanese history. In addition, a total of 79 women candidates ran for seats, and 39, nearly half of them, were elected. On May 3, 1947, the new Constitution became effective, and its Article 14 guarantees equal rights for women and men under the law. Furthermore, under the revised Civil Code issued in the same year, the patriarchal *ie* (family, household) system was abolished, and legal equality in marriage and the family was granted to women (Kaneko, 1995; Mackie, 2003). Regarding the progress in the status of women following World War II, the male-dominated Japanese media made a frequent reference that the democratization of the pre–World War II patriarchal social system, and the proven durability of nylon over silk, made women and nylon stockings the two most empowered objects in postwar Japanese society.

During the late 1940s and the early 1950s, two leading women's organizations were established. One is the Shufu Rengokai (the Federation of Homemakers), also known as Shufuren. Launched in 1948, Shufuren aims to reflect homemakers' perspectives in politics and consumer economics, and has become an influential lobby group for consumer safety. Another is Zenkoku Chiiki Fujin Dantai Renraku Kyogikai (the National Liaison Council of Regional Women's Organizations), commonly known as Chifuren, which was founded in 1952. With its membership of approximately 5 million and 50 women's organizations nationwide, Chifuren has been actively engaged in a wide range of political and social causes including equal rights for women, clean elections without corrupt practices, nuclear disarmament, and consumer protection, among others (Gelb, 2003).

In the 1960s, when an increasing number of women began to enter the labor force, the women's movement "retreated to the goal simply of promoting the full utilization of each woman's ability in the workplace" (T. Inoue, 1981, p. 179). As a result, the movement failed to address various complex issues surrounding women that were brought about both by rapid economic growth and social change in the 1960s. In addition, while many women activists joined the New Left movement and participated in student activism during this period, they were disappointed with the discriminatory treatment that they frequently received. Their disappointment, in turn, motivated these women to start a movement by and for women (Fujimura-Fanselow, 1995b; K. Tanaka, 1995a).

The second wave of feminism in Japan began in the early 1970s. It resulted from the failures in the women's movement in the 1960s, as well as the prevailing gender inequality and discrimination that women continued to experience in postwar "democratized" Japanese society

(Fujimura-Fanselow, 1995b; K. Tanaka, 1995a). The aim of the second wave of feminism was "to transform the entire cultural outlook from the standpoint of the oppressed segments of society through the consciousness-raising of women" (K. Tanaka, 1995a, p. 346). However, the feminist movement was viewed rather unfavorably, and was mostly ignored by the general public and the government alike (Fujieda, 1995). The male-dominated media was particularly harsh and critical of the feminist movement, treating it as no more than "a spree by some crazy young women" (Morley, 1999, p. 77).

In the mid–1970s, the feminist movement "changed its character from one that was targeted at bringing about changes in women's consciousness to one seeking visible changes in social institutions" (K. Tanaka, 1995a, p. 345). Furthermore, the feminist movement was legitimatized to some extent in 1975, which was designated as the United Nations International Year for Women. In November of that year, the Conference on Women's Problems for the International Year for Women was held in Tokyo under the sponsorship of the Japanese government. These developments that took place in the mid–1970s managed to attract media and public attention to a number of women's issues for the first time in Japanese history (Y. Sato, 1979; K. Tanaka, 1995a).

During the United Nations International Decade for Women (1976–1985), a number of women's centers were launched both at the national and local levels. In addition to offering resource materials and information for women, these multipurpose centers provide venues for various workshops, seminars, and training as well as meetings and activities of women's groups. For instance, the Kokuritsu Josei Kyoiku Kaikan (the National Women's Education Center) founded by the government has been holding an annual seminar on women's studies since 1980. Similarly, many centers established by local governments, including the Josei Sogo Senta (the General Center for Women) in Kanagawa located southwest of Tokyo, have continued to make significant contributions to promote the participation of women in society (Fujieda & Fujimura-Fanselow, 1995; Mackie, 2003).

Throughout the 1980s, a number of women's groups and associations were organized nationwide around diverse issues surrounding

5— Feminism in Japan

women, including domestic violence, sexism in the mass media, discriminatory treatment of women in the workplace, sexual harassment, and child care (K. Tanaka, 1995a). Since the mid–1980s more women have begun to make inroads into politics, and there has been a steady increase in the number of women candidates being elected to office at local as well as national levels. It is noteworthy that women in general have distanced themselves from the established male-dominated conservative parties such as the Liberal Democratic Party, and have associated themselves with small newly formed parties (Y. Sato, 1995; K. Tanaka, 1995a). The media declared that *onna no jidai*, the era of women, had dawned in 1990, when the Socialist Party led by its first female leader, Doi Takako, won a landslide victory in the national elections in the summer of 1989, ending the monopoly of the Liberal Democratic Party for over 30 years. Doi, a former law professor, was not only the first female leader of the Socialist Party in its over 40-year history, but also the very first female party leader in the history of Japanese politics.

Despite these advances, the number of women in Japanese politics remains rather small in comparison to other countries. According to The 2007 White Paper on Gender Equality issued by the Japanese government, the number of congresswomen in Japan was the second from the lowest among the 12 countries surveyed. While the percentage of congresswomen was the highest in Sweden (47.3 percent), followed by Norway (37.9 percent) and Germany (31.6 percent), Japan ranked 11th (9.4 percent) followed by Malaysia (8.9 percent). As for the percentage of women government officials, among the 10 countries where the relevant data was available, Japan ranked the lowest at 20 percent, compared to 9 other countries whose percentages ranged from 34 percent to 56 percent. Similarly, in regard to the number of high-ranking women officials, Japan ranked the lowest at 1.8 percent, while Singapore ranked the highest at 62 percent.

Although women are underrepresented in Japanese politics, they nevertheless have been making significant progress, particularly since the mid–1980s, as can be seen by the following statistics released by the Cabinet Office. In 2008, women accounted for 9.4 percent in the House of Representatives, a number that had increased nearly seven times from a mere 1.4 percent in 1986. Similarly, women accounted for 18.2 percent in the House of Councilors in 2008 — more than double the 8.7 percent in 1986. Women assembly members of 17 ordinance-designated major cities have also increased by over 50 percent from 11 percent in 1998 to 17.2 percent in 2007.

One of the significant developments in the 1990s was the adoption of the Policy toward Cooperative Participation of Men and Women (the Danjo Kyodo Sankaku Seisaku) by the Japanese government. In 1990, the Prime Minister's Office (the Cabinet Office since 2001) issued a report titled *Japanese Women Today*, which states, "Specifically, Japan must eliminate persistent, stereotyped concepts based on traditional sex roles, and provide a climate conducive to women's full participation in society" (K. Hara, 1995, p. 153).

Subsequently, the Law for Cooperative Participation of Men and Women in Society, also known as the Basic Law for a Gender-equal Society, passed in 1999. Its Article 3 reads in part that "the formation of a gender-equal society shall be promoted based on respect for the human rights of men and women, including: no gender-based discriminatory treatment of men or women, and the securing of opportunities for men and women to exercise their abilities as individuals" (Endo, 2004, p. 180). The stipulation of the adoption of a positive action policy for "the formation of a gender-equal society" and "no gender-based discriminatory treatment" by the Law was not only unprecedented in Japanese history, but was also considered a major landmark in the women's movement in Japan.

The passage of the Law resulted in the strengthening of the Council for Gender Equality (the Danjo Kyodo Sankaku Kaigi) as an advisory council for the Cabinet Office to promote policy on gender equality. Launched in 2001, the Council consists of 12 cabinet ministers as well as 12 experts including members of women's organizations, and is chaired by the Chief Cabinet Secretary. It is noteworthy that the term *danjo kyodo sankaku* (cooperative participation of men and women, gender equality) was used officially for the first time by the Japanese government in the 1990s (Gelb, 2003).

5—Feminism in Japan

Pending Issues and New Directions

The term *feminisuto* (feminist) has the following two definitions in the Japanese language: one refers to a chivalrous man who treats women with courtesy, as well as a man who has a soft spot for women; another refers to a person who advocates women's liberation as well as equal rights for women. The former, a chivalrous man, is the original definition for *feminisuto* in the Japanese language, and the latter, an equivalent to the English definition, has been a new addition since the 1970s, when the second wave of feminism began in Japan. Although the latter, an equivalent to "feminist" in English, has been steadily gaining public recognition in recent years, there remains some confusion about the term *feminisuto* among Japanese people, particularly those of the older generation. In fact, the vast majority of the Japanese language dictionaries continue to list two definitions for the term. In addition, the English terms such as *uuman ribu* (women's liberation) and *feminizumu* (feminism) started to make entry into Japanese language and society in the 1970s. For instance, the term, *uuman ribu* was one of the buzzwords of 1970 (Jiyukokuminsha, 2008). Similar to the term *feminisuto*, some dictionaries also list the following two definitions for *feminizumu*: one is an equivalent to "feminism" in English, and the other is "one's principle to have respect for women" (Kitahara & Taishukan, 2002–2008).

Since the 1990s, various publications on the Japanese women's movement have shown a marked tendency to trace the origins of the second wave of feminism in Japan to the Women's Liberation Movement in the United States (Buckley, 1997). In regard to this recent tendency, many Japanese feminists argue that the second wave of Japanese feminism had its distinct origins in Japan, and happened independently of the American Women's Liberation Movement that took place during the same period. They also point out that Japan's first exposure to American feminism in the late 1960s and 1970s was through the mass media focusing on such extreme incidents as bra-burning ceremonies and protests at beauty pageants. The male-dominated Japanese media not only negatively and pejoratively portrayed American feminists as eccentrics, but also set forth the constant criticism that the so-called *uuman ribu*

Part I: Representation of Women in Japanese Society

(women's liberation) movement in Japan was simply copying American feminism. As a result, Japanese feminists were concerned about their portrayals in the media, and were cautious not to identify themselves with their American counterparts (Aoki, 1997; K. Tanaka, 1995a).

This issue of identity is particular not only to Japanese feminists, but also to feminists in Asia. As Ueno (1997) asserts, the vast majority of Asian feminists are faced with the dilemma of "locating a female identity and a feminist movement in relation to questions of national and cultural identity" (p. 297). Ueno (1997) further explains that feminism in Asia is often considered and criticized as "a Western import"; therefore, Asian feminists are under constant pressure to separate themselves from their Western counterparts and define themselves independently in order to establish a distinctly indigenous feminist identity.

A number of comparative studies of Western and Japanese feminist models have also been conducted, the majority of which conclude that Western feminist models are not applicable to Japanese counterparts. For instance, Martinez (1987) claims that "the problem in Japan is not liberation in the Western sense, but reestablishing an identity outside the household which has value in a Japanese context" (p. 84).

There is no doubt that women have made considerable progress in Japanese society, particularly since the end of World War II. However, there remain a number of issues surrounding women that need to be resolved. The following are some of the major issues discussed earlier in Chapter 2: the 750th article of the current Civil Code requiring a married couple to choose the same surname, and the mandatory family registration system called *koseki seido* that supports the article. This mandatory family registration system, which played a vital role in the pre–World War II patriarchal *ie* system by recording detailed personal information for each family member, remains in present-day Japan, and has been criticized for the violation of privacy. In the following section, another major issue regarding single mother families is discussed.

A single mother family is called *boshi katei* (mother and child family) in the Japanese language. It has a negative and discriminatory undertone, which can also be seen in its English translation, "fatherless family," found in many Japanese-English dictionaries. Single mother families face a number of obstacles and discriminations socially as well as financially. For instance, the 2002 amendment in the Child-Care Allowance Law that took effect in 2008 adversely affected the finances of the majority of single mother families. The monthly child-care allowance for single mother families in 2008 varied from 9,850 yen ($98.50) to 41,720 yen ($417.20) per child depending on the household income. However, the amended law reduced the amount of the child-care allowance by 50 percent for households with annual incomes over 1.3 million yen ($13,000) that had received the allowance for over 5 consecutive years since a child became 3 years old. The survey conducted in 2006 by the Ministry of Health, Labor and Welfare on 1,500 single mother families nationwide reported that the average annual household income of single mother families in that year was 2.13 million yen ($21,300). It was 37.8 percent, slightly over one third of the average annual household income in Japan; nevertheless, the amended law does not exempt single mother families from the cut in child-care allowance if they meet the above-mentioned criteria. The Ministry of Health, Labor and Welfare estimated that this amendment would save over 10 billion yen ($100 million) in tax money ("Boshi Katei," 2007).

In another survey conducted in 2008 by Ashinaga Ikueikai, a private charitable organization, 83 percent of 1,000 single mothers who took part in the survey responded that the recession combined with the soaring consumer prices worsened their overall family finances. The average monthly income of these mothers was around 120,000 yen ($1,200) after taxes, a decrease by 10,600 yen ($106) compared to 2002. The survey also indicated that a mere 4 percent of single mother families were on welfare, while a much larger number of them were fully eligible for it. The survey ascribed this low percentage to the prevalent discrimination against single mother families. In fact, a number of single mothers reported the discriminatory treatment that they routinely received, including social workers' offensive, contemptuous, and hurtful remarks as well as the cold and condescending attitudes of the staff members of welfare agencies ("Bukka Daka," 2008).

Following the ratification of the United Nations Convention on the Elimination of All Forms of Discrimination against Women (CEDAW) in 1985, the Japanese government has begun to take more serious measures to eliminate discrimination against women (Kinjo, 1995). However, as briefly mentioned in Chapters 1 and 6, a number of blatantly insensitive and discriminatory remarks about women are frequently made by men who hold high-ranking and influential positions in the Japanese government and politics. The majority of these sexist remarks in recent years have been made in regard to the fertility of women because of the steady decline in the birth rate, which hit the record low of 1.26 per woman in 2005.

For instance, in 2007, in his speech at a local assembly, Yanagisawa Hakuo, the Minister of Health, Labor, and Welfare, referred to women between the ages 15 and 50 as "child-bearing machines (*kodomo o umu kikai*)" who had to make an earnest effort to reproduce ("Josei Wa," 2007). Yanagisawa's remark about women mirrors a similar one by Napoleon Bonaparte (1769–1821) who stated, "Women are nothing but machines for producing children" ("What Men," 2009). Similarly, earlier in the same year, Kan Naoto, the former Minister of Health and the acting leader of the Democratic Party of Japan, equated women's fertility with "productivity (*seisansei*)." Kan received counter criticism for this wording, when he criticized the remarks by his predecessor, Yanagisawa ("Seisansei Hatsugen," 2007). Earlier in 2003, former Prime Minister Mori Yoshiro commented that women who did not bear and raise children should not be entitled to receive pensions from the government, since social security ought to be acknowledged as a token of appreciation from the government to women who gave birth to children and raised them (Faiola, 2004).

Ishihara Shintaro, the Governor of Tokyo, who is known for his controversial remarks, made headlines with his notorious so-called *babaa hatsugen* (remarks on *babaa*, derogatory term for middle-aged and elderly women) in 2001. The following is the summary of his comment: "The worst and the most harmful creatures that civilization has brought about are *babaa* (derogatory term for middle-aged and elderly women). It is a waste and a sin for women without reproductive capability to live on. Men can reproduce even in their 80s and 90s, while women are not able to do so after menopause. And for these women to live long has an

5— Feminism in Japan

extremely harmful effect on the earth" (*Shukan Josei*, 2001). Although Ishihara insisted that he simply quoted Matsui Takafumi, a retired professor of geophysics at prestigious Tokyo University, Matsui denied ever making such a statement (*Shizen to Ningen*, 2003). The Japan Federation of Lawyers in its warning statement issued to Ishihara in 2003, also concluded that the derogatory comment was his own. Incidentally, Ishihara, who never apologized for his remark, was one of the adamant defenders of Yanagisawa, mentioned earlier, who called women "childbearing machines."

In 1985, Miura Shumon, the then head of the Agency for Cultural Affairs, made the following statement at the Education Committee meeting held during the 102nd session of the Diet, the national assembly in Japan: "While it is the most shameful for men to rape women, it is also shameful for men to be incapable of doing so." Later, Miura claimed that his statement was meant as a joke (Buckley, 1997). Furthermore, Sasagawa Takashi, the Secretary-General of the Liberal Democratic Party, is known for discriminatory comments he continues to make about women. In 2008, he stated that the US Government bailout plan was rejected because the speaker of the House of Representatives, Nancy Pelosi, was a woman ("Obuchi-shi Kodomo," 2008). Similarly, in the following year, Sasagawa concluded his congratulatory speech for a newly appointed woman mayor in the western part of Japan by commenting that women in politics were generally lacking in elegance and refinement ("Josei Giin," 2009). It should be noted that none of these men were forced to resign from their positions for their remarks, despite repeated protests by women's groups and feminist activists.

While a number of obstacles and challenges remain in Japanese society, women have continued to make steady progress in various spheres of life. This chapter concludes by presenting some of the significant accomplishments of Japanese women in recent years that also received much attention by the news media. In 2007, two women were appointed as new members of the Akutagawa literary award selection committee by the Japan Literature Organization. The Akutagawa literary award is one of the most prestigious awards given to up-and-coming authors, and is considered the gateway to literary circles in Japan. Its selection committee members were all male until 1987, when two women were appointed for the first time. The two newly appointed women are both highly-regarded best-selling authors, and recipients of numerous literary awards. With this latest addition, a total of four — nearly half of nine committee members — are women, which is the largest number ever in the history of the Akutagawa literary award ("Akutagawasho Senko," 2007).

In the field of science, two women have become astronauts since the 1990s. Mukai Chiaki, a medical doctor, was the first Japanese woman to be on board Space Shuttle Columbia in 1994, and Discovery in 1998. Yamazaki Naoko, an aeronautical engineer and mother of a young daughter, is expected to follow in Mukai's footsteps to be on board Atlantis in 2010. Moreover, in the field of medicine, traditionally dominated by men, two out of three obstetricians/gynecologists in their 20s, and one out of two pediatricians in their 20s are now women ("Josei Ishi," 2007).

The number of women has also continued to increase at a steady pace in the field of law. In 2008, women accounted for 17.2 percent of public prosecutors, 15.4 percent of judges, and 14.4 percent of attorneys. Since 1995, the increase is the largest among women public prosecutors whose numbers have more than tripled, while the numbers of women judges and attorneys have nearly doubled. These women are highly motivated, and continue to hold their positions after taking maternity and child-care leaves ("Josei Kenji," 2009). This is in clear contrast to the prevailing working pattern among Japanese women to leave the labor force for marriage, childbirth, and child care, which is explained in Chapter 4.

Women like these are true trailblazers who deserve recognition and respect. At the same time, the extensive media attention regarding women who defy traditions and gender stereotypes is a clear indication that the issue of gender inequality remains largely unresolved in Japanese society. The day when such women will no longer receive a great deal of attention by the media is much anticipated.

PART II
Representation of Women in the Japanese Language

6

Survey: Voices from Japanese Women

Vocabulary of a language is something like an index of the culture in which the language is used. The vocabulary that composes the structure of Japanese reflects the features of speech acts or mentality of the Japanese people, and the institution or the order of Japanese society [Haga, 1982, p. 83].

Method

Qualitative research is designed to understand various phenomena in their natural settings (Denzin and Lincoln, 1994). Being qualitative in nature, this research project aims to provide in-depth and detailed descriptions of Japanese women's perceptions of gender bias in language from a phenomenological perspective. Phenomenology seeks the perceptions of the individual as well as the meaning of a phenomenon or an experience in order to understand and describe an event from the participant's point of view. One of the distinctive features of phenomenology is placing subjective experience at the center of the inquiry (Mertens, 1998). As a phenomenologist with a similar background to the women who participated in this research project, I assume commonality with their experiences.

In order to closely examine the lived experiences of these women, this survey asked them to report their interpretations and perceptions of gender-related expressions in the Japanese language by responding to a questionnaire consisting of the following open-ended question presented in English translation:

> If there are any gender-related Japanese words or phrases that you find degrading to women, please list, and give explanation why you feel that way.

An open-ended question was chosen for the questionnaire because depth and detail of qualitative data are brought about by responses to open-ended questions. This, in turn, enables others to better understand the respondents' perceptions and interpretations of a phenomenon or an experience (Patton, 1980).

At the end of the questionnaire, participants were asked to provide demographic information on their age, education, and occupation. Anonymity and confidentiality were guaranteed to the participants in the cover letter attached to the questionnaire. Prior to distributing this questionnaire, the purpose of the survey was fully explained to the participants, and questions were answered in person as well as by e-mail. The questionnaire was then distributed to participants in person and by mail. The participants were asked to send their completed questionnaires back to me using the stamped and addressed envelopes provided.

The anonymous questionnaire was selected as a method of data collection by taking into consideration the way Japanese people express themselves. With a long tradition of living in close-knit and predominantly homogeneous communities, Japanese people have the inclination to value interpersonal harmony over self-assertion. For instance, *tatemae* (official stance and principles) is stated on occasions when expressing *honne* (candid opinions and honest feelings) is considered offensive or hurtful to others. Similarly, people tend to refrain from expressing their *honne* (candid opinions and honest feelings) that differ from others, and instead take *tatemae* (official stance and principles) to be in *wa* (harmony) with others (Lebra, 1976; Sugiura and Gillespie, 1993). The anonymous questionnaire was considered the most appropriate method of data collection for this project to obtain straightforward and candid responses from the participants, particularly those of the older generation who are more inclined to refrain from expressing their opinions in the presence of strangers.

Participants

In order to locate participants for this survey, I contacted six colleagues of mine residing in the Tokyo metropolitan area for cooperation.

6—Survey

My colleagues consisted of two instructors of Japanese and two instructors of English at private language schools, one college professor of Japanese literature, and one technical translator. After explaining the purpose of the survey to friends, acquaintances, students, and co-workers, my colleagues and I selected a total of 70 women who met the following criteria: (1) they are native speakers of Japanese, (2) they were born and raised in Japan, (3) they are of various age groups as well as educational and occupational backgrounds, (4) they have a keen interest in language. Table 1 presents in summary demographic information about the participants on their age, education, and occupation. A detailed list of the survey participants is provided in Appendix A.

Table 1. Demographic Information on the Survey Participants

Age Group	Number of Participants
20–29	12
30–39	12
40–49	12
50–59	12
60–69	11
70–79	11
Total	70

Highest Degree Earned	Number of Participants
High school diploma	12
AA/BA/BS	47
MA/MS/PhD	11
Total	70

Occupation Group	Number of Participants
Homemaker	18
Educator	15
Clerical worker	14
Professional	8
Retiree	7
Student	6
Housework helper	2
Total	70

As shown in Table 1, two women listed their occupation as "housework helper," which is the literal translation of the Japanese term *kaji tetsudai*. In Japan, *kaji tetsudai* refers to a single woman who, upon completion of her schooling, stays with her parents and family members until getting married. In addition to assisting them with household chores as *kaji tetsudai*, she takes lessons in cooking, flower arrangements, tea ceremony, calligraphy, and so forth in order to acquire various skills considered necessary and desirable for homemaking. In Japanese society, a woman who is *kaji tetsudai* is favorably viewed as a trainee bride who undergoes practical training called *hanayome shugyoo* (bridal training) to become a competent homemaker. Being *kaji tetsudai* is also associated with the affluent upper middle- to upper-class families who can afford such arrangements. In recent years, however, the number of *kaji tetsudai* is on the steady decrease, as more young single women are entering the labor force before getting married.

Results

The women who took part in the survey listed a total of 151 Japanese words and phrases that they found degrading to women along with explanations for their selections. The words and phrases listed by the women are grouped, based on their similarities, into the following seven categories shown in Table 2. The majority of these women also shared with me a number of thoughts, experiences, and concerns regarding gender-related expressions in the Japanese language, some of which are presented in Chapter 7.

Table 2. Distribution of Listed Words and Phrases by Category

Category	Total Number of Words and Phrases	Corresponding Percentage
Marriage	55	36%
Characterization	36	24%
Age	17	11%
Occupation	16	11%
Physical appearance	12	8%
Status	8	5%
Derogatory term	7	5%
Total	151	100%

6—Survey

Table 3 presents 45 frequently listed words and phrases with their English equivalents being placed in order of the total number of responses. Some of the English equivalents are quoted from the work by Cherry (1987). The following capitalized letters indicate the categories into which the words and phrases are grouped: M, marriage; C, characterization of women; A, age; O, occupation; P, physical appearance; S, status; and D, derogatory term. The entire list of words and phrases is provided in Appendix B.

Table 3. Words and Phrases Frequently
Listed by the Survey Participants

Total Number of Responses	Category	Japanese Words/Phrases (English Equivalent)
36	C	*onna no kuse ni* (after all she is a woman, though she is a woman)
28	M	*yome* (daughter-in-law, bride)
26	C	*memeshii* (like a woman, unmanly and effeminate man)
24	C	*onna datera ni* (unlike a woman, inappropriate for a woman)
22	C	some *kanji* (ideographic characters) composed of *onna hen* (the "female" radical)
22	P	*busu* (ugly woman)
21	C	*onna no kusatta yoona* (like a rotten woman, indecisive and cowardly man)
20	M	*oku-san* (Mrs. Interior, address term for married women) (Cherry, 1987)
20	M	*umazume* (stone woman, no-life woman, infertile woman)
20	C	*onna rashii* (feminine, womanly)
19	D	(*kuso*) *babaa* (derogatory term for elderly women)
18	O	*onna no ko* (girl)
17	M	*mekake* (mistress)
17	M	*shuutome* (mother-in-law)
16	M	*oorudo misu* (old miss, old maid)
16	M	*demodori* (returnee to one's parents' place, divorced woman)
16	M	*ikazu goke* (widow without marrying, single woman in her 30s)
16	O	*otsubone* (*-sama*) (elderly court woman, middle-aged female office worker)
15	M	*ikiokure* (late to marry, single woman in her 30s)
15	M	*yome o morau* (to receive a daughter-in-law/bride)

Part II: Representation of Women in the Japanese Language

Total Number of Responses	Category	Japanese Words/Phrases (English Equivalent)
15	M	*kanai* (house-insider, one's wife) (Cherry, 1987)
15	M	*gusai* (stupid wife, one's wife)
15	M	*shufu* (main woman, homemaker)
15	C	*Dakara onna wa dameda.* (That is why women are no good.)
15	A	*oba-san* (aunt, address term for middle-aged women)
14	S	*danson johi* (men superior, women inferior)
14	S	*onna kodomo* (women and children)
14	S	*Onna sangai ni ie nashi.* (Women have no home in the three realms of existence: the past, the present, and the future.)
14	C	*otoko masari* (superior to men, strong-minded and assertive woman)
14	C	*kawaii onna* (cute woman)
14	M	*urenokori* (unsold merchandise, single woman in her 30s)
14	O	*josei, fujin, joryuu, onna* (female, woman)
14	D	*ama* (derogatory term for women)
13	M	*yome ni iku* (to go as a daughter-in-law/bride, to marry into a husband's family)
13	M	*naijo no koo* (success from inside help, husband's success owing to the support and sacrifices of his wife) (Cherry, 1987)
13	M	*miboojin* (person who is not yet dead, widow)
13	M	*goke* (after family, widow) (Cherry, 1987)
13	M	*kyooiku mama* (education-conscious mother)
13	A	*obaa-chan* (granny, address term for elderly women)
13	A	*toshima* (years added, middle-aged woman) (Cherry, 1987)
13	A	*(o)nee-chan* (elder sister, address term for young women)
13	C	*shitoyaka* (modest, graceful, gentle)
13	P	*bijin* (beautiful person, beautiful woman)
13	S	*nyonin kinsei* (no females allowed)
12	C	*Onna san nin yoreba kashimashii.* (When three women get together, they make too much noise.)

In the subsequent section, I discuss representative words and phrases listed by the survey participants under the seven categories shown in Table 2. Quotations from the survey participants are also presented in English translation.

Marriage

Well over one third of all the words and phrases listed by the survey participants belong to the marriage category. Based on the similarities, these words and phrases are divided into the following three groups: various terms used for married women, fertility, and marital status.

Various Terms for Married Women

yome (daughter-in-law, bride)

Yome is the most frequently listed word in the marriage category. A number of expressions containing the word *yome* are also listed. The following are some of the frequently listed phrases: *yome ni iku* (to go as a daughter-in-law/bride, to marry into husband's family); *yome o morau* (to receive a daughter-in-law/bride); and *yome ni yaru* (to give a daughter as a bride, to marry off a daughter), which is often paraphrased as *katazukeru* (to get rid of, to dispose of, to marry off a daughter).

The etymology of *yome* dates back to the 12th century. There was a custom of matrilocal residence called *tsumadoikon* or *kayoikon* in Japan throughout the 10th century. A married couple maintained separate residences, and a husband made visits to his wife. By the Kamakura period (1185–1333) when the samurai class seized power and the notion of *danson johi* (men superior, women inferior) had developed, a custom of patrilocal residence called *yomeirikon* became prevalent. A woman married into her husband's family and assumed the lowest position of *yome* (daughter-in-law, bride) in his family to serve her husband and in-laws. This custom contributed to the establishment of the patriarchal *ie* (family, household) system in pre–World War II Japan. While the *ie* system was officially abolished shortly after the war, the custom of *yomeirikon* (patrilocal residence) has continued on to this day (Obayashi, 2005; Yoshizumi, 1995).

- I feel that the patriarchal family system is still very intact in present-day Japan: once a woman is married into her husband's

family, she becomes *yome* (daughter-in-law, bride), the most vulnerable member in his family (55-year-old office worker).
- Phrases like *yome o morau* (to receive a daughter-in-law/bride) and *yome ni yaru* (to give a daughter as a bride, to marry off a daughter) dehumanize women by treating them as commodities that are passed on from one family to another (48-year-old part-time English instructor).
- I find it troubling whenever I hear my friends nonchalantly use such expressions as *katazukeru* (to get rid of, to dispose of, to marry off a daughter) when their daughters are getting married, and *yome o morau* (to receive a daughter-in-law/bride) when their sons are getting married. We need to be more conscientious about making the right choice of words (45-year-old part-time interpreter).

shuutome (mother-in-law)

In patrilocal residence, the *shuutome* (mother-in-law) played a major role in passing family customs and traditions on to the *yome* (daughter-in-law, bride), who married into her husband's family. It was customary that the *yome* remained as an apprentice until the *shuutome* stepped down by transferring to the *yome* the position of *shufu* (main woman, homemaker) in the family. This transition was done by a ritual called *shakushi watashi*, in which the *shuutome* handed a rice-serving spatula called *shakushi* to the *yome*. In Japan, where rice is a staple diet, *shakushi* (rice-serving spatula) symbolizes the household work as well as the position of *shufu* in the family (Cherry, 1987).

In prewar patriarchal Japanese households where three generations customarily lived together, the *shuutome* exercised her authority and power over the *yome*, who was expected to serve and obey her husband as well as her in-laws. It was considered one of the many duties of the *yome* to endure frequent harsh treatment by the *shuutome* called *yome ibiri* (tormenting daughter-in-law, bride). With the abolishment of the patriarchal family system shortly after World War II, the *shuutome* is no longer an authoritarian figure in the household in most cases; nevertheless, the conflict between the *yome* and the *shuutome*, as well as the clash between the *yome* and the *kojuutome* (little mother-in-law, sister-in-law), has traditionally been one of the major causes of family dispute in Japan, where it is still relatively common for three generations to live together.

- My son is getting married, and I dread being called *shuutome* because it evokes a negative image of a mean old woman just like my own *shuutome* who mistreats *yome* (56-year-old office worker).
- I am single, and my sister-in-law is 3 years younger than I am. I cannot stand being called as her *kojuutome* (little mother-in-law, sister-in-law), which is written in *kanji* (ideographic characters) as "little old woman." How upsetting! (30-year-old graduate student).

oku-san/oku-sama (Mrs. Interior, address term for married women) (Cherry, 1987)

Oku-san (Mrs. Interior) (Cherry, 1987) and its more polite and formal term, *oku-sama* (Mrs. Interior) (Cherry, 1987), are used to address other men's wives both directly and indirectly. *Oku* means the recesses as well as the back of the house where a small family room is located, in contrast to *omote* meaning the front of the house where a spacious room to entertain guests is located.

The origin of the term *oku-san*, referring to a married woman, dates back to the Kamakura period (1185–1333) when the feudal system was established. Furthermore, the notion of *danson johi* (men superior, women inferior) had developed and prevailed, particularly in the privileged ruling samurai class. This notion to hold women in subjugation to men was based on Buddhist and Shinto beliefs, which associated women with impurity and sinfulness (Minamoto, 2005; Okano, 1995). While the term *oku-sama* was initially used exclusively for married women of privileged samurai families who had little autonomy, by the Meiji period (1868–1912) married women of all prominent families were addressed as such (Cherry, 1987).

Industrialization and the emergence of *sarariiman* (salary men, male office workers) in the Taisho period (1912–1926) promoted gender-based role division, which is aptly described by the phrase *otoko wa shigoto, onna wa katei* (men at work, women at home) (Rosenberger, 2001). It was also during this period when the term *oku-sama* lost its exclusiveness, and was used to connote any leisure-class married women. At the same time, the use of the more informal term *oku-san* became prevalent (Cherry, 1987). In present-day Japan, *oku-san* is the most commonly used term for addressing married women.

- I find it very depressing not only to be called *oku-san*, but also to call other married women as such. There should be much more respectful terms in the Japanese language to address married women, many of whom are very competent and successful in juggling numerous responsibilities both at home and at work (59-year-old homemaker).
- Although *oku-san* is the most commonly used address term for married women, I personally do not like its connotation that married women are supposed to stay in the background behind their husbands, and keep a low profile at all times (41-year-old office worker).
- The address term *oku-san* symbolizes the prevailing gender-specific role division in Japanese society, that is, a wife should stay home while a husband is at work. As a working woman, I much prefer gender-neutral terms like "spouse" in English (48-year-old graphic designer).

kanai (house-insider, one's wife)
(Cherry, 1987)

While *oku-san* is used to address other men's wives, *kanai* is used by Japanese men to refer to their own wives. *Ka* means house or home, and *nai* means inside as well as wife. Besides being used as an address term for married women, *kanai* is used in several compounds concerning family and household affairs such as *kanai anzen* (safety and well-being of one's family), *kanai koogyoo* (cottage industry), and *kanai roodoo* (subcontract work at home).

- Similar to the address term *oku-san*, *kanai* literally designates home as the place where married women should belong, and prevents them from developing their full potential in other spheres of life. What is more, there is no term to designate place for married men (70-year-old professor).
- I very much enjoy being a stay-at-home mother, and consider myself a quite competent *sengyoo shufu* (full-time professional homemaker). But I do not appreciate my husband referring to me as *kanai* to other people, because it makes me feel that I am less of a person than my husband (47-year-old homemaker).
- *Kanai* represents the longstanding notion in the Japanese society, "*otoko wa shigoto, onna wa katei* (men at work, women at home)," that a wife should stay home taking care of household chores as well as her children, and support her husband who works outside. With so many married women in the work force these days, *kanai* does sound outdated (38-year-old college lecturer).

nyooboo (court woman, one's wife)

In addition to *kanai*, *nyooboo* is used mostly among middle-aged to elderly Japanese men to informally refer to their wives. The origin of the term *nyooboo* dates back to the Heian period (794–1185), when it referred to high-ranking court women as well as their private living quarters. It was during the Kamakura period (1185–1333) when *nyooboo* was used by a samurai to refer to his wife, and its usage continues to this day (*Kojien*, 2008).

Nyooboo is also used in several compounds such as *furu nyooboo* (old wife) for a wife of many years, *anesan nyooboo* (big sister wife) for a wife who is older than a husband, and *oshikake nyooboo* (intruder wife) (Cherry, 1987) for an assertive woman who moves in with her boyfriend without his consent, and eventually becomes his wife. It should be noted that the equivalent term of right-hand man in the Japanese language is *nyooboo yaku* (one who plays wifely roles).

- I do not like to be called as *anesan nyooboo* not only because *nyooboo* sounds archaic, but also because it is nobody's business

if I am a few years older than my husband. An expression like this reflects the fact that Japanese people are very age-conscious, which I do not think is a good thing (50-year-old homemaker).
- My heart sinks every time when I overhear my husband of over 50 years referring me as *furu nyooboo* to his friends. How I wish there were a reciprocal term for an old husband so that he would know how I feel (77-year-old homemaker).
- *Anesan nyooboo* and *oshikake nyooboo* are the manifestations of age-old societal expectations as well as norms that a wife should be younger and less assertive than a husband (36-year-old graduate student).

gusai (stupid wife, one's wife)

In Japanese culture, speaking humbly about oneself and one's family members is one way to show deference to others. As a result, Japanese men of the older generation often use the humble term for their spouses, *gusai* and the humble term for their sons, *gusoku* (stupid son, one's son) when they talk about their wives and sons in formal situations. Incidentally, there is no humble term for one's daughter.

- It is very unpleasant to hear elderly men calling their wives *gusai* as an expression of humble-politeness to others. I believe that the virtue of modesty, which is highly praised in Japanese society, does more harm than good in many cases (43-year-old homemaker).
- To my dismay, my husband always calls me as *gusai* in front of other people. Whenever I tell my husband that I do not appreciate being called stupid, he dismisses my comment as an overreaction, because he is simply following the social protocol (75-year-old homemaker).

akusai (bad wife)

Compared to *gusai*, which is typically used as a humble-polite expression, *akusai* is used to criticize a married woman whose demeanor and behavior are considered not good enough for her husband. There are several expressions on *akusai*, out of which the most commonly used is "*Akusai wa isshoo no fusaku* (A bad wife ruins her husband's entire life)."

- My friends and I often complain about our husbands when they misbehave, but unfortunately, there is no reciprocal term of *akusai* that we can use for bad husband (71-year-old homemaker).
- I wonder why there is no corresponding expression of "*Akusai wa isshoo no fusaku* (A bad wife ruins her husband's entire life)." Isn't it true that wives are more often affected by their husbands' misconduct than the other way round? (72-year-old homemaker).

ryoosai (good wife), *naijo no koo* (success from inside help, husband's success owing to the support and sacrifices of his wife) (Cherry, 1987)

The opposite of *akusai* is *ryoosai*, as in the notion of *ryoosai kenbo* (good wives and wise mothers), which represented the ideal womanhood in the pre–World War II patriarchal Japanese society. Although not a term referring to a married woman, *naijo no koo* is commonly used to praise the support and sacrifices of a wife who helps her husband to succeed in life.

- Many expressions in the Japanese language are based on a male perspective. For instance, *ryoosai* unfairly judges a married woman on a male standard. The fact that there is no male equivalent to *ryoosai* speaks volumes about the traditional relationship between wife and husband in Japanese society (40-year-old homemaker).
- The phrase, *naijo no koo* (success from inside help, husband's success owing to the support and sacrifices of his wife) (Cherry, 1987) is commonly used in speeches at wedding receptions to emphasize the importance of wife's contribution to husband's success; however, I believe that a wife and a husband should help and support each other as equal partners (75-year-old homemaker).

Part II: Representation of Women in the Japanese Language

shufu (main woman, homemaker)

Homemakers in Japan are called *shufu* (main women). While those who devote themselves full-time to housework are called *sengyoo shufu* (full-time professional homemakers), those who juggle housework with either part-time or full-time employment are called *kengyoo shufu* (part-time adjunct homemakers). As described by these terms and other expressions such as *shufugyoo* (homemaker by trade) and *shufugyoo ni sennen suru* (to dedicate oneself to full-time homemaking), homemaking is regarded in Japan as a profession that consists of many responsibilities including housework, child-rearing, management of family finances, and care of elderly family members.

- *Shufu* symbolizes a societal expectation that it is a woman, not a man, who should take care of all the household chores and be responsible for the well-being of the entire family members (38-year-old homemaker).
- What the word *kengyoo shufu* connotes is that married working women like myself are not as capable and committed as *sengyoo shufu* in taking care of housework and child-rearing (30-year-old office worker).
- Despite the fact that full-time homemakers have a number of responsibilities such as household work, child-rearing and care for elderly parents and parents-in-law, the term, *sengyoo shufu* is often used to represent a misleading notion that full-time homemakers lead an easy life by staying home (46-year-old office worker).

kyooiku mama (education-conscious mother)

In Japan, mothers are primarily responsible for the education of their children due to the absence of fathers who often spend long hours at work. Although pejoratively called *kyooiku mama*, many mothers are committed to providing an optimal learning environment for their children to succeed in the society, where education and academic credentials are highly valued. Keeping track of their children's schoolwork, finding them qualified private tutors and appropriate preparatory schools as well as staying up late to serve them nutritious midnight snacks, are among the things *kyooiku mama* are willing to do for the academic achievements of their children.

- I make serious efforts to provide many opportunities for my children so that they will fully develop their potentials. It is hurtful whenever my in-laws and friends tease me about being a dedicated *kyooiku mama*. As a working mother, it is daunting and stressful to be solely responsible for the education of my children. It would be so nice and helpful if I could sometimes share some responsibilities with my husband who acts as "*kyooiku papa* (education-conscious father)" (32-year-old nurse).

Fertility

Kashite sannen konaki wa saru (A wife should leave her husband if she fails to bear a child within 3 years of marriage), *umazume* (stone woman, no-life woman, infertile woman)

Umazume (stone woman, no-life woman, infertile woman), referring to an infertile woman, and the phrase, "*Kashite sannen konaki wa saru* (A wife should leave her husband if she fails to bear a child within 3 years of marriage)," are infamous expressions which denote that women are responsible for infertility. These expressions became widely used from the late 12th to the late 19th centuries, when it was considered one of the most important roles of married women to maintain lineage by giving birth to children, particularly to boys who would become heirs to the family estate (Kaneko, 1995). Although these expressions are mostly outdated, there remains a persistent tendency, particularly among the older generation, to associate women with infertility. It is noteworthy that there are no expressions in the Japanese language to denote that men are responsible for infertility.

- As a woman who has been struggling to conceive, I cannot possibly think of any more dehumanizing expression for an

infertile woman than *umazume*. It is a huge relief that such a demeaning word has become mostly archaic (30-year-old homemaker).
- *Umazume* represents a lingering belief that childless women are not complete and fulfilled. What is worse, it wrongly places all the blame for infertility on women (62-year-old part-time sales clerk).
- I am so glad that both "*Kashite sannen konaki wa saru*" and *umazume* are now obsolete; however, women rather than men, are still often considered to be responsible for infertility (71-year-old homemaker).

onna bara, otoko bara (female womb, male womb, woman who gives birth only to girls, or only to boys)

A woman who gives birth only to girls or only to boys is pejoratively called *onna bara* (female womb), or *otoko bara* (male womb). The word *bara* is derived from *hara* which is a vulgar term for womb. There is a Japanese phrase called *ichi hime ni taroo* (first, a girl, next, a boy) that indicates an ideal birth order of children. A woman who has *onna bara* (female womb) or *otoko bara* (male womb), therefore, is often considered not as blessed as those who give birth to both girls and boys (Cherry, 1987).

- I find it outrageous that the *onna bara, otoko bara* mentality is prevalent in contemporary Japanese society. It devalues the contributions of women in childbearing by treating them like chickens laying eggs (57-year-old college lecturer).
- Expressions like *onna bara, otoko bara* not only convey absolutely no regard for women, but also literally reduce the status of women to child-bearing machines. No wonder the birth rate in Japan has been on a steady decrease (53-year-old speech therapist).

Marital Status

urenokori **(unsold merchandise, single woman in her 30s), *ikiokure* (late to marry, single woman in her 30s), *ikazu goke* (unmarried widow, single woman in her 30s), *oorudo misu* (old miss, old maid), *hai misu* (high miss, single woman in her 30s)**

In Japanese society, there is a prevailing notion of *tekireiki* (the period of marriageable age) ranging from mid- to late 20s for women, and late 20s to early 30s for men. Although the number of women who get married later has been steadily increasing in recent years, women rather than men are under frequent pressure from society, family, and peer groups to marry during *tekireiki*, before they become "too old" to find prospective partners. It should be noted that the Japanese language has many pejorative expressions for women who are single after *tekireiki*, while there are no reciprocal terms for their male counterparts.

- Expressions like *ikiokure* (late to marry, single woman in her 30s) and *ikazu goke* (unmarried widow, single woman in her 30s) are based on social expectations that women should get married before a certain age, and put great pressure on single women to marry before "it is too late" (20-year-old housework helper).
- The fact that there is no corresponding term of *urenokori* (unsold merchandise, single woman in her 30s) for men represents a widespread idea among Japanese people that single women ought to make themselves "available on the marriage market," and wait until selected by men (42-year-old nursery school teacher).

demodori **(returnee to one's parents' place, divorced woman)**

The term referring to a divorced woman, *demodori*, is derived from the verb, *demodoru* (to go back to one's parents' home, to divorce). Both of these expressions originate from the custom of patrilocal residence called *yomeirikon*, which became prevalent by the Kamakura period (1185–1333). During this period the notion of *danson johi* (men superior, women inferior) had developed, particularly among the privileged ruling samurai class where women's roles were mostly limited to producing male heirs (Kaneko, 1995). In the custom of *yomeirikon* (patrilocal residence), a woman married into her husband's family, and assumed the lowest position of *yome* (daughter-in-law, bride) in the family to serve her husband and in-laws (Obayashi, 2005). This custom has continued on to this day despite the fact that gender equality is guaranteed by the Constitution of Japan, having been proclaimed shortly after World War II.

The divorce rate in Japan was extremely low before the 1980s, when irreconcilable differences were not legally allowed as a reason for getting a divorce. Compared to men, women were far more adversely affected by divorce financially as well as socially, and they often had no option but to live with their parents. As the divorce rate has continued to increase since the 1980s, there is less social stigma attached to those who are divorced. However, women, particularly those with children, continue to experience financial difficulties after divorce, and some consider living with their parents a practical option to weather the hardship.

- There is no derogatory expression like *demodori* for a divorced man, which shows that traditionally there is far more stigma attached to divorced women than men in Japanese society (60-year-old homemaker).
- As a working single mother and a survivor of a divorce, I do not agree with the connotation of the word *demodori*— that divorced women are helpless with nowhere to go but back to their parents' home (35-year-old office worker).

miboojin (person who is not yet dead, widow), *goke* (after family, widow) (Cherry, 1987)

Miboojin (person who is not yet dead, widow) and *goke* (after family, widow) are the two most common terms for a widow. It is often pointed out that the term *miboojin* is based on a concept similar to that of the ancient custom in India called *sati*, in which a widow immolates herself on a husband's funeral pyre (Endo, 1995). *Miboojin* is a formal term as in *sensoo miboojin* (war widow), and is commonly used by the general public as well as by widows themselves.

Goke is a very informal term implying that a widow's family passes away with her husband (Cherry, 1987). Unlike *miboojin*, *goke* is not used by widows, nor can it be used in the presence of a widow because of its pejorative undertone.

- *Miboojin* is literally based on the primitive idea that a wife should follow her husband to the grave. It is unfortunate that widows have no choice but to continue to use this demeaning word (68-year-old professor emeritus).
- I think that the reason why there are far more terms referring to widows, such as *miboojin* and *goke*, than to widowers is because women are more often discouraged from remarrying than men (78-year-old retired office worker).

mekake (mistress)

Both *mekake* and *nigoo* (number two, mistress) as well as their more polite forms, *omekake-san* (mistress) and *nigoo-san* (number two, mistress) are used for a mistress in contrast to the terms for a lawful wife, *honsai* (true wife, lawful wife) and *seisai* (official wife, lawful wife). In addition, there are further contemptuous terms for a mistress such as *hikagemono* (person in the shadow, mistress) and *hikage no onna* (woman in the shadow, mistress). In recent years, however, the vast majority of these contemptuous terms are used exclusively among those of the older generation.

Until the late 19th century, it was legally acceptable for a husband to have one or more mistresses in order to maintain lineage, as well as to show off his wealth and masculinity. Although an illegitimate child was scornfully called *mekake bara* (mistress's womb, illegitimate child), an illegitimate son who was acknowledged by a husband had priority over legitimate daughters to inherit the family estate (Kaneko, 1995). Monogamy was adopted by the Civil Code of 1898; however, as symbolized by the phrase "*Uwaki wa otoko no kaishoo* (Affairs are proof of manliness)," the sentiment to justify a husband's extramarital affairs remains in present-day Japan.

As the number of married women and men who commit adultery has been rising since the 1980s (Yamada, 2008), various terms for a mistress have been replaced by the unisex term *aijin* (lover), particularly among those of the younger generation. Compared to belittling expressions that were used in the past for a mistress, the term *aijin*, referring to a mistress as well as a male lover, conveys much less negativity.

- I find it offensive that terms like *mekake* and *nigoo* continue to exist in the Japanese language, because it shows public acceptance of a husband's sexual relations with women other than his wife (56-year-old homemaker).
- While *mekake* and *nigoo* are used contemptuously against women, I feel that men who have *mekake* and *nigoo* are the despicable ones (72-year-old retired editor).

Characterization

Nearly a quarter of all the words and phrases listed by the survey participants are in regard to the characterization of women. Furthermore, 6 out of the 10 most frequently listed of all words and phrases belong to the characterization of women category. While almost all of the words and phrases in this category are used regarding the demeanor and character traits of women, a few expressions are used to criticize men whose demeanor and personality traits are considered "feminine."

onna no kuse ni (after all she is a woman, though she is a woman, in spite of being a woman)

The phrase, *onna no kuse ni* is by far the most frequently listed, not only in the characterization category, but also among all the words and phrases that are considered degrading to women by the survey participants. *Onna no kuse ni* is commonly used to criticize a woman who challenges or achieves what is traditionally reserved for men. It is also used to criticize the demeanor of a woman who defies the gender-based stereotypes. Many feminist scholars argue that *onna no kuse ni* connotes the violation of the acceptable range of behavior for women in Japanese society (Ide, 1997; Reynolds, 1990). Furthermore, it should be noted that there is a fundamental connotative difference between *onna no kuse ni* and its corresponding expression for men, *otoko no kuse ni* (after all he is a man, though he is a man). While *onna no kuse ni* connotes the breach of the socially acceptable range of demeanor as well as behavior for women, *otoko no kuse ni* is used simply to criticize the cowardice or weakness of a man, rather than his behavior being outside of what is considered acceptable for men (Ide, 1997).

- *Onna no kuse ni* overstates so-called disadvantages of being a woman, and restricts women's freedom of activities by designating certain fields off limits to them (37-year-old part-time public employee).
- Since I consider myself as hardworking as men, it is hurtful and offensive when some of my male clients and business partners say *onna no kuse ni* straight to my face (51-year-old office worker).
- It is a shame that the majority of men who suffer from superiority complexes treat women with the *onna no kuse ni* mentality, and undermine the achievements as well as potential of women (66-year-old part-time English instructor).

onna datera ni (unlike a woman, inappropriate for a woman)

Similar to *onna no kuse ni* in its connotation as well as its negative undertone, *onna datera ni* is also frequently listed among all the words and phrases. *Onna datera ni* is used to criticize the particular behavior of a woman which does not stay within the "femininity" code and parameters laid down by society. While *onna no kuse ni* is not generally used by women, *onna datera ni* is occasionally used by women of the older generation to criticize the demeanor and behavior of younger women.

Part II: Representation of Women in the Japanese Language

- I do not appreciate being frequently criticized by my relatives who use the expression *onna datera ni*. I feel that my individuality is ignored and denied by "femininity" that is considered socially and culturally desirable (35-year-old office worker).
- It is disheartening that *onna datera ni* is used by men as well as women to criticize independent, enterprising, and strong-minded women whom I admire (42-year-old translator).
- An expression like *onna datera ni* limits the potential of women by criticizing those who do not fit the stereotypical personality traits that are considered "feminine" in Japanese culture and society (52-year-old part-time high school teacher).

Dakara onna wa dameda. (That is why women are no good/useless.)

As with many other expressions, there is no expression for men corresponding to the phrase "*Dakara onna wa dameda*," which has a blatantly negative tone toward women.

- *Dakara onna wa dameda* is based on the assumption that women are inherently inferior to men. It is used to criticize women despite the fact that incompetence is not gender-specific (24-year-old college student).
- *Dakara onna wa dameda* is what male supervisors and colleagues in my workplace unanimously say whenever they are not pleased with the performance of female workers (26-year-old part-time office worker).

memeshii (like a woman, unmanly, effeminate man)

Unlike the majority of the words and phrases listed, *memeshii* is used exclusively for men whose personality traits as well as behavior are considered "feminine." *Memeshii* consists of two *kanji* (ideographic characters) representing woman, and is used to criticize men for being cowardly and unmanly. It is noteworthy that its reciprocal term, *ooshii* (like a man, manly) comprised of two *kanji* representing male, is used to praise men for being brave and manly.

- An expression like *memeshii* is based on prevailing gender-based stereotypes that women are weak, cowardly, small-minded, indecisive, and, therefore, inferior to men (68-year-old retired office worker).
- I do not understand why sensitive and caring men with so-called "feminine" personality traits are criticized as being *memeshii*. Personality traits are not gender-specific, and should not be treated as such (26-year-old office worker).
- *Memeshii* is the manifestation of unfounded negativity associated with women. It has been deeply ingrained in Japanese society since the late Heian period (794–1185), when women became subjugated to men (58-year-old assistant professor).

onna no kusatta yoona (like a rotten woman, indecisive and cowardly man)

Similar to *memeshii*, *onna no kusatta yoona* is used to criticize an indecisive and cowardly man. Despite their sexist undertones, both *memeshii* and *onna no kusatta yoona* are used not only by men, but also by some women to criticize the demeanor of men.

- *Onna no kusatta yoona* is an extremely insulting phrase for both women and men. Calling a man rotten has more than enough impact. I wonder why it has to make reference to *onna* (woman) (52-year-old part-time English instructor).
- Whenever I hear the expression *onna no kusatta yoona*, I simply wonder why women, not men, are considered rotten. My heart sinks every time I hear some women carelessly use this "rotten" phrase to criticize their sons, boyfriends, and husbands (61-year-old part-time office worker).
- Both *memeshii* and *onna no kusatta yoona* use woman as a point of reference to criticize what are considered socially negative traits of men (31-year-old junior high school teacher).

Part II: Representation of Women in the Japanese Language

onna rashii (feminine, womanly)

Unlike all the words and phrases listed, *onna rashii* has no overtly negative connotation; nevertheless, it is among those frequently listed. Japanese dictionaries in general define *onna rashii* as being gentle, delicate, emotional, submissive, and kind. Moreover, *onna rashii* is used in various contexts such as *onna rashii shigusa* (feminine behavior) and *onna rashii heaa stairu* (feminine hairstyle). In regards to *onna rashii hanashi kata* (feminine way of speaking), a female speaker of Japanese often has to adopt a nonassertive, indirect, polite, and deferential speech pattern that is considered appropriate for women (Reynolds, 1990).

- I feel that the definition of *onna rashii* is mostly based on the traits of young women, and does not include those of mature women such as the inner strength of motherhood (62-year-old homemaker).
- *Onna rashii* represents the stereotypical image of docile, quiet, passive, and submissive women, whom Japanese men of all ages appear to find desirable as well as ideal (76-year-old retired high school teacher).

shitoyaka (modest, graceful, gentle)

Similar to *onna rashii*, *shitoyaka* is listed although it does not have overtly negative connotations. *Shitoyaka* is the word that is most frequently used to describe what is *onna rashii*.

- My parents and relatives often tell me to be *shitoyaka* on the occasions when docility and passivity are required of women in the presence of men. Of course, I do not listen to them (29-year-old interpreter).
- While some women take it as a compliment to be called *shitoyaka*, I feel otherwise. What the word *shitoyaka* reminds me of is submissiveness and passivity, the personality traits that are very alien to me (32-year-old nurse).

kawaii onna (cute woman)

The adjective, *kawaii* (cute) can be used for both inanimate and animate objects. When used for inanimate objects, *kawaii* connotes being small, delicate, and pretty as in *kawaii fuku* (cute clothes) and *kawaii hana* (small and pretty flowers). When used for animate objects, *kawaii* connotes being pretty, loveable, and favorable as in *kawaii kodomo* (cute children) and *kawaii onna* (cute woman), whose vulnerability makes others protective of them. A number of surveys indicate that *kawaii* is what Japanese men, regardless of age, often look for in an ideal woman (Jiyukokuminsha, 2008).

- Personally, I am not interested in men who are looking for *kawaii onna*. It is unfortunate that so many men as well as some women feel that the greatest asset to women is cuteness, rather than other qualities such as inner strength and maturity, which I highly value (21-year-old college student).
- An expression like *kawaii onna* indicates that women are commonly judged by their physical appearances and demureness. Sadly, women who have other important qualities such as assertiveness and self-determination that are considered "masculine," are often criticized for not being "cute" (60-year-old junior high school teacher).

otoko nami (being on the level of men)

When a woman works hard to accomplish what is traditionally reserved for men, she is often ridiculed as being *okoto nami*, which implies that she has accomplished something at the cost of her femininity.

- Based on the age-old notion of *danson johi* (men superior, women inferior), *otoko nami* judges women's accomplishments by the male-as-the-norm perspective. As a hardworking woman, I find such male-oriented mentality very insulting (41-year-old part-time translator).

Part II: Representation of Women in the Japanese Language

otoko masari (superior to men, strong-minded and assertive woman)

Otoko masari has pejorative undertones similar to that of *otoko nami* (being on the level of men). *Otoko masari* refers to a woman who is strong-minded and assertive, and who excels over men intellectually as well as physically. Women in general prefer not to be called *otoko masari*, since it implies lack of femininity. The term, *otoko kaomake* (male loss of face) (Cherry, 1987) is also used in this context to ridicule a woman who surpasses men in her achievements.

- Expressions like *otoko masari* and *okoto nami* represent a prevailing attitude in society to consider strong-willed and self-assured women as not womanly, with which I totally disagree (46-year-old administrative assistant).
- I am often called *otoko masari*, and I do not appreciate its implication. It is only fair that women who are hardworking and capable be praised for their accomplishments like their male counterparts, rather than being criticized and ridiculed as not being "feminine" (27-year-old office worker).

otoko onna (mannish woman)

Despite its similarity to *okoto masari* in meaning, *otoko onna* has far more negative connotations, and is used to ridicule and belittle women who are mentally as well as physically strong.

- It is regrettable that many men, perhaps out of their own insecurities, use such a contemptuous word as *otoko onna* to equate feistiness and self-confidence of women with unattractiveness and lack of femininity (28-year-old graduate student).

kanji (ideographic characters) composed of *onna hen* (the "female" radical)

Although neither words nor phrases, some *kanji* composed of *onna hen*, are among the frequently listed items in the characterization of women category. *Kanji* consist of parts called *hen* (radicals), which are used to categorize and classify characters. Besides *onna hen* (the "female" radical), there are a number of radicals such as *ki hen* (the "tree" radical), *te hen* (the "hand" radical), and *san zui hen* (the "water" radical). However, it is noteworthy that the "male" radical does not exist.

It is believed that *kanji* were introduced to Japan from China between the 3rd and 4th centuries, and were used mostly by educated men. By the 8th century phonetic letters called *hiragana* were created from *kanji* in order to transcribe the Japanese language. Angular *kanji* were called "male-lettering (*otoko moji*)," while rounded *hiragana*, phonetic letters derived from *kanji* were called "female lettering (*onna moji*)," and were used mostly by women (Kitahara & Taishukan, 2002–2008).

Today, both women and men use *kanji* as well as *hiragana*; however, in Japanese society, a person's intellectual level is often judged by the number of *kanji*, "male-lettering (*otoko moji*)," that one knows. For this reason, *hiragana*, or "female lettering (*onna moji*)," is not highly regarded, although it is one of the key components of the Japanese writing system, and it is what children learn first. Furthermore, *kango*, words composed solely of *kanji* carry more prestige than those composed of *kanji* and *hiragana* (Cherry, 1987). *Kango* are typically used in formal writing and speech to convey authority.

- Gender bias in the Japanese language is symbolized by the fact that an overwhelming number of *kanji* composed of *onna hen* (the "female" radical) have negative meanings such as jealousy, hatred, illicit sexual relations, while there is no such thing as the "male" radical (72-year-old retired editor).
- Some *kanji* composed of *onna hen* convey stereotypical notions of women. For instance, *kanji* for *shuutome* (mother-in-law) is composed of *onna hen* and the character for old. Similarly, *kanji* for *yome* (daughter-in-law, bride) consist of *onna hen* and the character for house/family (23-year-old housework helper).
- The vast majority of *kanji* composed of *onna hen* have such negative connotations. Even those without negativity are based on bias against women. For instance, *kanji* for *musume* (daughter, young woman) is composed of *onna hen* and the character

for good. I wonder why only young women are considered good (33-year-old part-time sales clerk).

Age

Among 17 words and phrases about age, 8 concern young women, 5 refer to middle-aged women, and 4 are used to describe elderly women.

(o)nee-chan (elder sister, address term for young women), *oba-san* (aunt, address term for middle-aged women), *obaa-chan* (granny, address term for elderly women)

Japanese kinship terms are used in place of first names to directly address family members and relatives who are older than the speaker. Furthermore, the unique characteristic of Japanese kinship terms is that they can also be used as informal terms to address those outside the family and relatives, ranging from acquaintances to total strangers. For instance, *oba-san* (aunt) can be used to address a middle-aged woman, and *onee-chan* (elder sister) can be used to address a young woman. Kinship terms with the polite suffix *-san* convey formality as in *obaa-san* (grandmother), while those with the diminutive suffix *-chan* convey friendliness as in *obaa-chan* (granny) (Makino & Tsutsui, 1989; McClure, 2000).

- I do not mind being called *onee-chan* by my family members and relatives, but I find it very rude when total strangers, particularly older men, call me as such at the store where I work as a part-time clerk (24-year-old college student).
- I do not appreciate being addressed as *oba-san* by younger people that I do not know. It makes me feel that I am over the hill and no longer attractive (37-year-old part-time public employee).
- Every time my 80-year-old mother goes to the hospital, she is annoyed by nurses and doctors who address her as *obaa-chan* as a term of endearment. She says that since they are not her rela-

tives, they should call her by her name, with which I totally agree (54-year-old homemaker).

toshima (years added, middle-aged woman) (Cherry, 1987)

There are several Japanese terms referring to a middle-aged woman, the most commonly used being *chuunen josei* (middle-aged woman) and *toshima*. While *chuunen josei* has no overtly negative undertone, *toshima* has a definite negative connotation that aging works against women.

The origin of *toshima* dates back to the Edo period (1603–1867), when prostitutes who were past their prime were initially referred to as such. The usage then spread among the general public, and *toshima* became the term used for women in their early 20s. In addition, during the Edo period (1603–1867), two more expressions were derived from the term *toshima*: *chuudoshima* (medium *toshima*) for those in their mid- to late 20s, and *oodoshima* (grand *toshima*) for those older (*Kojien*, 2008). In modern Japanese, these two expressions are replaced with *toshima*.

- Unlike *toshima*, an unfavorable term used for middle-aged women, the terms for middle-aged men are mostly favorable such as *romansu gree* (romance gray, attractive middle-aged man with gray hair). This reflects the conventional belief that aging works for men, but not for women (60-year-old junior high school teacher).

hakoiri musume (daughter-in-a box, a young single woman who leads a sheltered life with her protective family)

A young single woman who has been raised by protective parents and leads a sheltered life with her family is called *hakoiri musume*. Having its origins in the late Edo period (1603–1867) (*Kojien*, 2008), *hakoiri musume* is now mostly a thing of the past because of a steady increase in the number of young women who live away from their family for education and career. However, based on the prevailing belief that young single women who live by themselves tend to "misbehave," Japanese companies often show preference to *hakoiri musume* by hiring young single women who live with their families. As a matter of fact, female college graduates who lived by themselves were not even qualified to apply for positions in the major Japanese corporations until the late–1980s. This prevailing practice did not change until 1985 when the Equal Employment Opportunity Law (EEOL) was enacted to ban such discriminatory practices.

- *Hakoiri musume* conveys the image of a helpless young woman with very little life experience who cannot be on her own, and is in need of protection at all times. I am so proud of not being one! (21-year-old college student).

roojo, rooba (old woman)

Elderly women are disparagingly called *roojo* and *rooba*, while there are no equivalent terms for elderly men. Despite their negative undertones, both *roojo* and *rooba* are sometimes used by the media when elderly women become victims of crime. The negative association with *rooba* can also be found in the expression *rooba shin* (the spirit of old woman), referring to the act of meddling and interfering. It is common among women and men, mostly of the older generation, to use the set phrase, "*rooba shin kara* (out of the spirit of old woman)" when they deferentially give advice to someone.

- Terms like *roojo* and *rooba* totally lack respect and courtesy toward elderly women. I certainly much prefer being called a woman of such-and-such age, which is customarily done with elderly males (76-year-old part-time Japanese instructor).

oni baba (devilish old woman)

Oni baba, an ogre disguised as a cruel and merciless old woman, is one of the evil characters that frequently appears in Japanese folk tales. *Oni baba* is also used as a derogatory term for an elderly woman. It should be noted that there is neither an ogre disguised as an old man in Japanese folk tales, nor an expression in the Japanese language for "a malicious and merciless old man."

- Just as in folk tales, there is no male equivalent for *oni baba* in the Japanese language, despite the fact that there are many nasty old men out there (77-year-old homemaker).

Occupation

Out of the 16 words and phrases listed in the occupation category, 8 refer to the occupations that are traditionally held by women, and 8 are regarding the status of women in the workplace.

onna no ko **(girl)**

The most frequently listed in the occupation category is *onna no ko*, which is routinely used by men to refer to an adult woman in the workplace. Similar usage of the word "girl" can be found in many other languages as well. Feminist scholars point out that the prevalent practice of using the term "girl" to refer to an adult woman leads to the misconception that women are childish and immature and cannot be taken seriously (Frank & Anshen, 1983).

- Although there are no children in the workplace, women are habitually called *onna no ko*, while men are rarely called *otoko no ko* (boy). It is a shame that some women also refer to this annoying word when they do not want to be held liable for their mistakes (56-year-old office worker).
- I have been working at one of the most well-known companies in the Tokyo metropolitan area for over 12 years. Despite the recent promotion that I received, my male supervisors and colleagues continue to call me *onna no ko*, which I find extremely demeaning (35-year-old office worker).
- The habitual use of *onna no ko* to refer to female workers is often justified by male workers as a term of endearment. However, what it implies is that women are not as competent as men, and should be in subordinate positions to men (46-year-old administrative assistant).

Part II: Representation of Women in the Japanese Language

otsubone(-sama) (elderly court woman, middle-aged female worker)

The second most frequently listed word in the occupation category is *otsubone* and its more condescending form, *otsubone-sama*. *Otsubone* consists of the polite prefix *o-* and *tsubone*, a deferential term for high-ranking women who served the Imperial Court from the Heian period (794–1185) throughout the Edo period (1603–1867) (Kitahara & Taishukan, 2002–2008).

In the present-day Japanese workplace, *otsubone* is used mostly among young female and male workers as a pejorative term for a middle-aged female worker who has been with the same company for a number of years.

- Malicious words against middle-aged women such as *otsubone* that are widely used in the workplace are one of the major factors to discourage young female workers including my granddaughter from seriously pursuing their careers (65-year-old retired high school teacher).
- I find it very troubling that an experienced and capable female colleague of mine whom I look up to, is often ridiculed as *otsubone-sama* behind her back by her immature and inexperienced subordinates (33-year-old part-time sales clerk).

josei, fujin, joryuu, onna (female, woman)

When women take up occupations and positions that are traditionally held by men, it is customary to add various terms which denote female and woman such as *josei, fujin, joryuu,* and *onna* as modifiers to these occupations and positions. *Josei* as in *josei giin* (congresswoman) is the most formal, with no overtly negative tone. *Fujin* mainly refers to married women, and has a slight pejorative undertone as in *fujin keikan* (woman police officer). *Joryuu* is typically used in the field of art, as in *joryuu sakka* (woman writer) with the connotation that women are secondary in the traditionally male-dominated field. *Onna* is the most casual, with a strong pejorative tone as in *onna shachoo* (woman CEO) and *onna shujin* (woman master/storekeeper). It should be noted that the practice to add gender markers as modifiers applies only to women. When men take up positions and occupations that are traditionally held by women, it is customary to create new gender neutral titles. For instance, *hobo* (protective mother), a term for female nursery school and kindergarten teachers, has been mostly replaced by *hoikushi* (licensed person for child care), although male nursery school and kindergarten teachers remain very small in numbers.

- The annoying custom of adding *josei*, *fujin*, and *onna* to male-dominated positions and occupations not only treats women like appendages to men, but also undermines the accomplishments of women (63-year-old Japanese instructor).

OL (office lady, female office worker)

OL stands for a female office worker who performs secondary and domestic functions in the Japanese workplace. Until the early 1960s, female clerical workers were called *BG* (business girl) in Japan. When its implication in English became publicly known, the term *OL* was coined and has been widely used since then (Kitahara & Taishukan, 2002–2008). Although a female office worker of any age can be technically called an *OL*, the term often refers to one who is young and single. These days, most women in Japan work full-time before marriage, more than two-thirds of them as *OLs* (Iwai, 1990; Nakano, 1984).

In addition to clerical work, *OLs* are generally responsible for a variety of domestic duties such as serving tea to their male colleagues, supervisors, and business clients, cleaning ashtrays, tidying up the kitchenette and the office space, to name but a few. In recent years, an increasing number of companies, particularly foreign-affiliated ones, spare *OLs* from performing domestic functions by introducing beverage dispensers and outsourcing housecleaning duties.

- Despite the popular image of *OLs* leading a carefree and affluent lifestyle, there is nothing glamorous about being one. *OL* is no more than a euphemism for an underpaid, disposable and unappreciated female worker like myself (26-year-old office worker).

Part II: Representation of Women in the Japanese Language

- Young women who enter the labor force should think twice about becoming *OLs* with dead-end career prospects. I would encourage them to look for the positions in which they can fully utilize their education and vocational training (72-year-old retired high school teacher).

shokuba no hana (flower in the workplace, young single female office worker)

While the term *OL* can be used for any female office worker regardless of her age and marital status, *shokuba no hana* refers exclusively to a female office worker who is young and single. Although not as commonly used as *OL* in recent years, *shokuba no hana* nevertheless is the term that symbolizes the ornamental and disposable status of young single female office workers in the Japanese workplace. Similar to *OL*, *shokuba no hana* engages in clerical and secretarial work as well as performs various domestic functions. The nature of her job responsibilities is often summarized as *ochakumi* (tea serving), and the duration of her service is described as *koshikake* (stool), which denotes a bar stool on which a guest sits for a short time. *Koshikake* also refers to a position or a job that a person holds temporarily while looking for something more permanent. Incidentally, marriage was often called *eikyuu shuushoku* (permanent employment) for women through the mid–1980s, when women had limited career prospects and the divorce rate was very low in Japan.

Although an increasing number of women continue to remain in the work force regardless of their marital status, single women in their late 20s to early 30s are more likely to experience *kata tataki* (a tap on the shoulder) from their male supervisors, who remind them of the short life span of *shokuba no hana*. There is also peer pressure on these single women to resign before they are ridiculed as *otsubone(-sama)* (elderly court women, middle-aged female office worker) who are considered too old to marry (Creighton, 1996; Lo, 1990).

- Treating young female workers as *shokuba no hana* to be replaced after several years of service remains a prevalent practice in the Japanese workplace. What a waste it is not to fully

utilize the potential of these women! (66-year-old homemaker).
- I finally decided to free-lance after spending many unhappy years in a big company where men, particularly those of the older generation, treat young single female workers as disposable *shokuba no hana* regardless of their skills and capabilities (29-year-old interpreter).

kotobuki taishoku / *kotobuki taisha* (congratulatory resignation, resignation of female workers because of marriage)

Kotobuki, meaning "auspiciousness" is the word which is commonly used in joyful and festive occasions such as weddings. *Kotobuki taishoku/kotobuki taisha* refers to the prevailing practice of female workers mostly in their mid– to late 20s who resign in preparation for upcoming weddings.

In Japan, women often leave the work force, either voluntarily or involuntarily, for full-time housework and child care at the time of marriage, or when they are expecting their first child. When their children reach school age, many women re-enter the labor force in order to earn supplemental household income by taking up low-wage part-time positions mainly in the manufacturing, sales, and service industries.

- Female workers should not be pressured into *kotobuki taishoku*, considering the limited career prospects for middle-aged women who re-enter the labor force (30-year-old homemaker).
- Based on my personal struggle to find a full-time position similar to what I had prior to marriage, I would urge young single women not to be lured into *kotobuki taisha*, and to hang onto their positions by all means (38-year-old homemaker).

kaseifu (housekeeper), *sooji no oba-san* (middle-aged cleaning woman), *otetsudai-san* (maid)

These three low-wage jobs with minimal security are representative of what is traditionally available for middle-aged and elderly women without access to adequate education and vocational training.

- *Kaseifu, otetsudai-san,* and *sooji no oba-san* not only represent limited career options available for underprivileged middle-aged women, but also connote a sense of contempt for unskilled and low-paid female workers (41-year-old office worker).

Physical Appearance

Among the 12 words and phrases listed regarding women's appearance, 6 refer to beauty, 5 refer to unattractiveness, and 1 refers to both.

busu, okame, okachi menko, subeta (ugly woman)

These four words referring to an ugly woman are also used as derogatory terms. *Busu* (ugly woman) is the most frequently listed in the physical appearance category, and it is the most commonly used in swearing, particularly at younger women. *Busu* not only refers to women's physical appearance, but also to their character and personality, as in *seikaku busu* (woman who has an unpleasant personality).

Okame (ugly woman) refers to a woman whose face resembles an unattractive female mask called *otafuku,* known for its round face with puffy cheeks and a flat nose. *Subeta* (ugly woman) originated in the Spanish and Portuguese words, *espada,* and has been used to refer to an unattractive woman since the Edo period (1063–1867). It also refers to a worthless card that does not count toward points in a Japanese card game called *hana fuda* (flower cards) (*Kojien,* 2008). Among the four words listed, *busu* and *okame* are far more commonly used than *subeta* and *okachi menko* (ugly woman), meaning a funny face.

- While there are countless words such as *busu* and *okame* to ridicule unattractive women, *buotoko* (ugly man) is the only one corresponding word for men that I can think of. What is more, in contrast to commonly used *busu* and *okame, buotoko* is rarely used (77-year-old homemaker).
- In the society where good looks are considered one of the

biggest assets to women, *busu* is an extremely cruel and hurtful word to ridicule women, particularly those who are young and self-conscious with their appearance (31-year-old junior high school teacher).

bijin (beautiful person, beautiful woman)

Bijin, referring to a woman with good looks, is listed in the physical appearance category, although it does not connote overt negativity. It is noteworthy that when *bijin* is used to refer to attractiveness other than good looks as in *koe bijin* (woman with beautiful voice) and *seikaku bijin* (woman with beautiful personality), it implies that these women compensate their lack of good looks with other assets.

While not as common as *bijin*, *bijo* (beautiful woman) is a formal term to refer to an attractive woman. Unlike most of the words listed with nonreciprocal expressions for men, *bijo* and *bijin* have male equivalents: *binan* (beautiful man) and *bidanshi* (beautiful man). However, in contrast to the very commonly used terms *bijin* and *bijo*, *binan* is rarely used, except in the compound, *binan bijo* (beautiful man and woman). Similarly, *bidanshi* sounds archaic, and is seldom used nowadays. Incidentally, the only instance when *bijin* is used in a unisex term is in the compound *happo bijin* (beautiful person in all directions). It has a negative undertone and refers to a person who tries to please everybody or who is affable to everyone.

- The vast majority of expressions for women's physical appearance in the Japanese language, such as *bijin* and *busu*, reflect the fact that unlike men, women are almost always judged by their looks rather than by other qualities (42-year-old translator).

biboo (beautiful looks, woman's beauty)

Similar to the majority of words listed in the physical appearance category, *biboo* is used exclusively for women's good looks. It should be noted that the word *yooboo* (looks, facial features), which does not denote beauty, is used to describe the looks and facial features of both women and men.

Part II: Representation of Women in the Japanese Language

- Physical appearance is something that a person was born with, and cannot change naturally. I feel that the frequent use of words like *busu* (ugly woman) and *bijin* (beautiful person; beautiful woman) among peer groups puts unnecessary pressure on younger women, and make them obsessed with their appearance to the point of resorting to cosmetic surgery in some extreme cases (72-year-old retired high school teacher).

Status

A total of five words and three phrases are listed in the status category. The most frequently listed in the status category are *onna kodomo* (women and children), *danson johi* (men superior, women inferior), and "*Onna sangai ni ie nashi* (Women have no home in the three realms of existence: the past, the present, and the future)."

onna kodomo (women and children)

The term *onna kodomo* is used to underestimate and belittle women by equating their status with that of children. Both *onna kodomo* and its more formal term, *fujoshi* (women and children), share the same connotation by equating the willpower and mental as well as physical strength of women to that of children. Furthermore, *Kojien* (2008), one of the highly regarded Japanese language dictionaries, says that the term *fujoshi* (women and children) is used to refer to those who are weak and effeminate.

- It is offensive and insulting that advertisers often use lines similar to what the term *onna kodomo* represents, claiming that their products are very simple and easy to operate even for women and children (38-year-old college lecturer).
- An expression like *onna kodomo* looks down upon the very existence of women by lowering their status to that of children. I am saddened to see some men treat women based on what this demeaning expression represents (27-year-old office worker).

danson johi (men superior, women inferior)

The notion of *danson johi* is based on the Buddhist and Shinto beliefs that associate women with impurity and sinfulness. This notion, which subjected women to subordinate positions to men as well as in society, developed in the 12th century. During the Edo period (1603–1867), it prevailed mostly in the ruling samurai class, and later, during the Meiji period (1868–1912), it became prevalent in all social classes (Minamoto, 2005; Okano, 1995). Furthermore, the notion of *danson johi* represented the ideology of the patriarchal *ie* (family, household) system, which was legitimatized by the Civil Code of 1898. The pre–World War II hierarchical structure of Japanese society, and the *ie* system that supported it, were both characterized by extreme gender inequality (Meguro, 1990; Uno, 1991). Although the Constitution enacted shortly after World War II guarantees gender equality, the residual effects of the notion of *danson johi* are observed in various spheres of life in present-day Japan.

- It is hard to believe that the *danson johi* mentality is still intact and prevailing in 21st century Japan, particularly among middle-aged and elderly men (50-year-old homemaker).

Onna sangai ni ie nashi. (Women have no home in the three realms of existence: the past, the present, and the future.)

"*Onna sangai ni ie nashi*" is based on a Buddhist sutra that defines the status of women as inferior and secondary to that of men. At the time of its arrival in Japan by way of Korea in the 6th century, Buddhism emphasized the importance of asceticism for monks, and strictly forbade their sexual relations with women, who were considered hindrances to ascetic monks. This negative view of women is expressed in many sutras including "*Onna sangai ni ie nashi*" (Minamoto, 1997; Ogoshi, Minamoto & Yamashita, 1990; Okano, 1995).

- I have heard that there is a similar expression to "*Onna sangai ni ie nashi*" in Arabic. I often think that there are many similarities between Japanese and Arab women in terms of their

Part II: Representation of Women in the Japanese Language

status in society as well as the discriminations against them (48-year-old part-time English instructor).

onna sanjuu no oshie (doctrine of three obediences for women: as a daughter, obey your father; once married, obey your husband; and when widowed, obey your son)

Another discriminatory concept of the "three obediences (*sanjuu*)" which define the secondary status of women was introduced to Japan in the sutras of Mahayana, one of the two major forms of Buddhism (Minamoto, 1997; Ogoshi, Minamoto & Yamashita, 1990; Okano, 1995). The Laws of Manu define the "three obediences (*sanjuu*)" as follows: "As a daughter, women must obey their father; once married, they must obey their husband; when widowed, they must obey their son. Women must not be independent" (Okano, 1995, p. 18).

- I cannot think of a more inhumane and insulting expression for women than *onna sanjuu no oshie* (doctrine of three obediences for women). It totally denies the autonomy and dignity of women. Although it is now considered archaic, similar sentiments still remain in Japanese society (70-year-old professor).

nyonin kinsei (no females allowed)

The notion of blood impurity originating in Buddhism as well as in Shinto associated women with sinfulness, and created the tradition of *nyonin kinsei*, which prevailed by the 12th century. Women were forbidden from Shinto and Buddhist rituals and festivals, Buddhist temples, Shinto shrines, and *reizan* (holy mountains) such as Mt. Fuji, which were revered in Shinto and Buddhism. Furthermore, women were banned in many secular places including fishing boats, construction sites, sake breweries, sumo rings, and behind the sushi counter.

Although this tradition was officially abolished in 1872, its residual effects remain in many spheres of life, and women are still excluded in a number of places and events in present-day Japan. For instance, women are prohibited from stepping up on the sumo ring based on the claim by the Japan Sumo Association that it maintains the sacredness of sumo, which developed as a Shinto ritual. Similarly, the Seikan Tunnel, the longest underwater tunnel in the world between the mainland and the northern island of Hokkaido, was completed in 1988 without the presence of any women on its site during its 16-year construction period (Asano, 2005).

- It is simply appalling that the notorious practice of *nyonin kinsei* not only lingers on in 21st century Japan, but also is maintained and even supported by both women and men as a deeply ingrained "tradition" in Japanese culture (68-year-old professor emeritus).

Derogatory Terms

Of seven derogatory terms listed, five concern sexual promiscuity and prostitution, one each for elderly women and for women of all ages. The most frequently listed in the derogatory term category is (*kuso*) *babaa*, a derogatory term used for elderly women.

(kuso)babaa (derogatory term for elderly women)

Babaa, as well as the more contemptuous term, *kuso babaa* (extremely derogatory term for elderly women), are by far the most frequently listed in the derogatory term category. *Babaa* is derived from *baba* (old woman), which has a much less negative undertone. Incidentally, the joker in a card game is called *baba* in the Japanese language, referring to what is worthless and unpleasant (*Kojien*, 2008).

While *babaa* has been commonly used for a number of years by both women and men to swear at elderly women, it received extensive media attention for the first time in 2001. As mentioned in Chapter 5, in the fall of that year, the Governor of Tokyo, Ishihara Shintaro, who is known for his highly controversial remarks, criticized the behavior of middle-aged and elderly women by commenting that *babaa* are the worst and the most hideous creatures that civilization has ever brought about

(*Shukan Josei*, 2001). An immediate outcry from women's as well as citizens' groups over the governor's statement was covered favorably by the Japanese media, who had not necessarily been sympathetic toward such protests in the past.

- The word *babaa* is bad enough; if someone calls me *kuso babaa* (extremely derogatory term for elderly women), I may punch her/him in the face. People should stop using such foul language (45-year-old part-time interpreter).
- *Babaa* is truly a disgusting word that also sounds horrendous. It is disheartening to hear those of the younger generation nonchalantly use such a hideous word without showing any respect or regard for elderly women (76-year-old retired high school teacher).

ama (nun, derogatory term for women)

Although *ama* literally means "nun," it is one of the worst derogatory terms for women, and is used exclusively by men to swear at women of all ages.

- Unfortunately, TV dramas and movies are full of derogatory terms such as *ama*, which makes me shudder. Also, there seem to be more derogatory terms that are used toward women than men. I think that the media should make a more conscientious effort to eliminate foul language (28-year-old graduate student).

abazure (audacious and impudent woman)

Although *abazure* is now used exclusively for women in the Japanese language, it originally referred to both women and men who are audacious and impudent (Kitahara & Taishukan, 2002–2008).

- Although *abazure* refers only to women, I personally feel that audaciousness and impudence are the personality traits that are more often associated with men than with women (36-year-old graduate student).

otoko gurui (nymphomaniac)

Unlike most of the words and phrases listed that do not have reciprocal expressions for men, *otoko gurui* has a male equivalent called *onna gurui*. However, *otoko gurui* is more commonly used than *onna gurui*.

- *Onna gurui* is much less frequently used than *otoko gurui*, which reflects the longstanding societal tolerance for the sexual promiscuity of men (42-year-old nursery school teacher).

Differences and Similarities by Age

Survey participants were divided into three age groups: 20 to 39, 40 to 59, and 60 to 79, in order to compare differences and similarities in the selections of words and phrases by age. The number of participants in each age group is 24 in their 20s and 30s, 24 in their 40s and 50s, and 22 in their 60s and 70s. The total number of words and phrases listed by each age group is 62 by those in their 20s and 30s, 82 by those in their 40s to 50s, and 92 by those in their 60s and 70s. The average number of words and phrases listed per participant of each age group is 2.6 for those in their 20s and 30s, 3.4 for those in their 40s and 50s, and 4.2 for those in their 60s and 70s, indicating that the older the age group, the more words and phrases are listed per participant. Table 4 summarizes the above findings.

Table 4. Distribution of Words and Phrases Listed by Age Groups

Age Group	Number of Participants	Total Number of Words and Phrases Listed	Average Number of Words and Phrases Listed per Participant
20–39	24	62	2.6
40–59	24	82	3.4
60–79	22	92	4.2

Part II: Representation of Women in the Japanese Language

As shown in Table 5, the following three words and phrases that belong to the characterization of women category are listed by all age groups: *onna no kuse ni* (after all she is a woman, though she is a woman) to criticize women who challenge or achieve what is traditionally reserved for men, *memeshii* (like a woman, unmanly and effeminate man), which is used to criticize the personality traits as well as behavior of men, and some *kanji* (ideographic characters) composed of *onna hen* (the "female" radical) that have negative meanings such as jealousy, adultery, and hatred.

Table 5. Words and Phrases Listed by All Age Groups

Category	Words and Phrases Listed by All Age Groups
Characterization	*onna no kuse ni* (after all she is a woman, though she is a woman)
	memeshii (like a woman, unmanly and effeminate man)
	some *kanji* (ideographic characters) composed of *onna hen* (the "female" radical)

At the same time, as presented in Table 6, a total of six words and phrases are listed exclusively by each age group.

Table 6. Words and Phrases Listed Exclusively by Each Age Group

Age Group	Category	Words and Phrases Exclusively Listed
20–39	Characterization	*shitoyaka* (modest, graceful, gentle)
	Occupation	*kotobuki taishoku/kotobuki taisha* (congratulatory resignation, resignation of female workers because of marriage)
40–59	Marriage	*oku-san* (Mrs. Interior, address term for married women)
	Occupation	*onna no ko* (girl)
60–79	Marriage	*miboojin* (person who is not yet dead, widow)
	Marriage	*Kashite sannen konaki wa saru.* (A wife should leave her husband if she fails to have a child within 3 years of marriage.)

Shitoyaka (modest, graceful, gentle), concerning the characterization of women, and *kotobuki taishoku* / *kotobuki taisha* (congratulatory resignation; resignation of female workers because of marriage), concerning occupation, are listed exclusively by women in their 20s and 30s. Some respondents argue that *shitoyaka* (modest, graceful, gentle) represents social and cultural preconditions of desirable traits in young women.

- In Japanese society, which remains largely patriarchal, *shitoyaka* is commonly used as one of the criteria for judging the value of young women as commodities (38-year-old college lecturer).

Others criticize that *kotobuki taishoku / kotobuki taisha* (congratulatory resignation; resignation of female workers because of marriage) is a euphemism for the prevailing discriminatory practice in the workplace to pressure young single female workers to resign upon marriage.

- *Kotobuki taishoku* reflects the societal expectation that women should get married, leave the work force, and become full-time homemakers (26-year-old office worker).

Oku-san (Mrs. Interior, address term for married women) (Cherry, 1987), relating to marriage, and *onna no ko* (girl), relating to occupation, are listed exclusively by women in their 40s and 50s. A significant number of respondents assert that the commonly used address term for married women, *oku-san*, would reinforce the existing gender-based role division in society by literally designating the place for married women.

- *Oku-san* represents the prevailing notion in society that a wife should always keep a low profile by staying behind her husband and rendering him full support (40-year-old homemaker).

Many respondents also point out the fact that *onna no ko* (girl) is customarily used in the workplace to refer to adult female workers regardless of their job experience and skills. In contrast, its corresponding term, *otoko no ko* (boy) is rarely used for adult male workers except as an occasional reference to those who are newcomers to the workplace.

Part II: Representation of Women in the Japanese Language

- The prevalent custom in the Japanese workplace to call an adult female worker *onna no ko* conveys a biased assumption that a woman is not capable of doing a man's share of the work (46-year-old office worker).

"*Kashite sannen konaki wa saru* (A wife should leave her husband if she fails to have a child within 3 years of marriage)," and *miboojin* (person who is not yet dead, widow), belonging to the marriage category, are listed exclusively by women in their 60s and 70s. Some respondents express their concern over the gender bias found in the literal meaning of *miboojin*.

- While *miboojin* is widely used even by widows themselves, what it stands for is an ancient primitive idea that a wife should follow her husband upon his death (70-year-old professor).

Others maintain that the lingering misconception about infertility is associated with the phrase, "*Kashite sannen konaki wa saru* (A wife should leave her husband if she fails to have a child within 3 years of marriage)," although it is now mostly archaic.

- An expression like "*Kashite sannen konaki wa saru*" proves the fact that women have been wrongly blamed for infertility (66-year-old homemaker).

Differences and Similarities by Education Levels

In order to compare the differences and similarities in the selections of words and phrases by education levels, survey participants were divided into the following three groups based on the highest degrees they earned: high school diplomas, associate and bachelor's degrees, and graduate degrees. The number of participants in each group is indicated in the parentheses: high school diplomas (12), associate and bachelor's degrees (47), and graduate degrees (11). The total number of words and phrases listed by each group is 31 by the group with high school diplomas, 118 by the group with associate and bachelor's degrees, and 29 by the group with graduate degrees. The average number of words and phrases listed per participant of each group is 2.6 for the group with high school diplomas, 2.5 for the group with associate and bachelor's degrees, and 2.6 for the group with graduate degrees. Table 7 summarizes the above-mentioned findings.

Table 7. Distribution of Words and Phrases Listed by Education Levels

Highest Degree Earned	Number of Participants	Total Number of Words and Phrases Listed	Average Number of Words and Phrases Listed per Participant
High school diplomas	12	31	2.6
AA BA BS	47	118	2.5
MA MS PhD	11	29	2.6

A total of 16 words and phrases are listed by all education levels. As presented in Table 8, these words and phrases belong to the marriage, characterization of women, age, occupation, and physical appearance categories. Words and phrases pertaining to marriage are *yome* (daughter-in-law, bride), *yome o morau* (to receive a daughter-in-law/bride), *oku-san* (Mrs. Interior, address term for married women) (Cherry, 1987), *kanai* (house-insider, one's wife) (Cherry, 1987), *gusai* (stupid wife, one's wife), *shufu* (main woman, homemaker), *ikiokure* (late to marry, single woman in her 30s), and *urenokori* (unsold merchandise, single woman in her 30s). Relating to the characterization of women are *onna no kuse ni* (after all she is a woman, though she is a woman), *memeshii* (like a woman, unmanly and effeminate man), some *kanji* (ideographic characters) composed of *onna hen* (the "female" radical), *onna no kusatta yoona* (like a rotten woman, indecisive and cowardly man), and *onna rashii* (feminine, womanly). *Obaa-chan* (granny, address term for elderly women) is related to age, *onna no ko* (girl) belongs to the occupation category, and *busu* (ugly woman) is concerning physical appearance.

Part II: Representation of Women in the Japanese Language

Table 8. Words and Phrases Listed by All Education Levels

Category	Words and Phrases Listed by All Education Levels
Marriage	*yome* (daughter-in-law, bride)
	yome o morau (to receive a daughter-in-law/bride)
	oku-san (Mrs. Interior, address term for married women)
	kanai (house-insider, one's wife)
	gusai (stupid wife, one's wife)
	shufu (main woman, homemaker)
	ikiokure (late to marry, single woman in her 30s)
	urenokori (unsold merchandise, single woman in her 30s)
Characterization	*onna no kuse ni* (after all she is a woman, though she is a woman)
	memeshii (like a woman, unmanly and effeminate man)
	some *kanji* (ideographic characters) composed of *onna hen* (the "female" radical)
	onna no kusatta yoona (like a rotten woman, indecisive and cowardly man)
	onna rashii (feminine, womanly)
Age	*obaa-chan* (granny, address term for elderly women)
Occupation	*onna no ko* (girl)
Physical Appearance	*busu* (ugly woman)

As shown in Table 9, no words and phrases are listed exclusively by the groups with high school diplomas and graduate degrees, while *toshima* (years added, middle-aged woman) (Cherry, 1987), concerning age, is exclusive to the group with associate and bachelor's degrees.

Table 9. Words and Phrases Listed Exclusively by Each Education Level

Highest Degree Earned	Category	Words and Phrases Exclusively Listed
High school diploma	n/a	0
AA BA BS	Age	*toshima* (years added, middle-aged woman)
MA MS Ph.D.	n/a	0

Many respondents with associate and bachelor's degrees point out that *toshima* (years added, middle-aged woman) (Cherry, 1987) reflects

6—Survey

the prevailing notion that unlike men, aging does not work for women.

- While there are a number of negative expressions for middle-aged women such as *toshima* in the Japanese language, there is virtually none for middle-aged men. I guess it is a universal notion that aging works against women (56-year-old homemaker).

Differences and Similarities by Occupation

Survey participants were divided into the following three occupational groups in order to compare the differences and similarities in the selection of words and phrases by occupation. The total number of participants in each occupational group is indicated in the parentheses: homemakers (18), educators (15), and clerical workers (14). The remaining 23 participants consisted of 8 professionals, 7 retirees, 6 students, and 2 housework helpers were excluded from the comparison due to their lack of adequate representation. The total number of words and phrases listed by each group is 50 by homemakers, 39 by educators, and 39 by clerical workers. The average number of words and phrases listed per participant of each group is 2.8 per homemaker, 2.6 per educator, and 2.8 per clerical worker. The above findings are summarized in Table 10.

Table 10. Distribution of Words and
Phrases Listed by Occupation Groups

Occupation Group	Number of Participants	Total Number of Words and Phrases Listed	Average Number of Words and Phrases Listed per Participant
Homemaker	18	50	2.8
Educator	15	39	2.6
Clerical Worker	14	39	2.8

A total of six words and phrases are listed by all occupational groups, out of which three are related to marriage, and another three are related to the characterization of women. As presented in Table 11, three words

Part II: Representation of Women in the Japanese Language

concerning marriage are *urenokori* (unsold merchandise, single woman in her 30s), *oku-san* (Mrs. Interior, address term for married women) (Cherry, 1987), and *kanai* (house-insider, one's wife) (Cherry, 1987). Two phrases and one word concerning the characterization of women are *onna no kusatta yoona* (like a rotten woman, indecisive and cowardly man), *onna no kuse ni* (after all she is a woman, though she is a woman), and *memeshii* (like a woman, unmanly and effeminate man).

Table 11. Words and Phrases Listed by All Occupation Groups

Category	Words and Phrases Listed by All Occupation Groups
Marriage	*urenokori* (unsold merchandise, single woman in her 30s) *oku-san* (Mrs. Interior, address term for married women) *kanai* (house-insider, one's wife)
Characterization	*memeshii* (like a woman, unmanly and effeminate man) *onna no kusatta yoona* (like a rotten woman, indecisive and cowardly man) *onna no kuse ni* (after all she is a woman, though she is a woman)

As shown in Table 12, *gusai* (stupid wife, one's wife), pertaining to marriage, is listed exclusively by homemakers, while no words and phrases are listed exclusively by educators and clerical workers.

Table 12. Words and Phrases Listed Exclusively by Each Occupation Group

Occupation Group	Category	Words and Phrases Exclusively Listed
Homemaker	Marriage	*gusai* (stupid wife, one's wife)
Educator	n/a	0
Clerical Worker	n/a	0

A number of homemakers express their concern about the use of *gusai* (stupid wife, one's wife) as a humble term for one's wife, which is particularly prevalent among men of the older generation. Using humble terms for oneself as well as one's own family members is a customary practice among Japanese people in order to be deferential to others.

- Among a number of demeaning terms for wife, *gusai* is probably the worst of all. I have heard my father referring to my mother as such on many occasions, to her dismay. It is simply beyond my comprehension that a husband would call his wife stupid in order to be humbly polite to others (28-year-old homemaker).

Summary of the Survey Results and Discussion

The voices of women in this survey validate many instances of gender bias in the Japanese language. A total of 151 words and phrases that are found degrading to women by the survey participants are characterized by one or more of the following features: gender asymmetry, dehumanizing as well as stereotypical descriptions of women, and an element of the notion of *danson johi* (men superior, women inferior). This notion to subjugate women to men developed among the ruling and privileged samurai class in the Kamakura period (1185–1333), prevailed in all classes by the Meiji period (1868–1912), and became an indispensable element to support the hierarchical structure of pre–World War II patriarchal Japanese society (Kaneko, 1995; Kinjo, 1995).

Gender asymmetry is typically found in such words and phrases as *gusai* (stupid wife, one's wife), *katazukeru* (to dispose of, to marry off a daughter), *demodori* (returnee to one's parents' place, divorced woman), "*Akusai wa isshoo no fusaku* (A bad wife ruins her husband's entire life)," and "*Dakara onna wa dameda* (That is why women are no good)," all of which do not have reciprocal expressions describing males. Prototypical examples of dehumanizing as well as stereotypical descriptions of women include *miboojin* (person who is not yet dead, widow), *urenokori* (unsold merchandise, single woman in her 30s), *umazume* (stone woman, no-life woman, infertile woman), *onna bara / otoko bara* (female womb / male womb, woman who gives birth only to girls / boys), and *kanai* (house-insider, one's wife) (Cherry, 1987). The longstanding *danson johi* (men superior, women inferior) mentality is reflected in such words as *onna no ko* (girl), a term routinely used by men to refer to an adult

Part II: Representation of Women in the Japanese Language

woman in the workplace, and *onna kodomo* (women and children), which equates the status of women with that of children, as well as in some terms denoting female and women including *josei*, *fujin*, and *onna*, which are used as modifiers to occupational and positional terms. These modifiers are customarily added when women take up traditionally male-dominated occupations and positions, as in *josei giin* (congresswoman), *fujin keikan* (woman police officer), and *onna shachoo* (woman CEO). Phrases that reflect the *danson johi* mentality include *naijo no koo* (merit of inside help) (Cherry, 1987), a commonly used phrase to praise the support and sacrifices of a wife who helps her husband succeed in life, and "*Onna sangai ni ie nashi* (Women have no home in the three realms of existence; the past, the present, and the future)," which is based on a Buddhist sutra to define the status of women being inferior to that of men.

Furthermore, among age, level of education, and occupation, age is a decisive factor in differences in the participants' selections of words and phrases. As presented in Table 6, certain words and phrases are listed exclusively by each age group, which indicates that the participants perceive gender bias in the language that is specifically related to their age. For instance, *shitoyaka* (modest, graceful, gentle), listed by those in their 20s and 30s, is one of the most frequently used words in the Japanese language to describe femininity, particularly of younger women. A commonly used address term for married women, *oku-san* (Mrs. Interior) (Cherry, 1987), is listed by those in their 40s and 50s, while *miboojin* (person who is not yet dead, widow), the term widely used not only by the general public but also by widows themselves, is listed by those in their 60s and 70s.

Well over one third of all the words and phrases that the survey participants find degrading to women are in regard to marriage, which is commonly considered in Japan as "a means of conferring legitimacy and status to both men and women" (Fujimura-Fanselow, 1995a, p. 141). A number of the participants assert that *yome* (daughter-in-law, bride), the most frequently listed word in the marriage category, along with its derivatives such as *yome ni iku* (to go as a daughter-in-law/bride, to marry into a husband's family) and *yome o morau* (to receive a daughter-in-law/bride) describe women as commodities to pass on from one family

6—Survey

to another. Aoki (1997) and Yoshizumi (1995) make similar claims by pointing out that the concept of the pre–World War II patriarchal family system remains intact in present-day Japan, where upon marriage, a woman not only becomes the wife of her husband, but also assumes a vulnerable position of *yome* (daughter-in-law, bride) in his family. Traditionally, *yome* is under many obligations to her husband's family, including taking up her husband's surname, looking after household chores, giving birth to children (preferably boys who would succeed the family name as well as estate), and caring for her parents-in-law through their advanced age, among others.

The survey participants also comment that there are a number of words including *urenokori* (unsold merchandise), *ikiokure* (late to marry), and *ikazu goke* (widow without marrying) to belittle and ridicule women who remain single after *tekireiki* (the period of marriageable age in their mid– to late 20s). Words like these confirm that the compulsion and expectation for Japanese people, particularly women, to marry by a certain age remains prevalent in Japanese society, which is observed by Creighton (1996), Lo (1990), and Morley (1999), among others. In addition, a number of the survey participants express their concern over expressions, including *umazume* (stone woman, no-life woman, infertile woman), which connote that women are responsible for infertility. While these expressions are becoming mostly obsolete, many participants assert that there remain sentiments that associate women with infertility and hold them responsible for it.

Out of the 10 most frequently listed words and phrases, 6 belong to the characterization of women category. The most frequently listed of all the words and phrases is *onna no kuse ni* (after all she is a woman, though she is a woman), a commonly used phrase to criticize a woman who challenges or achieves what is traditionally reserved for men. It is also used to criticize the demeanor of a woman who defies gender-based stereotypes. Feminist scholars including Ide (1979) and Reynolds (1990) argue that the implication of *onna no kuse ni* is that women should know better and stay within the acceptable range of behavior and demeanor for women defined by Japanese society, rather than stepping out of line only to be criticized.

Similar to *onna no kuse ni* in its connotation and negative undertone, *onna datera ni* (unlike a woman, inappropriate for a woman) is also frequently listed. In general, *onna no kuse ni* is used to criticize not only the accomplishment as well as challenge of a woman who defies gender stereotypes, but also her demeanor and behavior. *Onna datera ni* on the other hand, is used to criticize a woman for her specific behavior that is considered not "feminine." For instance, Endo (2004) explains that some Japanese language dictionaries define drinking heavily, or sitting cross-legged as unfeminine behavior. Moreover, *onna no kuse ni* is used exclusively by men, while *onna datera ni* is occasionally used by women of the older generation to criticize the behavior of women of the younger generation.

It is noteworthy that unlike all the other expressions to degrade and deride women, two frequently listed expressions, *memeshii* (like a woman, unmanly and effeminate man) and *onna no kusatta yoona* (like a rotten woman, indecisive and cowardly man), are in regard to the characterization of men. Both are commonly used by men as well as by women to criticize a man whose demeanor and personality traits are considered "feminine," that is, being indecisive, cowardly, weak-minded, infirm, weak-willed, and so forth. The participants point out that such expressions as *memeshii* and *onna no kusatta yoona* are based on a biased perspective to associate women's personality traits with negativity. This makes a clear contrast to expressions such as *okoto masari* (superior to man, strong-minded and assertive woman) and *otoko nami* (being on the level of men), which are based on the male-as-the-norm notion to judge and ridicule women.

Although neither a word nor a phrase in the characterization category, some *kanji* (ideographic characters) composed of *onna hen* (the "female" radical) are listed by the survey participants. *Kanji* consist of parts called radicals, which are used to categorize and classify characters. The participants point out that the majority of *kanji* composed of *onna hen* have negative connotations such as hatred, jealousy, adultery, mistress, malice, lewdness, to name but a few. The studies conducted by Wong (1991) and by Hio (2000) also discuss the negativity commonly associated with *kanji* composed of *onna hen*. For instance, a character consisting of three "female" radicals are read as either *kan* or *kashimashii* depending on the context, *kan* meaning "adultery," and *kashimashii* meaning "noisy" as in the frequently listed set phrase, "*Onna san nin yoreba kashimashii* (When three women get together, they make too much noise)." Similarly, Nakamura (1990) and Takahashi (1991) argue that unlike other terms to denote females in the Japanese language, *onna*, which is used in *onna hen* (the "female" radical), often conveys negative connotations.

In the age category, the participants listed various kinship terms including *(o)nee-chan* (elder sister, address term for young women), *oba-san* (aunt, address term for middle-aged women), and *obaa-chan* (granny, address term for elderly women). Japanese kinship terms are used to directly address family members and relatives who are older than the speaker. Furthermore, the unique characteristic of Japanese kinship terms is that they can also be used as informal terms to address those outside the family and relatives, ranging from acquaintances to total strangers. For instance, *oba-san* (aunt) can be used to address a middle-aged woman, and *onee-chan* (elder sister) can be used to address a young woman. Kinship terms with the polite suffix *-san* convey formality as in *obaa-san* (grandmother), while those with the diminutive suffix, *-chan* convey friendliness as in *obaa-chan* (granny). Although it is customary in Japan to use kinship terms to address non-family members, a number of the participants are offended by being addressed in such a manner by total strangers, and express their strong preference to be called by their names instead.

The participants also assert that expressions concerning middle-aged and elderly women, such as *toshima* (years added, middle-aged woman) (Cherry, 1987), have overwhelmingly negative undertones due to the general perception that aging works for men, but against women. Moreover, by reflecting the value that is placed on youth, the number of terms for mature women with positive connotations is much fewer than those for younger women.

As for the words and phrases regarding occupation, the survey participants claim that expressions like *OL* (office lady, female office worker), *shokuba no hana* (flower in the workplace, young single female office worker), and *onna no ko* (girl), a term routinely used by male workers to refer to adult female workers, indicate limited career prospects for women as well as their secondary status in the Japanese workplace. Furthermore, the participants state that the discriminatory practices against women in the Japanese labor force are symbolized by such expressions as *kotobuki taishoku / kotobuki taisha* (congratulatory resignation, resignation of female workers because of marriage), and *otsubone* (elderly court woman, middle-aged female office worker) along with its more condescending term, *otsubone-sama*, which are used by younger workers to ridicule an older female worker behind her back.

Iwai (1990) and Nakano (1984) also report that most Japanese women work full-time before marriage, more than two thirds of them as *OLs* (office ladies, female office workers). They typically perform secondary and domestic functions in the office including *ochakumi* (tea serving) to their male colleagues and supervisors, as well as to company clients. Due to the tradition of strict gender-based role division in Japanese society, the vast majority of *OLs* leave the work force upon marriage to become full-time homemakers and mothers. When their children reach school age, many women re-enter the labor force by taking up part-time positions, mostly in manufacturing, sales, and service industries, in order to earn supplementary household income. Saso (1990) similarly asserts that single *OLs* in their late 20s to early 30s are likely to experience the pressure to resign by *kotobuki taishoku / kotobuki taisha* (congratulatory resignation, resignation of female workers because of marriage) before they become too old to be *shokuba no hana* (flowers in the workplace, young single female office workers).

In the physical appearance category, the survey participants comment that there are a large number of scornful expressions to ridicule women for their looks, all of which are also used to swear at women, particularly those who are young. The most frequently listed word is *busu* (ugly woman), which is followed by *okame* (ugly woman). Although *busu* is mostly used to make fun of women's looks, it can also be used to criticize women's personality and character as being unpleasant, as in *seikaku busu* (woman with an unpleasant personality). Expressions for women's good looks without overtly negative connotations such as *bijin* (beautiful person, beautiful woman) and *biboo* (beautiful looks, woman's beauty) are also listed. It is noteworthy that when the word *bijin* is used to describe attractiveness other than good looks as in *koe bijin* (woman with beautiful voice) and *seikaku bijin* (woman with beautiful personality), it implies that these women compensate for their lack of good looks with other assets.

The participants assert that regardless of the undertone being positive or negative, all the expressions pertaining to women's physical appearance are a clear manifestation of the prevailing perception that women are judged by their looks and that one of the most important assets for women is good looks. This assertion by the survey participants is verified by the differences in usage between *yooboo* (looks, facial features) and *biboo* (beautiful looks, woman's beauty). While *yooboo* with gender neutral denotation is used in regard to the looks of both women and men, *biboo*, is used exclusively for the good looks of women.

As for the words and phrases regarding status, the survey participants state that the age-old notion of *danson johi* (men superior, women inferior), which developed in the Kamakura period (1185–1333), remains intact in present-day Japanese society. For instance, they point out that this notion to define the status of women being secondary to that of men is reflected in the commonly used expression *onna kodomo* (women and children), which equates the status of women with that of children. Similarly, the phrase listed by the participants, "*Onna sangai ni ie nashi* (Women have no home in the three realms of existence: the past, the present, and the future)," although mostly archaic, is based on the Buddhist sutra that considers women inherently inferior to men. In addition, another phrase listed by the participants, *onna sanjuu no oshie* (doctrine of three obediences for women: as a daughter, obey your father; once married, obey your husband; and when widowed, obey your son), is also derived from the Buddhist sutra advocating women's unconditional obedience and submission to men (Okano, 1995).

Furthermore, the survey participants listed the tradition of *nyonin kinsei* (no females allowed). This tradition was created from the notion of blood impurity in Shinto that originated in Japan as well as in Buddhism that was introduced to Japan in the 5th century by way of Korea

Part II: Representation of Women in the Japanese Language

and prevailed by the 12th century. Women were considered sinful and were forbidden from participating in Shinto and Buddhist rituals and festivals, as well as from entering many secular places including fishing boats, construction sites, sake breweries, and sumo rings. Although this tradition was officially abolished in 1872, women are still excluded in a number of places and events in present-day Japan (Minamoto, 2005; Okano, 1995). Lebra (1984) and Okano (1995) maintain that women were relegated to a secondary status due to male supremacy embedded in Shinto, Buddhism, and Confucianism, which not only promoted the development and maintenance of gender-based role division, but also gender inequality in Japanese society.

In the derogatory term category, the most frequently listed is *babaa* (derogatory term for elderly women) and its more insulting version, *kuso babaa* (extremely derogatory term for elderly women). The survey participants express their concern that derogatory expressions like these are totally lacking in respect and regard for elderly women. Moreover, out of seven derogatory terms listed, five are in regard to sexual promiscuity and prostitution. This coincides with the argument by Stanley (1977) that the majority of sexual insults are applied to women because woman's sex, unlike man's sex, is commonly treated as if it were her most noticeable characteristic, which becomes the basis of defining women.

7

Women and the Japanese Language: The Present and the Future

Language enters into women's lives in complex, varied, and subtle ways. Women, in turn, breathe life into language [McConnel-Ginet, Borker & Furman, 1980, p. xv].

Prospects for Changes in Gender Bias in the Japanese Language

Continuous efforts to materialize the fairer representation of genders in the Japanese language have been made by a number of women's groups, feminist activists and scholars alike, particularly since the mid–1970s as a result of the second wave of feminism, which began in the early 1970s. Although gender bias remains prevalent and deeply rooted in the Japanese language, these ongoing efforts have had a significant impact on bringing about a change for the better. In this chapter such existing instances of gender bias in the Japanese language are discussed by themes, along with any relevant changes and reforms that have taken place or are underway. Some suggestions in regard to future language reform are included as well. As mentioned in Chapter 6, the majority of women who took part in the survey also shared with me their various thoughts on gender bias in the Japanese language. Where applicable, some of their specific comments are presented in English translation.

Male-Female Word Order

The male-female word order is the norm of the modern Japanese *kanji* (ideographic characters) compounds, in which the characters rep-

Part II: Representation of Women in the Japanese Language

resenting males precede those representing females. For instance, in regard to the two most commonly used compounds referring to married couples, *fuufu* (husband and wife) and *fusai* (husband and wife), the character which represents husband precedes the one that represents wife. Similarly, in such compounds as *danjo* (man and woman) and *fubo* (father and mother, parents), the characters representing man and father precede those representing woman and mother. This male-female word order can also be found in English; when putting the genders in order, males commonly precede females as in husband and wife, men and women, his and hers, and he or she (Simmonds, 1995).

- To the best of my knowledge, characters that represent males are always followed by those that represent females in Japanese *kanji* compounds as in the case of *fuufu* (husband and wife) and *sofubo* (grandfather and grandmother, grandparents). I consider such word order as one of many examples of the long-standing male supremacy in Japanese society (52-year-old part-time high school teacher).
- I feel that the age-old notion of *danson johi* (men superior, women inferior) underlies the prevailing male-female word order that is found in many Japanese compounds such as *danjo* (man and woman), *fubo* (father and mother, parents), and *fusai* (husband and wife), to name just a few (31-year-old junior high school teacher).

As pointed out by these quotations, it is fair to consider the male-female word order found in many Japanese *kanji* compounds to be one of the many instances of the residual effects of the notion *danson johi*. This notion to subjugate women to men prevailed in all social classes during the Meiji period (1868–1912), and became one of the fundamental elements to support the hierarchical structure of the pre–World War II patriarchal Japanese society (Kaneko, 1995).

While the male-female word order is customary in *kanji* compounds in modern Japanese, the reverse female-male word order did exist through the early Kamakura period (1185–1333) before the notion of *danson johi* had fully developed. It is not only thought-provoking but also inspiring to find this female-male word order in a number of well-known literary works of the late Nara period (710–794) through the early Kamakura period (1185–1333). For instance, a compound referring to parents is written in the order of "mother and father" in *Manyoshu* (*The Collection of Ten Thousand Leaves*), the oldest anthology of poetry in Japan, completed in the 8th century (Endo, 1995). Furthermore, in *Konjaku Monogatari* (*The Tales of the Present and the Past*), the oldest anthology of ancient tales in Japan, comprised in the early 12th century, a compound referring to a married couple, *meoto*, appears as "woman and husband" as well as "wife and husband." In addition, another term for a married couple called *meotoko* is written as "woman and man" in *Ujishui Monogatari* (*The Supplementary to the Tales of Uji Dainagon*), a representative anthology of tales of the Kamakura period (1185–1333), which was completed in the early 13th century. Similarly, another term referring to a married couple, *meo*, appears as "woman and man" as well as "wife and husband" in *Hosshinshu* (*The Collection of the Tales of Attaining Enlightenment*), an anthology of Buddhist tales also compiled in the early 13th century (*Kojien*, 2008).

There ought to be more flexibility on the part of language users to choose either the female-male word order found in many classical literary works, or the prevailing male-female word order in modern Japanese to suit our needs and personal preference, as well as particular context. Such an approach will not only add more variations in the word order of *kanji* compounds, but would also provide a major step forward to eliminate the legacies of *danson johi* and overall gender inequality that are embedded in the Japanese language.

Invisibility of Women

Women are invisible in many *kanji* compounds that refer to both women and men. For instance, *kyoodai*, the compound meaning siblings, consists exclusively of characters that represent males — "elder brother" and "younger brother" — without any representation of female. The same can be said about the term *fukei*, meaning parents or guardians, which consists entirely of characters representing males—"father" and "elder brother." As a result, PTA (Parent-Teacher Association) meetings used to be called *fukeikai* (fathers' and elder brothers' association meetings) despite the fact that the vast majority of the active members are mothers.

Invisibility of women is not particular to the Japanese language. For instance, in English it can be found in the use of "generic masculine" or "pseudo-generic," that is, the use of the masculine to refer to human beings in general. Such usage can be found in expressions including mankind, man-made, man-hour, and manpower, to name but a few (Stanley, 1978). Particularly prevalent is the use of "he" as the generic-masculine; according to an estimate by some scholars, the average American is exposed to "he" used as the generic masculine a million times at the minimum in a lifetime (MacKay, 1983). Many grammarians and linguists argue that the use of "generic masculine" is one of the many instances of "marking" in the language which include women, and therefore, is not gender biased (Greenberg, 1966). However, a number of studies suggest that "he" and other masculine terms are rarely used generically, and in fact cause gender bias in people's interpretation (Hamilton, 1988; Harrison, 1975; Henley, et al., 1985; MacKay, 1980a, b; Martyna, 1978).

Because of language reform in recent years, *fukeikai* (fathers' and elder brothers' association meetings), referring to PTA (Parent-Teacher Association) meetings, has been mostly replaced by *fubokai* (fathers' and mothers' association meetings), the term that fairly represents the presence of women, as well as *hogoshakai* (guardians' association meetings), the gender neutral term. However, it remains customary to use *fukei* (fathers and elder brothers), the term without any representation of female, to address parents and guardians of both genders in formal settings.

- I always felt that the term *fukeikai* (fathers' and elder brothers' association meetings) was misleading and unfair, since its regular attendees were mothers, not fathers. I am very happy to learn that the terms to fairly represent both women and men,

such as *fubokai* (fathers' and mothers' association meetings) and *hogoshakai* (guardians' association meetings), are being used instead these days. I am also interested to see if changes in language like this will lead to changes in other areas of the male-oriented Japanese society (72-year-old retired high school teacher).
- I cannot help but feel excluded and alienated as a woman when I have no choice but to use the *kanji* (ideographic characters) compound composed exclusively of characters representing men. For instance, when asking a woman about her siblings, *kyoodai* (elder and younger brothers) is the only appropriate term that can be used. I wish there were more gender inclusive terms to represent the presence of women in the Japanese language (26-year-old part-time office worker).

As described by these quotations, the presence of women is completely disregarded in many commonly used *kanji* compounds that consist entirely of characters representing men. Many feminist scholars point out that such prevalent male dominance in the Japanese language has resulted from the pre–World War II social system based on patriarchy, as well as the notion of *danson johi* (men superior, women inferior) that supported such a social system (Endo, 1995; Nakamura, 1990; Swanger, 1994).

It should be noted that young women and girls are also invisible in a number of expressions in the Japanese language, as in the case of the word *shoonen* (boys), which not only refers to boys, but also to young children regardless of gender in Japanese legal terms. According to the Juvenile Law, literally called Shoonen Ho (the Boys' Law) in Japan, *shoonen* is defined as both girls and boys under 20 years of age. Although there is a unisex term, *jidoo* (young children), referring to young girls and boys, *shoonen* is often used in place of *jidoo*. For instance, according to Jidoo Fukushi Ho (the Child Welfare Law), the term *jidoo* is defined as children under 18 years of age. They are further divided into the following two categories: *yooji* (infants, small children) for those who are under 6 years of age, and *shoonen* for those who are under 18 years of age, regardless of gender. Similarly, the period of childhood in Japanese is called *shoonenki* (the period of boyhood) as well as *jidooki* (the period of childhood).

The same invisibility of young women can also be found in the term *seinen* (young men), which is commonly used to refer to both young women and men. For example, in developmental psychology *seinen* are defined as those in their early-teens to their mid–20s regardless of gender. Likewise, adolescence is called *seinenki* (the period of young manhood), and *seinen jidai* (the days of young manhood) refers to one's youth for both women and men. Moreover, the Junior Chamber (JC) in Japan, which is the local chapter of the Junior Chamber International (JCI), is called the Seinen Kaigisho (the Chamber of Young Men), and its members are referred to as *seinen keizaijin* (young men in the business community). Although the membership of the Junior Chamber (JC) in Japan is open to both women and men, none of these terms represent the presence of its women members. In addition, the junior board system that was first adopted in the United States by McCormick and Company in 1932 translates as *seinen juuyakukai seido* (board system for young men) in Japanese. Furthermore, the Japanese volunteer organization similar to the Peace Corps in the United States is called the Seinen Kaigai Kyoryoku Tai (The Japan Overseas Cooperation Corps of Young Men)—without any reference to female members, who are as active and dedicated as their male counterparts.

Considering a large number of expressions in the Japanese language that reflect male dominance, it is certainly a welcome trend that one of the prototypical patriarchal terms, *fukeikai* (fathers' and elder brothers' association meetings), has been replaced by the gender inclusive term *fubokai* (fathers' and mothers' association meetings). While it does have the male-female word order, *fubokai* (fathers' and mothers' association meetings) accurately describes the presence of women. What is even more encouraging is the emergence of a gender neutral term called *hogoshakai* (guardians' association meetings), which is being used in place of *fukeikai* (fathers' and elder brothers' association meetings). A change such as this which increases the visibility of women in language may seem rather small; nevertheless, it does have a significant effect on the realization of fairer representation of genders in the Japanese language.

Occupational and Positional Terms for Women

When women take up occupations and positions that have been traditionally held by men, various terms to denote females are customarily added as modifiers to these occupations and positions. The same practice used to be found in English, in which neutral occupational terms took on female modifiers as in "woman writer" and "woman doctor" (Minh-ha, 1989). The most commonly used terms in the Japanese language have been *fujin, josei, joryuu,* and *onna / jo,* as in *fujin keikan* (woman police officer), *josei kisha* (woman reporter), *joryuu sakka* (woman author), *onna shachoo* (woman CEO), and *joi* (woman doctor). Among these four terms, *josei* is the most neutral with the least gender bias, followed by *fujin,* the term commonly used for older married women. In contrast, both *joryuu,* which is predominantly used in the field of art, and *onna / jo,* connote strong gender bias, implying that women who are holding traditionally male dominant occupations and positions are not as competent and capable as their male counterparts.

It should be noted that unlike other terms denoting female, *onna* is not only used with occupational and positional terms, but is also commonly used with the names of well-known male figures when describing the accomplishments of women in the relevant fields. For instance, when the Japanese women's softball team won the gold medal for the first time in history at the 2008 Beijing Olympic Games, a member who was the driving force behind the accomplishment was referred to as *onna* (female, woman) *Ichiroo,* a well-known Japanese fielder of the Seattle Mariners.

In addition to *fujin, josei, joryuu,* and *onna / jo,* there are other various terms to denote females that are used as modifiers to describe activities, positions, and occupations held by women. For instance, *mama-san* (mother, mom) is routinely used with activities and positions held by married women with children. Some of the common expressions include *mama-san koorasu* (mothers' chorus groups), *mama-san baree* (mothers' volleyball teams), and *mama-san rannaa* (women runners who are married with children). The latest creation is *mama-san uchuuhikooshi* (mother astronaut), referring to Yamazaki Naoko, the second Japanese woman astronaut mentioned in Chapter 5, who is scheduled to be on board Space Shuttle Atlantis in 2010. Yamazaki is referred to as such, since unlike her predecessor, she is the first woman astronaut who is married with a young daughter. As described earlier, a large number of Japanese words and phrases are characterized by gender asymmetry. Likewise, the term *mama-san* (mother, mom) does not have a reciprocal term like *papa-san* (father, dad), that can used as a modifier to activities or positions held by married men with children. Although *mama-san* as a modifier is commonly considered a term of endearment, such usage does have an undertone of mockery and ridicule in regard to activities, occupations, and positions held by married women with children.

Another term, *shufu* (main woman, homemaker), is also used as a modifier for activities and positions held by homemakers as in *shufu sakka* (homemaker/author). Compared to *mama-san*, *shufu* is a much more formal term, and is not as frequently used; however, it conveys the similar negative and biased assumption that homemakers are secondary as well as mediocre in what they do besides household work.

Furthermore, the term *joshi* (girl), referring to a young woman, is widely used with occupational and positional terms. Expressions composed of *joshi* as a modifier include *joshi koosei* (female high school student), *joshi daisei* (female college student), *joshi shain* (young female office worker), and *joshi ana* (young female TV announcer), among others.

Incidentally, the usage of the term *joshi* referring to an adult woman can be traced back to ancient China in the most important scriptures of Confucianism called *Lun-yu* (*The Discourses of Kong-zi*), which was canonized during the Han dynasty (206–220 B.C.). *Lun-yu* is the oldest collection of the teachings of Kong-zi (551–479 B.C.), the Chinese scholar and theorist who was the founder of Confucianism. According to *Nihon Shoki* (*The Chronicles of Japan*), the oldest historical record of Japan, completed in 720, *Lun-yu* was introduced to Japan in the 5th century. It won much popularity among the Japanese, and a number of its annotated editions were published throughout the Edo period (1603–1867) (Hane, 1991).

One of the well-known quotations from Kong-zi (551–479 B.C.)

found in *Lun-yu* includes the term *joshi* referring to an adult woman. It reads in the Japanese translation, "*Joshi to shoojin towa yashinai gatashi* (Women as well as those who are narrow-minded and are lacking in virtue, are hard to deal with; if you keep them close to you, they become rude, while if you stay away from them, they become vengeful)" (*Kojien*, 2008). Such unfavorable views of women in Confucianism are reflected in many quotations from *Lun-yu* as well as in a number of Confucian maxims for women.

Among the four terms to denote females, *fujin*, *josei*, *joryuu*, and *onna* / *jo* that were mentioned earlier, both *joryuu* and *onna* / *jo* have been less frequently used in recent years because of their implication that women are secondary to men in male dominant occupations and positions. This change has taken place as a result of the nonsexist language reform led by women's groups and feminist activists to promote gender free occupational and positional terms. Similarly, *fujin*, the term typically used for older married women, has been mostly replaced with *josei*, which refers to adult women in general, regardless of their age and marital status. For instance, in the spring of 1999, the Osaka Prefectural Police, the second largest police force next to the Tokyo Metropolitan Police, abolished the term *fujin keikan* (woman police officer) altogether, and adopted *josei keikan* instead.

Nowadays, *josei* (woman, female) is the most frequent modifier used with occupational and positional terms traditionally held by men. The latest such creations include *josei kanbu* (woman executive), *josei jieikan* (female member of the Japanese Self-Defense Forces), *josei shichoo* (woman mayor), and *josei kenkyuusha* (woman researcher), among others. Compared to other terms, *josei* has the least sexist undertone; however, the prevailing practice of adding the terms to denote females as modifiers to male-dominated positions and occupations is a manifestation of gender bias and inequality in the Japanese language that treats women as secondary to men. It should be noted that the results of the survey conducted in the early 1980s indicated that the general public had mixed feelings about this practice. Over 30 percent of women and men who took part in the survey responded that it was not necessary to use terms to denote females as modifiers to occupational and positional terms.

Part II: Representation of Women in the Japanese Language

The percentage was even higher among women of the younger generation: 45 percent of those in their 20s, and 41 percent of those in their 30s (Endo, 1995).

- I feel that the custom of adding such terms as *onna*, *josei*, and *joryuu* to male dominant occupations and positions like appendages symbolizes the prevailing notion in Japanese society that women are less important than men, and do not deserve much recognition. This notion is also reflected in the practice to create new terms every time men enter the professions traditionally held by women (65-year-old retired high school teacher).
- As a working woman, I do not appreciate the vast majority of occupational terms for women including *josei keieisha* (woman manager), *joryuu kishi* (woman, Japanese chess player), and *onna shachoo* (woman CEO), to name but a few. Terms like these are often used by men to undermine and ridicule various accomplishments of women in the work force, which I find a shame (48-year-old part-time English instructor).
- New occupational terms such as *kangoshi* (nursing specialist, nurse) and *hoikushi* (licensed person for child care, preschool and kindergarten teacher) are routinely created even when a small number of men take up occupations in which women are predominantly engaged. In addition, all these new terms, without any exception, sound much more professional and formal than *kangofu* (nursing woman, female nurse) and *hobo* (protective mother, female preschool and kindergarten teacher) as if to imply that the presence of men adds authority to these professions (39-year-old adjunct college lecturer).

Gender-based differences concerning occupational and positional terms that are mentioned in these quotations can be interpreted as yet another residual effect of the notion of *danson johi* (men superior, women inferior). As pointed out by the survey participants, when men take up occupations and positions traditionally held by women, new, mostly gen-

7—Women and the Japanese Language

der inclusive terms are routinely created. For instance, *hobo* (protective mother) used to be the term for female nursery school and kindergarten teachers. In the late 1970s when a small number of men of the younger generation began to take up the occupation for the first time, they were initially called *hofu* (protective fathers). Following the amendment of Jidoo Fukushiho Shikorei (the Enforcement Act of the Child Welfare Law) in 1998, *hofu* was replaced by the much more professional and formal term, *hoikushi* (licensed person for child care), which was created in 1999 to represent both female and male nursery school and kindergarten teachers.

A similar process took place in the creation of the unisex term for nurse, *kangoshi* (nursing specialist, nurse), despite the fact that men consist of less than 5 percent of the entire number of nurses in present-day Japan. In the past, the term, *kangofu* (nursing woman) was used for female nurses, while men who began to take up nursing as a profession were called *kangonin* (nursing person). In 1968, with the amendment of Hokenfu, Josanpu, Kangofu Ho (the Public Health Nurses, Midwives, and Nurses Law), the new term, *kangoshi* (nursing man) was created for male nurses. Subsequently, in 2002, the Japanese government approved the legislation under which both female and male nurses are designated by the new term, *kangoshi* (nursing specialist, nurse). As explained in the following section, *kangoshi* (nursing man) and *kangoshi* (nursing specialist, nurse) are homonyms consisting of different *kanji* (ideographic characters) of *shi*; therefore, the former, *kangoshi* (nursing man) is a term exclusive to men, while the latter, *kangoshi* (nursing specialist; nurse) is a gender inclusive term.

The coinage of these gender inclusive occupational terms is a welcome development; however, it takes place only when men take up traditionally female-dominated occupations, not vice versa. Moreover, some of the coined occupational terms consist of the *kanji* that are not gender inclusive. For instance, as mentioned in the previous section, there are two characters sharing the same sound, *shi*, that are commonly used in occupational terms. One character refers to master regardless of gender, and is etymologically gender inclusive. Occupational terms consisting of this character include *kangoshi* (nursing specialist, nurse), *biyooshi* (hairdresser, beautician), *rihatsushi* (barber), *yakuzaishi* (pharmacist), *choorishi* (chef), *kyooshi* (teacher), *bokushi* (priest), and *ishi* (medical doctor), among others. In contrast, another character refers to male as well as samurai, and is etymologically exclusive to men. Occupational terms such as *kangoshi* (nursing man, male nurse), *hoikushi* (nursery school teacher, kindergarten teacher), *eiyooshi* (dietician), *bengoshi* (lawyer), and *daigishi* (assembly member) are among those made up of this character. It is, therefore, crucial to look carefully into the etymological background of *kanji* so that appropriate terms are coined in order to fairly represent genders.

Since the 1980s, there have been a surge of occupations that are transcribed by *katakana*, the phonetic letters used to transcribe words of non–Japanese origin. Some of these occupations include *serapisuto* (therapist), *kaunseraa* (counselor), *sutairisuto* (stylist), *purogramaa* (programmer), *directaa* (director), *purodyuusaa* (producer), *insutorakutaa* (instructor), *baiyaa* (buyer), *fotogurafaa* (photographer), *aatisuto* (artist), *myuujishan* (musician), *shefu* (chef), and *somurie* (sommelier). Occupations like these are literally called *katakana shokugyoo* (occupations), and are commonly found in the fashion and the high-tech industries as well as in show business. *Katakana shokugyoo* are particularly popular among the younger generation, who tend to consider such occupational terms of non–Japanese origin as being trendy and stylish. It is noteworthy that unlike traditionally male dominant occupational terms in the Japanese language, these new terms of non–Japanese origin are gender inclusive, and do not take various terms to denote female and woman as modifiers.

A significant increase in the usage of *katakana*, the phonetic letters to transcribe words of non–Japanese origin, as well as the popularity in *katakana shokugyoo* since the 1980s, is not favorably received, mainly by the older generation who consider such phenomena as the decay in the Japanese language. Nevertheless, the gender free notion that these occupational terms connote is a positive development not only for women in the work force, but also for overall nonsexist language reform.

In recent years, there has also been a welcome change in the use of titles. In the Japanese language, commonly used titles consist of three suffixes, *-shi*, *-sama*, and *-san* that are used after surnames to indicate levels of formality as well as respect: *-shi* and *-sama* are transcribed in *kanji* to convey a higher level of formality and greater degree of respect than *-san*, which is transcribed in *hiragana*, phonetic letters derived from *kanji*. Unlike their English counterparts, Japanese titles do not mark gender or marital status; however, there was gender-based asymmetry in their usage: *-shi* used to be frequently used with men's names, and *-san* with women's names (Endo, 1995; Takahashi, 1991). Because of the ongoing nonsexist language reform, this practice is not as prevalent. Nowadays, *-shi* and *-san* are used equally with both women and men depending upon the formality of the settings.

Single Women

There are a large number of words and phrases to ridicule and belittle single women past *tekireiki* (the period of marriageable age, in their mid– to late 20s) in the Japanese language. Some of the most commonly used derogatory expressions include *urenokori* (unsold merchandise), *ikiokure* (late to marry), and *ikazu goke* (widow without marrying), to name just a few. They have existed long before modern times; for instance, the origin of the term *urenokori* (unsold merchandise) dates back to the Edo period (1603–1867) (*Kojien*, 2008). Derogatory terms such as these are becoming less frequently used in urban areas with a relatively large population of single women in their 30s. On the other hand, in rural areas, these terms remain widely used against single women past *tekireiki*, whose number is rather small. Furthermore, various terms to deride single women are often used not only by their peer groups, but also by their family members as a reminder that women should marry during *tekireiki* before they become "too old." The gender asymmetry in many expressions in the Japanese language is also reflected by the fact that there are no pejorative terms in regard to single men past *tekireiki*.

Part II: Representation of Women in the Japanese Language

- Whether to marry or stay single is a very personal matter; however, it is not regarded as such in Japanese society. It is simply appalling that there are so many derogatory Japanese words and phrases referring to single women in their 30s. While some become old-fashioned, new ones are constantly created. I often wonder whether a situation like this also exists in other countries and languages (37-year-old part-time public employee).
- In the mostly homogenous Japanese society, there is strong emphasis on conformity at the cost of individuality. This can be seen in the prevailing notion of *tekireiki* (the period of marriageable age), particularly for women, as well as in a large number of both old and new expressions in the Japanese language to deride women who are single past *tekireiki* (76-year-old part-time Japanese instructor).

As pointed out by these quotations, in addition to *urenokori* (unsold merchandise), *ikiokure* (late to marry), and *ikazu goke* (widow without marrying), various expressions to belittle single women past *tekireiki* continue to be coined on a regular basis. For instance, *kurisumasu keeki* (Christmas cake) is a coinage from the 1980s, which likens single women to fancy cakes that people in Japan consume on or before Christmas day. They are both much in demand until the 25th, and then are unwanted afterwards. Throughout the 1980s, 25 was considered the crucial age for single women, as described in the commonly used phrase, "*25-sai wa ohada no magarikado* (The age of 25 is the turning point of the skin)." Originally used in an advertisement by a well-known cosmetics company in Japan, this phrase became another source of pressure on single women in their 20s.

As the number of single women past *tekireiki* has increased steadily, such terms as *toshikoshi soba* (buckwheat noodles consumed on New Year's Eve) took the place of *kurisumasu keeki* (Christmas cake) in the 1990s. In this case, single women are likened to buckwheat noodles that Japanese people traditionally consume on New Year's Eve for longevity. Similar to what *kurisumasu keeki* connotes, nobody wants *toshikoshi soba* or single women after the 31st. Another expression with a similar connotation, *31-sai make gumi* (the loser group of 31-year-old single women) was coined in the 2000s, referring to the age of 31 as the latest for a single woman to find a marriage partner. While both *toshikoshi soba* and *31-sai make gumi* have gained popularity to some extent, they are hardly as prevalent as the latest coinage, *makeinu* (loser, underdog, single woman in her 30s without children), which has been the most commonly used derogatory term since the early 2000s to ridicule and deride single women in their 30s without children.

Makeinu (loser, underdog, single woman in her 30s without children) was coined by a popular essayist, Sakai Junko, who herself was in her 30s, single, and without children at the time her book, *Makeinu no Toboe* (*Grumbling of the Loser*) was published in 2003. In her book, Sakai (2003) asserts that single women in their 30s without children are better off if they are resigned to being labeled as *makeinu* (loser, underdog) regardless of their professional and personal accomplishments or their assets, including good looks and attractive personalities. Based on her own experience, Sakai (2003) believes that such a mindset on the part of single women in their 30s would make it easier for them to get on in life, considering the prevailing negative reactions of the general public toward single women past *tekireiki* who are content with their lifestyles.

With its provoking title, *Makeinu no Toboe* (*Grumbling of the Loser*) not only became a bestseller and received many literary awards, but also the coinage *makeinu* by Sakai (2003), made the top 10 buzzwords of the year in 2004 (Jiyukokuminsha, 2008). It is unfortunate that since then the term *makeinu* has become one of many derogatory and demeaning expressions for single women in their 30s, despite the original intention of Sakai (2003) to give moral support to single women who share backgrounds similar to her own. Many critics, as well as Sakai (2003) herself, also point out that her account has been badly distorted by the sensational press coverage on the title of her book rather than on its content.

Single women in their 30s are not the only ones under close scrutiny: single women in their 20s are in a similar situation. The parents of young single women and those of the older generation frequently use the phrase *yomeiri mae no musume* (young woman before marrying into another family as *yome*, daughter-in-law/bride), although it is perceived as rather old-fashioned, particularly by those of the younger generation. This phrase is used when reminding young single women of their status as brides-to-be, and when criticizing certain demeanors and behaviors that are not considered appropriate for young single women prior to becoming *yome*, such as being ill-mannered or too outspoken, staying out late at night, wearing revealing clothes, and drinking heavily.

In present-day Japan, it is more common than in the past for young single women to lead an independent lifestyle and to leave their families for education and employment. As a result, it has become increasingly difficult in recent years to find young single women who can be labeled as *hakoiri musume* (daughter-in-a-box, young single woman who leads a sheltered life with her protective family). Nowadays, many Japanese people consider that such young single women have virtually gone out of existence.

However, *hakoiri musume*, the term whose origin dates back to the late Edo period (1603–1867) (*Kojien*, 2008), continues to be used mostly by elderly men when making references to nonhuman objects that are grown with utmost care. For instance, in one recent newspaper article, a 57-year-old gardener referred to the orchids that he grew as *hakoiri musume*. He further commented that it would be best to send them off to market when they are about to bloom, just like parents would marry off their daughters while they are attractive ("Ran No," 2008).

As pointed out by the quotations of women that were presented earlier, single women, particularly those past *tekireiki*, have been traditionally subjected to blatant ridicule, scorn, and criticism in the homogeneous Japanese society where conformity is highly valued. A large number of both old and new derogatory expressions for single women in their 30s are manifestations of such prevailing attitudes in society. It is time that women who have been subjected to various unfair treatment and offensive remarks should be treated fairly in society, as well as in language, regardless of their marital status and lifestyles.

Incidentally, there is one particular term related to single women and the institution of marriage, *nyuuseki* (entry into the family registers, marriage registration), which has been under much criticism in recent years. It is a commonly used term that refers to the marriage registration system in Japan. Under the existing *koseki seido* (family registration system), when a couple gets married, a woman's name is typically deleted from her family register, and is transferred into her husband's family register in order to officially document and legalize their marriage. This custom is called *nyuuseki*, and originated in the Meiji period (1868–1912) when the *koseki seido* was established.

Many feminist scholars and activists assert that the term *nyuuseki* is based on longstanding gender bias and should be eliminated altogether. They point out the historical fact that *nyuuseki* is one of the fundamental elements of the *koseki seido* which was created to support the pre–World War II patriarchal *ie* (family, household) system characterized by extreme gender inequality. Under the *ie* system, a woman married into her husband's family by *nyuuseki*, and literally became a part of her husband's household. She assumed the lowest position in his family as *yome* (daughter-in-law/bride), who served her husband as well as her in-laws. Furthermore, under the Civil Code of 1898, a wife was not only a legally unrecognized person without any rights, but also was considered an incompetent (Mackie, 2003; Sievers, 1983). Based on their assertion, feminist scholars and activists alike have proposed that legal terms without gender bias, such as *konin todoke* (marriage registration) and *konin todoke o dasu* (to submit marriage registration), should be used as nonsexist alternatives to *nyuuseki* and *nyuuseki suru* (to make an entry into the family registers, to register marriage).

Various Terms for Spouses

The Japanese language has a number of terms for wife and husband. The most frequently used terms referring to wife are *oku-san* (Mrs. Interior) (Cherry, 1987), *kanai* (house-insider) (Cherry, 1987), and *nyooboo* (court woman). While both *kanai* and *nyooboo* are used exclusively by a husband when referring to his wife, *oku-san* is used by women and men to refer to someone's wife. *Oku-san* is also used as an address term for married women in general. The terms used exclusively by a wife to refer to her husband are *shujin* (master), *teishu* (master, owner, head), and *danna* (master). Among these terms, *shujin* is the most formal, while *teishu* and *danna* are very casual. *Shujin, teishu,* and *danna* can also be used by women and men when referring to someone's husband. In this case, these terms take either the polite prefix *go-*, or the title *-san* as in *go-shujin* (master), *go-teishu* (master, owner, head), and *danna-san* (master).

- The vast majority of the Japanese terms that refer to wives and husbands such as *oku-san, kanai, shujin,* and *teishu,* not only sound very old-fashioned, but also reflect and foster existing gender-based role division. I personally do not want to use any of these when I get married. They need to be replaced with more modern terms that are free from gender bias (26-year-old part-time office worker).
- I do not like most of the Japanese terms for wife and husband because they are based on gender stereotypes. So, instead of referring to my husband as *shujin*, I use either his name in casual settings, or *otto* (husband) in formal settings. The problem is that I have no choice but to use the term *go-shujin* when addressing someone's husband. How I wish there were alternative terms that are more appropriate (39-year-old adjunct college lecturer).

As described by these quotations, commonly used Japanese terms referring to wife and husband are based on gender stereotypes, and define the traditional division of labor between wife and husband. However, there are some formal unisex terms for spouses that do not convey gender bias. For instance, a legal term called *haiguusha* (spouse) is among them, although it is extremely formal, and rarely used in everyday conversation. Other legal terms, *tsuma* (wife) and *otto* (husband), can be used to refer to one's spouse in formal settings, but they cannot be used to address the spouses of other people. Incidentally, in *Manyoshu* (*The Collection of Ten Thousand Leaves*), the oldest anthology of poetry in Japan completed in the 8th century, the term *tsuma* (wife, husband) was used gender inclusively to refer to one's spouse as well as others (*Kojien*, 2008).

In addition, there are both old and new informal gender neutral Japanese terms that are not based on gender stereotypes. Unlike the formal legal terminologies mentioned above, these informal terms can be used to refer to one's spouse as well as to address the spouses of other people. *Tsureai* (partner, mate), whose origin dates back to the Edo period (1603–1867), is one such term that is predominantly used by those of the older generation and by many feminist activists and scholars. Although perceived by many as old-fashioned, *tsureai* (partner, mate), derived from *tsureau* (to accompany someone), denotes spouse as a companion of one's journey without any element of gender stereotypes or bias. Another more recent term is English in origin: *paatonaa* (partner). It is used primarily by women of the younger generation who tend to prefer trendy and contemporary expressions of non–Japanese origin. In casual settings, many young couples also use first names or nicknames of spouses in place of various terms for spouses.

Considering the lifestyles, roles, and expectations of married couples that continue to evolve, particularly among the younger generation, most of the existing Japanese terms for spouses are undoubtedly out-of-date. As a matter of fact, the origin of the term for wife, *oku-san* (Mrs. Interior) (Cherry, 1987), dates back to the Kamakura period (1185–1333) when the feudal system was established. Married women of privileged samurai families who were addressed as such had little autonomy, and their roles were mostly limited to producing male heirs (Kaneko, 1995). Furthermore, the terms for husbands, including *shujin* (master) and *teishu* (master, owner, head), symbolize male supremacy based on the notion of *danson johi* (men superior, women inferior) that had developed and prevailed, particularly in the privileged ruling samurai class during this period. Similarly, the terms for wives, *kanai* (house-insider) (Cherry, 1987) and *oku-san* (Mrs. Interior) (Cherry, 1987), literally represent the place traditionally designated for wives in Japanese society. It should also be noted that in the Japanese language, there are a number of expressions including *gusai* (stupid wife, one's wife) and *akusai* (bad wife), which refer to a wife with negativity, while there is virtually no negative term for a husband.

It is reassuring that there are both old and new terms for spouses, *tsureai* (partner, mate) and *paatonaa* (partner) that do not convey gender bias. Furthermore, an encouraging development in recent years is the steady increase in the number of coinages to defy gender stereotypes, some of which are presented and discussed in the following section. In addition to the popularity of words of non–Japanese origin among the younger generation, such as *paatonaa*, that are free of gender bias, there are good prospects for the creation of more terms for spouses without any element of gender inequality and stereotypes.

Changes in the Japanese Language: Redefined and Coined Expressions

The ongoing nonsexist language reform that started in the mid–1970s, together with overall changes in Japanese society and in people's perceptions of gender issues, have resulted in the redefinition and creation of a number of gender-related expressions in the Japanese language, particularly since the 1980s. These expressions are redefined and coined to defy the notion of traditional gender-specific roles and stereotypes that have been prevalent in Japanese society for many centuries. Furthermore, these new additions to the Japanese language are often characterized by innovative approaches to coinage, as well as by a great deal of wit and humor, which make them appealing to the younger generation and the general public alike.

As a matter of fact, many of the redefined and coined expressions listed in this book either won the Trendy Word Grand Prix, or were selected among the top 10 buzzwords of the year. The Trendy Word Grand Prix is a popular annual event that was started in 1984 by Jiyukokuminsha, one of the major publishing companies in Japan, known for its yearly publication *Gendai Yogo no Kiso Chishiki* (*The Encyclopedia of Contemporary Words*). Since its first issue launched in 1948, *Gendai Yogo no Kiso Chishiki* has defined itself as "the compass of wisdom" (Jiyukokuminsha,

2008, p. 2), which provides its readers with sources to understand social phenomena by means of vogue words. Over the years it has earned a reputation as one of the most reliable and comprehensive references of the latest trends in the Japanese language. Representatives of its readership are invited every year to nominate a total of 60 trendy words and phrases, out of which a grand prize and the top 10 buzzwords are selected by committee members composed of editors of *Gendai Yogo no Kiso Chishiki*, authors, journalists, and scholars, among others. An award ceremony held in December is one of the most popular events in the publishing industry, and is covered extensively by the media. The fact that many recently redefined and coined expressions that defy gender-based roles and stereotypes have been selected as buzzwords is a very encouraging development, and certainly has a positive effect on ongoing language reform.

In the following section, some of the representative gender-related expressions that have been redefined and coined since the 1980s are presented, and are discussed along with relevant etymological information.

shufu (main husband, house husband)

A term for a house husband, *shufu*, was created in the 1980s, when an increasing number of couples of the younger generation began to share housework despite the age-old tradition of strict gender-based role division. In some instances, this has led to the reversal of the traditional gender-specific role that is symbolized by the phrase "*Otoko wa shigoto, onna wa katei* (Men at work, women at home)." As a result, some husbands have decided to leave the labor force and opted to stay home as full-time homemakers, while their wives either take up or continue to engage in full-time employment. The number of *shufu*, however, remains extremely limited in Japan.

It should be noted that although the term *shufu* shares the same pronunciation as its female counterpart, *shufu* (main woman, homemaker), they are different *kanji* (ideographic characters) compounds. The term *shufu* referring to a house husband is a compound consisting of characters representing main and husband, while *shufu* referring to a homemaker consists of characters that represent main and wife. In addition, the term *shufu* (main woman, homemaker) tends to be perceived unfavorably by some women and men because of its close association with domesticity; on the other hand, some women of the younger generation with full-time employment tend to have favorable perceptions of men who are *shufu* (main husbands, house husbands) as being open-minded and liberated enough to take up a reversed role.

hai misutaa (high mister, single man in his mid–30s or older)

As the number of single women in their 30s has increased at a steady pace since the 1980s, so has the number of single men past *tekireiki* (the period of marriageable age, in their late 20s to early 30s). This trend resulted in the emergence of the new term *hai misutaa* (high mister), referring to a single man in his mid–30s or older. It was created jokingly in the 1980s as a reciprocal expression of the Japanese English coinage, *hai misu* (high miss, single woman in her 30s), which had existed long before. Similar to many pejorative expressions for single women, *hai misu* has a definite tone of mockery. In contrast, its male counterpart, *hai misutaa*, coined as a wordplay, is spared such a negative tone. Furthermore, there has been no other coinage similar to *hai misutaa* since the 1980s, while new terms to belittle single women in their 30s have continued to be coined on a regular basis. Gender-based differences in regard to coinages as well as their connotations clearly reflect the prevalent differences in public perceptions of single women and of single men in Japanese society.

ikemen (great face, good-looking young man)

Reflecting a popular belief that good looks are the greatest asset to women, there are a large number of Japanese terms that are commonly used for attractive women, such as *bijin* (beautiful person, attractive woman) and *bijo* (beautiful woman); on the other hand, there used to be very few terms that referred to men with good looks. Among these terms, *hansamu* (handsome) has been by far the most widely used, and the rest, including *otokomae* (handsome, good-looking), *binan* (beautiful man), and *bidanshi* (beautiful man) are rather obsolete.

However, this has changed in recent years, as there has been a steady increase in men, particularly of the younger generation, who are very conscious of their appearance. It is not uncommon for these men to use various skin care products, wear make-up, dye their hair, and visit aesthetic salons for facials in order to keep up their looks (Miller, 2006). The emergence of such young men has resulted in a number of coinages for a man with good looks, out of which *ikemen* (great face, good-looking young man) has gained the most popularity. It was originally a buzzword that was coined among those of the younger generation in the late 1990s, but it later spread to the general public through frequent use by the media (Kitahara & Taishukan, 2006).

The term *ikemen* was created by combining *ikeru* (very good), as well as *iketeiru* (cool), with "*men*," which means face in Japanese, and "men" in English. The coinages are often made up in this manner by combining Japanese words with non–Japanese words, mostly from English. Despite the Japanese saying, "*Otoko wa nakami de shoobu suru* (Man's worth is judged by his substance, not by his looks)," which represents the prevailing attitude with regard to looks among men of the older generation, younger men these days are flattered to be labeled as *ikemen* (great face, good-looking young man).

While there are a large number of expressions in the Japanese language that are used to ridicule unattractive women, traditionally there are very few of those for their male counterparts. The coinage of *busamen* (plain face, unattractive young man) as an antonym of *ikemen* defies such tradition, although *busamen* has not yet gained as much popularity as *ikemen*. As in the case of *ikemen*, the term *busamen* was coined by combining *busaiku* (plain-looking) with "*men*," meaning face in Japanese, and "men" in English. According to the 2006 edition of *Minna de Kokugo Jiten! (The Japanese Language Dictionary by All of Us!)* (Kitahara & Taishukan, 2006), *busamen* refers to a man in his late teens to early 30s whose appearance is not trendy and refined.

gyakutama (reverse *tamanokoshi*, man who manages to achieve high social status by marrying a wealthy woman)

The coinage *gyakutama* (reverse *tamanokoshi*) originates from the phrase "*tamanokoshi ni noru*," whose literal translation is "to ride the jeweled palanquin" (Cherry, 1987). Both the phrase and its shortened form, *tamanokoshi* (jeweled palanquin) (Cherry, 1987), refer to a woman who manages to achieve high social status by marriage to a well-to-do man. As pointed out by Cherry (1987), its English equivalents, including gold digger and fortune hunter, convey overt negativity as well as contempt toward such women. In contrast, a woman referred to as *tamanokoshi* is not only admired and perceived favorably in Japanese society, but also thought of as one in an enviable position by most single women.

The term *gyakutama* (reversed *tamanokoshi*, man who manages to achieve high social status by marrying wealthy woman) was coined by the media in the 1990s, when there was an increase in younger men, typically those with good looks, getting married to wealthy women who were often older, mostly in the entertainment industry. Representing the reverse of traditional gender-based stereotypes and roles, *gyakutama* has gained much popularity among women of all generations. As in the case of a woman referred to as *tamanokoshi*, who manages to acquire an enviable position by marriage, a man referred to as *gyakutama* is also considered lucky to be in such a position.

Incidentally, the gender neutral term *kakusakon* (marriage with disparity), was coined in the early 2000s, and has been frequently used along with *tamanokoshi* and *gyakutama*. Being more formal and inclusive than these two terms, *kakusakon* refers to a couple who differ not only in social and economic status, but also in physical appearance and occupation (Jiyukokuminsha, 2008).

tanshin katei (single parent family)

Prior to the 1980s, single parent families in Japan consisted predominantly of *boshi katei* (mother and child family, single mother family) because of the very low number of women who remarried. The steady rise in the divorce rate since the 1980s is the major factor in the overall increase in the number of single parent families in Japan, and the term *fushi katei* (father and child family, single father family) was coined later as the number of such families began to increase in the 1980s. Although both of these terms are commonly used in official documents as well as in formal settings, they are discriminatory in nature: *boshi katei* is typically associated with economic hardship, while *fushi katei* is associated with a lack of home environment. They are also often used both in public and in private with an undertone of pity and contempt toward single parent families. This is evidenced by the English translation of these terms in dictionaries, in which *boshi katei* is listed as "fatherless family," and *fushi katei* as "motherless family" (*Progressive Japanese-English Dictionary*, 1986).

The term *tanshin katei* (single parent family) was coined in the late 1990s against such a social climate as an alternative to *boshi katei* and *fushi katei*. In the past, a single parent family was often referred to as *kesson katei* (deficient family), in contrast to the term *seijoo katei* (normal family), made up of both parents and children. Such an extremely discriminatory term was also replaced by *tanshin katei*. However, *boshi katei* and *fushi katei* have continued to be widely used by the media and the general public alike, and the discrimination and prejudice against single parent families remain. Nevertheless, the coinage of *tanshin katei* (single parent family) without negativity and without a discriminatory tone symbolizes the change in traditional family structures in Japan. It also conveys the message that a single parent family is simply one of many variations of families, and should be fairly treated as such.

kaishun (buying lust, engaging in sexual act by offering money or goods)

Among a number of derogatory Japanese terms for prostitutes, the most frequently used in formal settings is *baishunfu* (woman who sells lust). It is derived from *baishun* (selling lust, prostitution), which refers to the act of prostitution. On the other hand, there used to be no expression in the Japanese language with regard to men engaging in sexual acts by offering money or goods. Such instance of gender-based imbalance in language was corrected with the coinage of the term *kaishun* (buying lust, engaging in sexual act by offering money or goods). It was created in the mid-1970s shortly after an increasing number of Japanese men began to take part in organized sex tours to South Korea and Southeast Asian countries, mostly Thailand, and the Philippines. Many women's groups both in Japan and in these countries joined together to protest against sex tours as a form of economic exploitation of women, and against Japanese men who took part in such tours to exploit women in the sex industry.

Unlike the creators of the vast majority of coinages, who are often difficult to locate, the term *kaishun* was coined by Matsui Yayori, a senior staff writer of the Asashi Shinbun, a major newspaper company in Japan. One of very few women at the editorial level in the male-dominated news media, Matsui is well-known for her publications on gender issues, specifically the impact of Japan's economic growth on the lives of women in Asia. In addition, she has been organizing and participating in various activities and events of the Ajia no Onnatachi no Kai (the Asian Women's Association) as one of its founding members. Launched in 1977, the association aims to create stronger relationships between women in Japan and those in Asian countries (Buckley, 1997). Matsui (1997) recalled that it was during the demonstration that she had organized against Japanese male sex tours to Korea that she coined the term *kaishun*. She further comments:

> In Japanese, prostitution is called *baishun*, written with two characters meaning "sell spring." I changed the characters so that it meant "buy spring." I wanted to change attitudes toward and concepts of prostitution. Traditionally, women who sold their bodies were blamed, while men who bought their sex were not condemned. Therefore, the word had to be changed. It may seem a rather small thing, but it is revolutionary to shift the responsibility from women to men. Those who buy sex are to be condemned more than those who sell [p. 153].

Since then, the term *kaishun* has gained wide recognition and has been routinely used by the media to report various instances of sexual exploitation of women by men. As Matsui (1997) states, the coinage is revolutionary and epoch-making in Japanese society where prostitution has been traditionally viewed only from the women's perspectives.

hikon (unmarried by choice)

In the 1990s, when the number of single women and men continued to increase, the unisex term *hikon* (unmarried by choice) was coined to describe the lifestyle of those who opt to be single. It was taken from the title of the book *Hikon Jidai* (*The Era of Unmarried by Choice*), published in 1993 by a well-known journalist, Yoshihiro Kiyoko, which gained particular popularity among young women. A series of books on the single lifestyle were published during this period, and the concept of single life by choice became known to the public. Prior to the 1980s, *mikon* (not yet married), which connotes the intention and expectation to marry was one of the most frequently used terms to describe the status of singles. For this reason, the coinage of *hikon* is epoch-making in Japanese society where single people, particularly women, have long been considered oddities, and have been subjected to frequent ridicule and criticism. In contrast to the prevailing social convention to marry, the term *hikon* not only connotes the intention of both women and men who opt to remain single without any negative undertone, but also denotes it as an alternative lifestyle.

shinguru (single, single person)

While the numbers are limited, there are several Japanese terms such as *dokushin* (lone self, single), *hitori mono* (one person, single), and *hitori* (by oneself, single), that refer to both single women and single men without overtly negative connotations. These terms can also be used by those who are single, when asked about their marital status. The one that is most frequently used in formal settings is *dokushin*. Unlike a number of terms that are used to ridicule and deride single women past *tekireiki* (the period of marriageable age, in their mid- to late 20s), *dokushin* does not convey any negativity for those who are single regardless of gender or age. For instance, there is a coined term called *dokushin kizoku* (aristocratic singles) referring to single people who have freedom, large disposable incomes, and spare time to enjoy a carefree lifestyle. Those who are married with children, who long for such a lifestyle, often use the term *dokushin kizoku* with envy for those of the similar age group who are single. In contrast, other expressions, like *hitori mono* and *hitori*, which are mainly used in casual settings, tend to convey a feeling of pity toward single women as well as single men by those who are married.

In the 1980s, the number of both single women and men past *tekireiki* began to increase at a steady pace for the first time in Japanese history. It was during this period when the English word *shinguru* (single) gained popularity among single women of the younger generation as a trendy alternative to the Japanese terms *dokushin*, *hitori mono*, and *hitori*. As in the cases of many words of non–Japanese origin, *shinguru* conveys a gender free notion without any negative connotation.

The use of the term *shinguru* became prevalent in the 1990s, particularly since it appeared in the subtitle of the book *Hikon Jidai: Onnatachi no Shinguru Raifu* (*The Era of Unmarried by Choice: Women's Single Life*), which was mentioned earlier. The book was based on the interviews that the author, Yoshihiro Kiyoko, also a well-known journalist, conducted with a total of 56 women who opted to be single by defying social conventions. Because this book, published in 1993, was one of the few that documented the lifestyles and voices of single women in Japan, it not only gained huge popularity, particularly among women in their 20s and 30s, but also received extensive media coverage.

Moreover, the prevalence of the word *shinguru* in the 1990s resulted in the Japanese English coinage *parasaito shinguru* (parasite singles). According to Yamada Masashiro, a sociologist who coined the term in 1997, *parasaito shinguru* refers to those who are single, stay with their parents in their adulthood, and are dependent on them in every aspect of their lives including finances. The term *parasaito shinguru* is also used to criticize those who, instead of getting married, continue to live in comfort at their parents' home not only after the completion of schooling, but also after being employed. The number of such cases has been steadily rising since the late 1990s. As a matter of fact, *parasaito shinguru* was selected among the top 10 buzzwords of the year 2000 (Jiyukokuminsha, 2008).

batsu ichi (one cross/mark against them, a person who is divorced once)

The divorce rate was very low in Japan prior to the 1980s, when incompatibility was not allowed as the reason for divorce, and women's career choices were very limited. There was a strong social stigma attached to those who were divorced, particularly to women, as can be seen by a discriminatory and contemptuous term, *demodori* (returnee to one's parents' place), referring to a divorced woman. What this term implies is that upon divorce, a woman without means to support herself has no place to go but back to her parents' home to weather the hardship.

As the number of divorces has continued to increase at a steady pace since the 1980s, less stigma is attached to those who are divorced. This has resulted in the coinage of the unisex term *batsu ichi*. Compared to *demodori*, which was commonly used until around the early 1980s to look down upon divorced women, *batsu ichi* is used for both women and men without the undertone of negativity that was associated with divorce in the past. It also conveys a laid-back attitude, particularly among the younger generation, to deal with divorce as one of many ups and downs in life, which is an unprecedented phenomenon in Japanese society.

kafu (lone woman, widow)

Although it is one of the most discriminatory expressions in the Japanese language, *miboojin* (the person who is not yet dead, widow) has been the term that has been most frequently used by widows themselves as well as by the general public. This is because *miboojin* was customarily used in a formal context, as in *sensoo miboojin* (war widow), for a number of years. In contrast, other terms for widows such as *goke* (after family) (Cherry, 1987) are not suitable to use in the presence of widows because of a pejorative undertone. As a result, the misleading perception that *miboojin* was the most appropriate term to refer to a widow became prevalent.

Since the mid-1970s, when nonsexist language reform became known to the public, the term *miboojin* has been under frequent criticism by women's groups who have proposed alternative expressions without gender bias. Among them is a gender neutral term, *yamome* (widow, widower), whose origin dates back to the Heian period (794–1185). *Yamome* does not have an undertone of negativity; however, it is a colloquial expression, and can be used only in casual settings. Therefore, a rather formal *kanji* (ideographic characters) compound, *kafu* (lone woman), is used nowadays as an alternative term for a widow, although it cannot be used by widows as a term to refer to themselves. The elimination of *miboojin*, one of the most derogatory and discriminatory terms used for women, is certainly among the many important contributions of nonsexist language reform in recent years.

Incidentally, the term *kafu* refers not only to a widow but also to a divorced woman, and consists of the *kanji* that represent lone and woman. As in the cases of many *kanji* compounds sharing the same pronunciation that were mentioned earlier, the term referring to a widower and a divorced man is also called *kafu* (lone man); however, it consists of the characters representing lone and man. It is noteworthy that the term *kafu* (lone man, widower, divorced man), which does not have any discriminatory tone, has been used alongside *miboojin* in formal settings as well as in official documents for a number of years.

dansei funin (male infertility)

In the past, there was no expression in the Japanese language with regard to male infertility, while there were a number of discriminatory words and phrases to denote that women were exclusively responsible for infertility. The two most commonly used such expressions were *umazume* (stone woman, no-life woman, infertile woman), and "*Kashite sannen konaki wa saru* (A wife should leave her husband if she fails to bear a child within 3 years of marriage)." They were widely used from the late 12th to the late 19th centuries, when bearing children, particularly male heirs to succeed the family estate and to maintain family lineage, was considered the most important role of women (Kaneko, 1995). Although these expressions became mostly archaic by the mid– to late 20th century, the tendency to associate women, not men, with the causes of infertility remains among Japanese people, particularly those of the older generation.

It is, therefore, a major progress in recent years that these extremely derogatory expressions for female infertility have been replaced by medical terms such as *funin* (infertility) and *funinshoo* (infertility, sterility). Moreover, the gender-specific terms, *josei funin* (female infertility) and *dansei funin* (male infertility) are backed by medical research, which verifies that the causes of infertility are equally shared by women and men. Considering the long history in Japanese society to wrongly place all the blame for infertility on women, it is certainly a relief to see the creation of the term *dansei funin*, although it is long overdue.

ara saa (around 30, woman around 30), *ara foo* (around 40, woman around 40)

There are very few Japanese words and phrases to denote the age of women, particularly those in their 30s and older, without negative undertones. These two new terms, *ara saa* and *ara foo*, are created by English words, and are written in *katakana*, the phonetic letters used to transcribe words of non–Japanese origin. As in the majority of coinages of non–Japanese origin that are transcribed in *katakana*, both of these terms not only denote trendiness, but also do not connote gender related bias or negativity.

According to the 2008 *Gendai Yogo no Kiso Chishiki* (*The Encyclopedia of Contemporary Words*) (Jiyukokuminsha, 2008), *ara saa* was originally coined by a fashion magazine and was used mostly in the clothing industry before it gained popularity among the general public in the mid–2000s. The women referred to as *ara saa* are fashion-conscious, and set a number of trends in Japan in the mid–1990s. They are also interested in making various personal investments in order to enrich their lifestyle, rather than getting married or giving birth to children. In recent years, a number of companies in Japan have been specifically targeting the women of the *ara saa* generation who have strong purchasing power with large disposable incomes.

Following the coinage of *ara saa*, another age-related expression, *ara foo*, was created in 2008. It was taken from the title of the TV drama series called *Around 40*, which aired in the spring of that year, depicting the ups and downs in the life of a single medical professional in her 40s. As one of the very few TV dramas about women in their 40s, *Around 40* won a lot of popularity, particularly among women of that age group, and the coinage *ara foo* also won second place among the top 10 buzzwords of 2008 (Jiyukokuminsha, 2008).

In the extremely age-conscious Japanese society, where it is traditionally considered that aging works for men, but against women, the coinages of *ara saa* and *ara foo* without negative tones are certainly revolutionary developments and also have a liberating effect on women. These two terms have given women in their 30s and 40s new ways of expressing their age, not only openly, but also in a trendy manner, rather than hiding it.

seiteki iyagarase, seku hara (sexual harassment)

The English term sexual harassment was introduced to the public in 1988 by citizens' groups in Japan, and won the Trendy Word Grand Prix in the following year of 1989 (Jiyukokuminsha, 2008). The Japanese term, *seiteki iyagarase* (sexual harassment), was also coined during this period. Various developments, including the completion of the outline of the Legislative Bill on the Prevention of Sexual Harassment by the government in 1991, led to the increase in public awareness of sexual harassment. At the same time, another coinage, *seku hara* (sexual harassment), an abbreviated form of the English term, sexual harassment, has gained popularity over the rather formal original Japanese coinage, *seiteki iyagarase*.

Furthermore, in order to stop sexual harassment among the institutions of higher education, an organization called the Campus Sexual Harassment Nationwide Network was launched in 1997, which was followed by the coinage of the term *aka hara* (academic harassment). It refers to sexual harassment as well as a broader range of harassment and abuse of power by professors toward their colleagues, subordinates, and students. Similarly, other Japanese English terms such as *pawa hara* (power harassment) and *mora hara* (moral harassment) were coined. The coinages of these terms have played a significant part in increasing public understanding that any form of harassment, whether sexual or not, is a violation of human rights (Ueno, 2008). Unlike the victims of *seku hara* who are generally women in Japan, the victims of other forms of harassment consist of both women and men.

In the Japanese workplace, women have traditionally been considered secondary and subordinate to men, and have been subjected to frequent sexual harassment. Prior to the coinage of *seku hara*, sexual harassment was typically referred to as *seiteki karakai* (sexual joke) or *itazura* (prank), and was not taken seriously (Ueno, 2008). Furthermore, sexual harassment was routinely justified by a number of expressions, out of which one of the commonly used terms was *sukin shippu* (skinship), a Japanese English coinage, referring to intimate physical contact, as between mother and child, without a negative tone. Another frequently used phrase was *sake no ue no dekikodo* (incident happened under the influence of alcohol), representing the overall tolerance in Japanese society for the misbehavior of men who are drunk. In the past, women who expressed their concerns or complained about sexual harassment were routinely ignored, criticized, or told that they were simply overreacting.

Consequently, this prevailing mentality among Japanese companies to overlook the seriousness of sexual harassment led to the sexual harassment and discrimination lawsuit filed against Mitsubishi Motor Company by the Equal Employment Opportunity Commission (EEOC) in the United States in 1996. Subsequently, the Guidelines to Prevent Sexual Harassment were proclaimed by the Ministry of Labor in 1998, and a number of lawsuits have continued to be filed by women, which is unprecedented in Japanese labor history (Mackie, 2003). The coinages of *seiteki iyagarase* (sexual harassment) and *seku hara* have an immeasurable effect on women who have been suffering in silence for many years, as well as on some men who have been physically and verbally abusive to women without thinking about the grave consequences of their behavior.

Overview of the Progress of Nonsexist Language Reform in Japan

The second wave of feminism, which began in the early 1970s, generated considerable interest among linguists and language professionals worldwide in re-examining the ways languages represent, define, and treat women and men. This has become the area of study known as sexism in language or linguistic sexism, and has led to the movement called nonsexist language reform. Nonsexist language reform aims to expose the linguistic bias that is "in favor of the representation of the man, the male,

Part II: Representation of Women in the Japanese Language

and the masculine as the norm, and against the woman, the female, and the feminine" (Pauwels, 1998, p. 9). It also aims "to rid language of sexism by eliminating sexist practices from language use, and by replacing them with nonsexist ones or, by creating new ways of expression which avoid gender bias" (Pauwels, 1998, p. 9).

The concept of nonsexist language reform became known to the general public in Japan in the mid–1970s. Following the designation of 1975 as the United Nations International Year for Women, the Conference on Women's Problems for the International Year for Women was held in Tokyo in the fall of that year under the sponsorship of the Japanese government. These developments had a positive effect on increasing public awareness regarding various women's issues, including sexism in the Japanese language (K. Tanaka, 1995a). As a matter of fact, it was also during that same year when an incident in regard to nonsexist language reform received extensive media coverage for the first time in Japanese history.

It all started with a TV commercial for instant noodles by one of the major food companies in Japan. In the commercial, a young woman was busy preparing the noodles for her boyfriend in the kitchen, and said to him, "*Watashi tsukuru hito* (I am the one who cooks)." And her boyfriend, who was waiting at the table, said to her, "*Boku taberu hito* (I am the one who eats)," in response. About a month after the commercial was first aired, several members of the Kokusai Fujinnen o Kikkake to shite Kodo o Okosu Onnatachi no Kai (the Group of Women Who Take Action on the Occasion of the International Women's Year) visited the company headquarters in Tokyo to request the discontinuation of the commercial.

The members protested that not only the visual image presented, but also the language used in the commercial would further promote the existing gender-based role division to designate women for household work and child care, and men for employment outside the home. Although the company countered their protest by insisting that there was no intention of discrimination against women in the commercial, it nevertheless went off the air after 2 months. This incident attracted so much public and media attention that the phrases used in the commercial,

"*Watashi tsukuru hito*" and "*Boku taberu hito,*" were selected among the top 10 buzzwords of that year (Jiyukokuminsha, 2008).

Moreover, the Kokusai Fujinnen o Kikkake to shite Kodo o Okosu Onnatachi no Kai, during the same year of 1975, held a meeting with senior managers of Nihon Hoso Kyokai (Japan Broadcasting Corporation), a public broadcasting system in Japan also known as NHK. The group submitted a list of questions and demands regarding the representations of women in the male-dominated Japanese media. The elimination of sexist language such as *shujin* (master, husband) and discriminatory expressions against women was included in their demands, along with the diverse portrayal of women and men in nontraditional roles, and the overall increase in the number of women among staff members as well as in important positions in programs, to name but a few (Yukawa & Saito, 2004).

The Kokusai Fujinnen o Kikkake to shite Kodo o Okosu Onnatachi no Kai was launched in 1975 as a grass-roots organization and as an advocate group for women's rights. Its members consisted of women of diverse backgrounds, including legislators, lawyers, educators, office workers, students, and homemakers. For the next 2 decades, the group continued to run a number of campaigns together with its subgroups on nonsexist language reform and fairer representations of women in the media as well as on a wide range of women's issues including equality in education and employment, among others. It successfully attracted the attention of the general public and the media with its highly visible campaign style by means of demonstrations and sit-ins. In 1986, following the United Nations International Decade for Women, the group shortened its name to the Kodo Suru Onnatachi no Kai (the Group of Women Who Take Action), and remained active through 1996, when it disbanded upon achieving its initial goals (Endo, 2004; Mackie, 2003).

A series of protests against the gender stereotypes and discrimination in the media by the Kokusai Fujinnen o Kikkake to shite Kodo o Okosu Onnatachi no Kai during the United Nations International Year for Women in 1975 made an immeasurable contribution to nonsexist language reform. It attracted public and media attention to sexism and gender bias in the Japanese language, which continued to grow throughout the following United Nations International Decade for Women from 1976 to 1985.

Furthermore, the Ratification of the United Nations Convention on the Elimination of All Forms of Discrimination against Women (CEDAW) in 1985, and the subsequent introduction of Danjo Koyo Kikai Kinto Ho (the Equal Employment Opportunity Law) in 1986 to prohibit discrimination against women in the Japanese workplace, had a significant effect on advancing nonsexist language reform. One of the well-known organized efforts by women's groups took place in 1989, when the Nihon Joseigaku Kenkyu Kai (the Japan Women's Studies Association) demanded that commercial and public broadcasting stations nationwide should eliminate the use of sexist language to belittle women and to foster existing gender inequality (Endo, 2004; Mackie, 2003).

At the same time, a series of inquiries into the representation of genders in the Japanese language were made by feminist scholars and researchers during the 1980s and the 1990s, which contributed substantially to further promote nonsexist language reform. One such pioneering study was carried out by the Kotoba to Onna o Kangaeru Kai (the Group to Think about Language and Women) whose founding members consist of several women educators and scholars. In 1983, the group launched a project to closely examine the representation of genders in Japanese language dictionaries. Detailed content analysis was conducted on entries, definitions, and illustrative sentences of a total of eight highly regarded and widely used Japanese language dictionaries that were published or revised in the early 1980s. The results of the analysis were presented in 1985 in the group's publication entitled, *Kokugojiten ni Miru Josei Sabetsu* (*Sexism in the Japanese Language Dictionaries*) (Kotoba to Onna o Kangaeru Kai, 1985).

The group concluded that the definitions and illustrative sentences of the Japanese language dictionaries were saturated with gross gender stereotypes and gender-based asymmetry. Based on these findings, the group made a series of suggestions about revisions which would eliminate the gender discrimination, and proposed that lexicographers as well as publishers make serious concerted efforts to eliminate sexism. It should be noted that some publishers were willing to accept the group's proposal, and revised their dictionaries accordingly. The group continues to conduct content analysis on dictionaries when new editions are published, and to evaluate the extent of the revisions whenever they are made by the publishers.

Another significant study was conducted by the Media no Naka no Seisabetsu o Kangaeru Kai (the Association to Think about Gender Discrimination in the Media) also known as GEAM. It is one of the most influential groups that have been playing an active role in challenging the prevalent sexism in the male-dominated Japanese media. While other groups and associations mentioned earlier are located in the Tokyo metropolitan area, this association, since it was founded in the early 1990s, is located in Toyama prefecture, away from the urban area. In order to promote nonsexist language reform in the media, the association not only organizes and participates in various activities and events nationwide, but also maintains close ties with the community by holding study groups, workshops, and meetings with local journalists, as well as with residents, on a regular basis.

In addition to examining the representation of genders in the media by conducting extensive content analysis on newspaper articles, the association continues to make proposals for expressions that can be used in place of those embedded with sexism (Saito, 1997; Yukawa & Saito, 2004). In 1996, the association and Ueno Chizuko, a noted feminist scholar, collaborated to publish *Kitto Kaerareru Seisabetsugo: Watashitachi no Gaidorain* (*Sexist Language that can be Certainly Changed: Our Guidelines*), in which their own *jendaa gaidorain* (gender guidelines) are included. These were the first guidelines issued specifically for the media, and they exerted considerable influence. As a matter of fact, a part of the guidelines proposed by Ueno and the association (1996) were adopted by some of the news media. For instance, Kyodo Tsushinsha, the largest nonprofit news agency in Japan, added a section on sexist expressions for the first time in its *Kisha Handobukku Dai 8 Han* (*Reporters' Handbook the 8th Edition*) which was compiled the following year in 1997. Further details on the revisions of the handbook are presented in the following section on nonsexist language reform and the Japanese media.

The overall progress of nonsexist language reform since the mid–

1970s can be summarized by the following quote from Ide (1997), who is a full-time academic and a feminist linguist known for her research on Japanese women's language:

> In 1979, when I wrote my book *Women's Language, Men's Language*, I think there was a purpose to listing in detail the types of sexist language common in Japan. It was a strategy suited to that period. I have to admit, however, that when I recently canvassed students in order to look at the contemporary use of discriminatory language, I was surprised to find how much change there has been. There has also been an obvious improvement in the major daily newspapers [p. 45].

Nonsexist Language Reform and the Japanese Government

It is fair to say that a local, self-governing organization in Kanagawa prefecture located southwest of the Tokyo metropolitan area, took the initiative in carrying out nonsexist language reform at the government level. In 1982, a comprehensive prefectural plan to improve the social status of women, called the Kanagawa Josei Puran (the Kanagawa Women's Plan) was developed, and was promoted by the Fujin Kikakushitsu (the Women's Project Office), which was established in the same year as a part of the Kanagawa prefectural office. Nonsexist language reform was among a number of objectives stated in the plan, which made a specific request that the publications by Kanagawa prefecture be reviewed and revised if they contained any of the following: "(1) language that discriminates against or derogates women, (2) passages that implicitly valorize traditional, fixed gender roles, and (3) words and phrases for family, married couples, women, and men that evoke the old patriarchal family system (Endo, 2004, p. 180)." This action on language reform initiated by a local women's office had a ripple effect throughout the entire nation, and resulted in extensive reviews and revisions of publications by local governments.

Another major reform was undertaken by the Danjo Kyodo Sankaku Shingikai (the Council for Gender Equality), which was set up in 1994 as an advisory body to the Prime Minister for the realization of a society based on gender equality. In 1996, the Council completed the Vision for Gender Equality, which was followed by the issuance of the Plan for Gender Equality in the Year 2000. Language reform was included in the plan, which calls for "the promotion of the use of nonsexist phrases in all informational and other publications produced by public agencies" (Endo, 2004, p. 180). Furthermore, the plan made a recommendation that local governments should draw up their own detailed guidelines to promote nonsexist language reform. As a result, a series of *handobukku* (handbooks) and *gaidorain* (guidelines) were produced by local governments nationwide, and have made a considerable contribution to further raise public awareness about language reform aimed at eliminating sexism and gender bias embedded in the Japanese language.

In 2001, the Danjo Kyodo Sankaku Shingikai (the Council for Gender Equality) changed its name to the Danjo Kyodo Sankaku Kaigi (the Conference on Gender Equality), and became a part of the influential Cabinet Office headed by the Prime Minister. This development was viewed by many as a positive indication that the Japanese government has begun to enact serious efforts toward promoting gender equality in society. This, in turn, will certainly have a favorable effect on successful nonsexist language reform in the future.

Nonsexist Language Reform and the Japanese Media

As mentioned in Chapter 5, prior to the mid–1970s, the male-dominated Japanese media was very harsh and critical of the women's movement, repeatedly referring to it as "a spree by some crazy young women" (Morley, 1999, p. 77). Sexism was prevalent in the media in its use of language as well as its portrayal of women. However, a series of nonsexist language reforms undertaken by a number of feminist activists and women's groups since the mid–1970s, along with language reform at the government level starting in the mid–1980s, has had considerable influence on sexist language use by the media.

Part II: Representation of Women in the Japanese Language

Newspaper companies as well as news agencies in Japan routinely provide reporters with instruction and reference manuals to serve as guidelines in writing articles. These instruction and reference manuals include a section regarding various discriminatory terms and offensive expressions. Precise examples informing reporters how to handle these terms and expressions properly in order to write articles that do not offend readers are shown in this section. Discriminatory terms and offensive expressions in this section are listed under a number of categories, such as physical and mental disabilities, illnesses, occupation, status, race, and ethnicity, among others; however, there was no specific category on gender bias and discrimination until the late 1990s.

In 1997, for the very first time in the history of the Japanese media, gender discrimination was added to the categories in this section in the handbook compiled by Kyodo Tsushinsha, the largest nonprofit news agency in Japan, which consists of major newspapers and Nihon Hoso Kyokai (Japan Broadcasting Corporation), a public broadcasting system. The following are the guidelines on gender discrimination that appeared in *Kisha Handobukku Dai 8 Han* (*Reporters' Handbook the 8th Edition*) published by Kyodo Tsushinsha:

- Avoid the term, *joryuu* (female style, used as a female modifier to a male-dominated occupation, particularly in art, as in *joryuu sakka* referring to a woman author) except in proper nouns such as *joryuu bungakushoo* (female literary award) and *joryuu meijin* (female master). Simply state the name of the occupation without adding *joryuu*, along with the surname of the woman who holds the occupation.
- Replace *-joshi* (woman who has fame as well as high social status, used as a title with the surname of such a woman) with the gender neutral title, *-san*.
- Note: Whenever possible, avoid such expressions which place a particularly unfair emphasis on woman as follows: *joketsu* (woman hero, strong and feisty woman), *otoko masari* (superior to man, strong-minded and assertive woman), *jojoofu* (female equivalent of excellent and talented man, strong and feisty

7—Women and the Japanese Language

woman), *onna datera ni* (unlike a woman, inappropriate for a woman), and *onna no tatakai* (fight between women).
- Note: Make an effort to use the same titles (either *-san* or *-shi*) for both women and men, particularly in the same setting.

In addition to these first revisions in the 8th edition, the following are excerpts from the guidelines that were included in *Kisha Handobukku Dai 9 Han* (*Reporters' Handbook the 9th Edition*) issued by Kyodo Tsushinsha 4 years later in 2001:

- Avoid the following terms: *teishu* (master, owner, head, husband), *shujin* (master, husband), *oku-san* (Mrs. Interior, address term for married women) (Cherry, 1987), and *kanai* (house-insider, one's wife) (Cherry, 1987).
- Replace *fujin keikan* (woman police officer) and its shortened form, *fukei*, with *josei keiken*.
- Avoid the term *miboojin* (person who is not yet dead, widow). Specify as *ko X-san no tsuma* (wife of the late Mr. so-and-so), X *fujin* (Mrs. so-and-so), or X-san.
- Replace *kikoku shijo* (sons and daughters who are returnees from abroad) with *kikoku jidoo* (children who are returnees from abroad).
- Replace *nyooboo yaku* (one who plays a wifely role, assistant, aid) with *hosa yaku* (one who assists, assistant, aid).
- Replace *nyuuseki suru* (to make an entry into the family registers, to have a marriage registered) with *konin todoke o teishutsu suru* (to submit a marriage registration).
- Replace *fujoshi* (women and children, discriminatory term to put women and children in the same category) with *josei to kodomo* (women and children).
- Note: Avoid expressions which place unfair emphasis on women such as *shokuba no hana* (flower in the workplace, young single female worker), *saien* (talented woman), *saijo* (talented woman), and *saishoku kenbi* (woman who is intelligent and attractive).

- Note: Avoid expressions that represent male dominance in society such as *fusho fuzui* (husband leads, wife follows) and "*Otoko wa dokyoo, onna wa aikyoo* (Men should be daring, women should be charming)."
- Note: Avoid expressions that promote gender inequality and bias such as *onna no asajie* (women's shallow wits), *onna no kuse ni* (after all she is a woman, though she is a woman), *memeshii* (like a woman, unmanly and effeminate man), *onna no kusatta yoona* (like a rotten woman, indecisive and cowardly man), and *otoko no kuse ni* (after all he is a man, though he is a man).

There is no doubt that the male-dominated Japanese media needs further reform and improvement regarding nonsexist language use and fairer representation of women; nevertheless, the voluntary guidelines issued by the media such as those found in *Kisha Handobukku* (*Reporters' Handbook*) (Kyodo Tsushinsha, 1997, 2001) that have continued to be revised on a regular basis since 1997, have proven to be very effective in significantly reducing the instances of sexist language use in the media.

Nonsexist Language Reform in Japanese Language Dictionaries

A number of feminist scholars and women's groups point out that the progress toward nonsexist language reform in dictionaries has been very slow, and has certainly lagged behind that in the media (Endo, 2003; Hio, 2000; Swanger 1994). For instance, Swanger (1994) discusses gender bias found in Japanese language dictionaries by making a reference to the expression, "*onna datera ni* (unlike a woman, inappropriate for a woman)." It is a very commonly used phrase to criticize the particular behavior of a woman which does not stay within the "femininity" code and parameters set by society. As a matter of fact, this phrase was listed by well over one third of the survey participants in Chapter 6, and is ranked third among a total of 151 offensive and degrading expressions for women. The following is the argument by Swanger (1994):

> In a society where in most workplaces female employees are still expected to serve tea and, worse, where educated women can be heard agreeing with men that the tea surely tastes better when served by a pretty girl, who could find it unusual that the expression *onna datera ni* (unlike a woman, inappropriate for a woman) is still commonly found in Japanese language dictionaries? Similar examples reflecting Japanese society's tendency to automatically associate women with marriage and home, not to mention chattering, meddling, and other undesirable behaviour, are all too easy to find in dictionaries published in Japan [p. 4].

In addition to Japanese language dictionaries, many instances of gender bias can also be found in *kanji* (ideographic characters) dictionaries in their interpretations as well as definitions of the compositions and meanings of *kanji*. For instance, there is a character called *fu* that refers to a woman, a daughter-in-law, a bride, or a wife. It is used in various *kanji* compounds such as *fujin* (adult woman) and *fuufu* (husband and wife). The character *fu* is composed of *onna hen* (the "female" radical) and the component that represents broom. *Kanjigen* (*Kanji Sources*), a widely used *kanji* dictionary published in 2006, says that the character *fu* symbolizes a woman holding a broom. It further states that the character *fu* refers to a bride or a wife who takes care of household chores such as cleaning, and snuggles up to her *shujin* (master, husband) like an appendage.

Dictionaries are the most respected and authoritative sources that people turn to for definitions of words and phrases (Graham, 1975). Despite the ongoing nonsexist language reform which started in the mid–1970s, the majority of Japanese language dictionaries maintain the status quo and continue to list entries as well as definitions embedded with gender bias. However, some conscientious lexicographers and publishers have started to make conscious efforts to eliminate sexism and promote fairer representation of genders in dictionaries. Along with the definitions of the entries with gender bias, these new types of dictionaries that are oriented toward nonsexist language reform typically provide additional explanations of the nature of the gender bias associated with the entries. Such an innovative approach is evident among some dictionaries published or revised since the mid–1990s.

In the following section, comparisons are made between the 6th edition of *Kojien*, one of the most highly regarded Japanese language dictionaries, revised in 2008, and the 2002–2008 edition of *Meikyo Kokugo Jiten* (*Meikyo Japanese Language Dictionary*) (Kitahara & Taishukan), one of the new dictionaries oriented toward nonsexist language reform. Some representative entries and definitions, as well as additional explanations where applicable, are presented below in English translation. Capitalized letters K and M stand for *Kojien* (2008) and *Meikyo Kokugo Jiten* (*Meikyo Japanese Language Dictionary*) (Kitahara & Taishukan, 2002–2008), respectively.

onna no ko (girl)

K: girl, young woman
M: young woman as in *kaisha no onna no ko* (young woman in the company)
   This term is used to show affection as well as disrespect for young women.

hai misu (high miss, single woman in her 30s)

K: slightly old unmarried woman
M: woman who is single past *konki* (marriageable age, in her mid– to late 20s)
   This Japanese English coinage is a discriminatory term that is based on the assumption that women should get married during *tekireiki* (marriageable age, in their mid– to late 20s).

otoko masari (superior to man, strong-minded and feisty woman)

K: woman who, despite being a woman, is almost feistier than man
M: woman who is feisty and almost stronger-minded than man
   This term is based on the gender stereotype that men are stronger than women.

busu (ugly woman)

K: woman with ugly facial features
M: woman who does not have a pretty face
   This discriminatory term is also used to swear at women.

onna datera ni (unlike a woman, inappropriate for a woman)

K: unlike a woman as in *onna datera ni tanka o kiru* (inappropriate for women to speak defiantly), *onna no kuse ni* (after all she is a woman, though she is a woman)
M: unlike a woman as in *onna datera ni oozake o nomu* (inappropriate for women to drink heavily)
   This term is based on the stereotyped notion that women should be *shitoyaka* (modest, graceful, ladylike).

demorodi (returnee to one's parents' place, divorced woman)

K: woman who was once married, got divorced, and returned to her parent's home
M: woman who returns to her parents' home after divorce
   This term is based on the notion that a woman should get married and stay with the family that she has married into.

urenokori (unsold merchandise, single woman in her 30s)

K: woman who remains unmarried after *konki* (marriageable age, in her mid– to late 20s)
M: woman who remains single past *konki* (marriageable age, in her mid– to late 20s)
   This discriminatory term is commonly used for a single woman.

umazume (stone woman, no-life woman, infertile woman)

K: woman who is not able to bear children
M: archaic expression used for a woman who is not able to conceive
    This discriminatory term places all the causes of infertility solely on women.

okame (woman's face that resembles an unattractive female mask also called *otafuku*, unattractive woman)

K: mask of *otafuku*, woman whose face resembles the mask of *otafuku*
    This term is used to ridicule an ugly woman.
M: female mask with a round face, a flat nose, and high cheekbones and forehead, woman whose face resembles such a mask
    This term is also used to deride a woman about her facial features.

oorudo misu (old miss, single woman in her 30s)

K: woman past *konki* (marriageable age, in her mid– to late 20s) who remains unmarried, *roojoo* (old unmarried woman)
M: single woman past *konki* (marriageable age, in her mid– to late 20s)
    This discriminatory term is based on the assumption that women should get married during *tekireiki* (marriageable age, in their mid– to late 20s). There is a tendency among native speakers of English to avoid the term "old maid," which is an English equivalent of *oorudo misu* (old miss), a Japanese English coinage.

fujin (woman)

K: adult woman, woman who married into husband's family
M: adult woman
    Compared to *josei* (woman, female), *fujin* (adult woman)

is slightly archaic. Nowadays there is a tendency to avoid using the term *fujin* (adult woman) because of its discriminatory tone, when it is used as a modifier to positional and occupational terms that are traditionally dominated by men.

komusume (little girl)

K: young girl
   This term referring to young girls is used with contempt.
M: young girl who is 14 to 15 years of age
   This term is often used when looking down upon young women.

As can be seen from the above comparison, there are striking differences between these two dictionaries. Compared to *Meikyo Kokugo Jiten* (*Meikyo Japanese Language Dictionary*) (Kitahara & Taishukan, 2002–2008), which provides fairly detailed information on the gender biases of its entries, the definitions and additional information on the entries, if any, provided by *Kojien* (2008) mostly reflect gender stereotypes and biases. It is regrettable that *Kojien* (2008), one of the highly regarded dictionaries, includes such an obsolete and extremely discriminatory term, *roojoo* (old unmarried woman), in the definition of *oorudo misu* (old miss, old maid). Furthermore, since its 5th edition, published in 1998, there were no additions or revisions made to these representative entries listed above in the latest 6th edition of *Kojien* published a decade later in 2008.

Some dictionaries oriented toward nonsexist language reform have taken further steps by providing additional detailed explanations for the gender biases of their entries in the form of supplementary notes. The following is one instance of such notes found in *Meiji Shoin Seisen Kokugo Jiten* (*Meiji Shoin Selected Japanese Language Dictionary*), one of the innovative Japanese language dictionaries published in 1994. The note is in regard to the commonly used phrase, *onna datera ni* (unlike a woman, inappropriate for a woman) that Swanger (1994) made a reference to in her argument which appeared earlier in this section.

> [*Onna datera ni* is] A term used to express the feeling that something is not appropriate for a woman to do. It is used to confine women within a narrow framework [of "suitable" activities], and to ridicule or deride

those women who attempt to move beyond that framework [Endo, 2004, p. 174].

Detailed and informative notes on gender biases that are embedded in the entries are still not commonly found even among the dictionaries with innovative approaches. Nevertheless, providing additional information on the gender biases of the entries, regardless of the length, is extremely helpful in making users aware of the pervasiveness of sexism in the Japanese language. It is also a positive development in realizing the fairer representation of genders in Japanese language dictionaries. Although the number of dictionaries with innovative approaches remains very limited, conscientious efforts by the lexicographers and publishers of such dictionaries have certainly set the standard for nonsexist language reform in dictionaries, which can be followed by more, hopefully in the foreseeable future.

Nonsexist Language Reform in Japanese School Textbooks

While nonsexist language reform has made steady progress in Japan since the mid–1970s, its effect has not yet been widely reflected in many areas, including Japanese language dictionaries (mentioned in the previous section) and Japanese school textbooks. It should be noted that the implementation of nonsexist language reform, particularly since the 1970s, has been the most comprehensive and successful in English, which is the most extensively studied language in terms of linguistic sexism. For instance, in the United States, scholastic organizations including APA as well as a number of publishers such as McGraw-Hill Book Company, and Scott, Foresman and Company have continued to revise guidelines since the 1970s to identify the areas of sexism, and to suggest alternative expressions for authors and editors to consider when writing or approving new materials (DeShazer, 1981; Gershuny, 1977, 1989; Nielsen, 1988; Worby, 1979). In contrast, neither the publishers of textbooks nor scholastic organizations in Japan, including one of the most influential, the Japanese Language Society, have proposed or issued such guidelines to eliminate gender bias and stereotypes.

Furthermore, in 1971 the National Council of Teachers of English (NCTE) in the United States organized a committee on the Role and Image of Women in the Council and the Profession, and in 1975 created the first detailed guidelines for nonsexist language use in its publications. In addition, a lot of research and a number of academic surveys have been conducted on sexism in English textbooks including ESL and EFL materials (Florent & Walter, 1988; Hartman & Judd, 1978; Hellinger, 1980; Porreca, 1984; Sunderland, 1992). Because of all these efforts, English education textbooks have been reported to be significantly more advanced than those of other disciplines in eliminating sexism from illustrative sentences and prose passages (Gershuny, 1977).

In Japan, there is a textbook inspection and authorization system administered by the Ministry of Education, Culture, Sports, Science and Technology; however, the use of nonsexist language is not included in its guidelines and criteria. Similarly, the government agencies such as the Subcommittee on the Japanese Language of the Japanese Culture Council, and the National Research Institute of the Japanese Language do not include nonsexist language use in their recommendations for reform in the Japanese language. This official stance, adopted by the government and its agencies, does not take into consideration a storm of criticism directed at the gender inequality embedded in school textbooks. Since the 1970s, feminist scholars and educators have regularly conducted a number of content analyses on Japanese textbooks, and have continued to point out that sexist language as well as the stereotypical portrayal of women and men remains prevalent in the vast majority of textbooks, despite the progress of nonsexist language reform in recent years (Saito, 1994; Sasaki, 1994; Y. Sato, 1978; Ujihara, 1997a, 1997b). Together with feminist scholars and educators, the Japan Federation of Lawyers has also taken initiative, and has issued a series of recommendations in order to eliminate gender bias in school textbooks (Kameda, 1995; Owaki, 1991).

School textbooks are used repetitively by children, and exert immeasurable influence on their perceptions of gender relations. In order to promote fair gender ideology among schoolchildren, there is an urgent need to create specific guidelines for nonsexist language use and unbiased representation of genders in Japanese school textbooks (Owaki, 1991). To this end, influential guidelines similar to those formulated and revised by the National Council of Teachers of English (NCTE) in the United States can serve as a reference point. The Constitution of Japan and the Basic Law of Education that were enacted shortly after World War II guarantee equal opportunity for women and men to receive education for the first time in Japanese history. It is essential that the spirit of these laws be embodied in school textbooks.

Various Views on Nonsexist Language Reform

As briefly stated in Chapter 6, the majority of the survey participants voiced their various thoughts and concerns regarding gender-related expressions as well as the overall representation of women in the Japanese language, in addition to listing and commenting on words and phrases that were considered offensive and degrading to women. Among all the thoughts and concerns of the participants, the most frequently mentioned was in regard to the feasibility and effectiveness of changing or eliminating such offensive gender-related expressions. While the survey participants unanimously agree that gender bias is embedded in the Japanese language, their opinions on nonsexist language reform differ widely. The following are some of the representative quotations from the survey participants presented in English translation:

- Having been a Japanese language professional for over 50 years, I feel it is truly a shame that there are so many expressions to belittle and insult women in the Japanese language. These expressions have existed for a very long time; in some cases, they were widely used before I was even born. As much as I would like to see these expressions disappear, I do not think it is feasible to change them, let alone to eliminate them (76-year-old part-time Japanese instructor).
- There is no doubt that the Japanese language has a variety of offensive and degrading expressions for women; however, I am

not certain if getting rid of such sexist words and phrases is a practical solution to the problem. I think that language would change by itself as a result of the change in the society where women would be treated equally with men (28-year-old homemaker).
- Although the power of language is often underestimated and overlooked, language has a significant influence on the perceptions of its users. It is, therefore, crucial to initiate the process of eradicating gender bias from the Japanese language. This, in turn, will promote the realization of gender equality in Japanese society (53-year-old speech therapist).
- I believe that the concerted effort to eliminate gender bias in the Japanese language is not only meaningful to those who are concerned, but also very effective in making the general public aware of the overall seriousness and pervasiveness of sexism in Japanese society (39-year-old adjunct college lecturer).

As can be seen by these quotes, some survey participants question the necessity and feasibility of language reform, while others support it. It is often pointed out that these variations in opinions regarding nonsexist language reform reflect the differences in the views of individuals on the relationship between language and reality (Penfield, 1987). Generally speaking, there are three views that are typically used for the argument on language reform. The view that language reflects reality is most frequently used to argue against the feasibility of reform, while the linguistic determinist view and the interactionist view are commonly used to argue in favor of it (Pauwels, 1998). In the following section, these views are presented in summary.

Those who hold the view that language reflects reality are doubtful whether language could cause social change; therefore, they do not have a strong preference for language reform. They argue that the discriminatory treatment of women and their subordinate status are simply reflected in gender bias in language, rather than are caused by it. As a result, in order to realize gender equality, they give preference to organized efforts that promote social change over nonsexist language reform.

Lakoff (1975), who supports this view, insists that language change is created by social change, not the other way around. Similarly, Martynyuk (1990) claims that since language change takes longer than social change, feminist language reform is feasible only when there is sufficient awareness and urgency in society. It should be noted that those who hold the view that language reflects reality do not totally deny the necessity for language reform. As a matter of fact, a large number of advocates of official guidelines for nonsexist language use such as Miller and Swift (1980) support this view. However, they argue in favor of language reform based on their stance that language change lags behind social change (Miller & Swift, 1991; Sorrels, 1983).

The linguistic determinist view on the relationship between language and reality maintains that language not only influences, but also determines the way people construct and examine reality. Spender (1980), an advocate of this view, asserts that the world people live in becomes meaningful through language. According to those who support this view, sexist language is the cause of the oppression of women, since language is a leading force in creating and maintaining gender inequality in society. They further argue that men in a patriarchal society have total control in the creation of a language that constructs and presents reality solely from male perspectives. This so-called "man-made" language, lacking in female perspectives, alienates women, and as a result, creates women's subordinate status in society. Advocates of this view believe in the benefit of nonsexist language reform based on their assertion that language is an instrument of women's oppression as well as liberation (Gibbon, 1999; Pauwels, 1998; Penfield, 1987). For instance, Spender (1980) asserts that with perseverance, language can be reformed and modified in favor of women.

Those who hold the interactionist view of the relationship between language and reality claim that language not only reflects reality, but also helps to construct it (Pauwels, 1998; Van Den Bergh, 1987). This view does not make an attempt to determine the direction of influence or effect between language and reality. Rather, it focuses on the mutual influence between the two. Advocates of this view argue in favor of nonsexist language reform, claiming it is helpful in making people aware of the pervasiveness of sexism not only in language, but also in many other aspects of life. Van Den Bergh (1987) further asserts that since language often serves as a mirror that reflects the extent of gender inequality and power imbalances in society, it is possible to make use of language as a powerful and effective instrument for social change. Pauwels (1998) also points out that a majority of feminist language critics opting for linguistic action can be aligned with the interactionist view, because they "believe that linguistic action may give women an opportunity to express their perspectives and experiences, and that linguistic action can increase people's awareness that language is not a neutral medium for transmitting ideas and values" (p. 92).

While I respect a wide range of views on nonsexist language reform, personally I am inclined toward the interactionist view. I also believe that reform will not only bring forth the fairer representation of genders in language, but also make the world a better place where women and men coexist in harmony based on mutual respect and understanding.

This section concludes by presenting the views on nonsexist language reform expressed by feminist scholars in Japan, who have actively engaged in varied research for many years in order to eliminate sexism from the Japanese language; much can be learned by their insights.

> A representation of the Japanese appreciation of the norm of male domination can be seen in the terms designating women and men. How women and men are defined or represented in Japanese can be evidence for how women and men are treated in male-dominated Japan (Hio, 2000, p. 163). Every time we converse and especially when we write, this inequality underlying Japanese is repeated. Not surprising then that we often accept, without questioning, social habits, conventions, and customs that favor men.... I expect that even in the 21st century, many people will still feel inequality in social habits, conventions, and customs as is felt today unless the Japanese language is changed [Hio, 2000, p. 169].

* * *

> What is crucial to feminist linguistic practice is to constantly attempt to reform male definitions, believing that the meanings in a language are ultimately changeable by the conscious language use [Nakamura, 1990, p. 160].

* * *

Part II: Representation of Women in the Japanese Language

It is often argued that as long as there is gender discrimination in society, gender bias in language continues to exist; therefore, it is meaningless to reform language alone. Such an argument certainly makes sense, and we have to continue making efforts to change society. However, there is a way to do so through language. As long as sexist language continues to exist, society will not change, either. There are instances in which language changes people's perceptions. Language is a product of society, and at the same time, there is something that language can produce in society. We cannot afford to make language an obstacle to progress in society [Endo, 1985, p. 236].

Future Prospects of Nonsexist Language Reform and the Japanese Language

Some critics have asserted that the emphasis on conformity in Japanese society and the Japanese people's strong inclination to avoid confrontation of any kind could be potential obstacles to the advancement of nonsexist language reform.

For instance, Okano (1995) points out that Japanese society is a "maternal society (*bosei shakai*)," where conformity is the norm, and the status quo precedes changes. The term "maternal society" became a buzzword in the Japanese media in the late 1970s. It was coined by Kawai Hayao (1928–2007), a psychologist and former chief of the Agency for Cultural Affairs in the Ministry of Education, in his 1976 best-selling book titled *Bosei Shakai Nihon no Byori* (The Pathology of Japan's Maternal Society) (Jiyukokuminsha, 2008). Okano (1995) further explains that in Japanese "maternal society" there is a tendency "to accept everything without analysis or criticism" (p. 26), and "to harmonize both the good and the bad" (p. 26). Seeking changes by analyzing and criticizing language is likely to encounter resistance as well as opposition.

In addition, Farnsley (1995) makes reference to one of the inclinations of the Japanese people as follows:

> To focus on self-promotion, especially through conflict, is viewed as selfish behavior.... The priority of group well-being over self-satisfaction on the part of most Japanese, particularly, women, may result in slowed

discovery of linguistic ways in which to improve women's social status [p. 3].

At the same time, Farnsley (1995) discusses another inclination of Japanese people which makes it feasible for further language reform to occur:

> Most Japanese are concerned for the well-being of society as a whole; if they can see that the entire society, not only women, would benefit from changes in the way women speak and are spoken of, these modifications could take place [p. 4].

When the concept of nonsexist language reform was first introduced to the general public in Japan in the mid–1970s, it was perceived primarily as an issue related to feminist activists and women's groups. However, the past 3 decades have witnessed the increasing involvement of the government and the media with the reform, which has produced many tangible results including a number of guidelines issued to eliminate gender bias in the Japanese language. These guidelines, in particular, have a significant effect on changing the public perceptions of nonsexist language reform from a women's issue to a societal issue. Based on this development, it can be concluded that further language reform in Japan will be feasible, which coincides with the second quotation from Farnsley (1995) presented above.

The survey results presented in Chapter 6 indicate that among age, education levels, and occupation, age is a decisive factor in differences in the participants' perceptions of gender bias in the Japanese language. As shown in the following, the younger the age group, the fewer expressions considered offensive and degrading to women were listed; the average number of words and phrases listed per participant of each age group is 2.6 for those in their 20s and 30s, 3.4 for those in their 40s and 50s, and 4.2 for those in their 60s and 70s. Moreover, it is noteworthy that out of 70 participants, 2 who did not list any words or phrases at all were in their 20s. Both of the participants stated that they were simply not familiar with any such expressions. While it is premature to make any inferences based on these findings, they cannot be totally unrelated to the positive effect of nonsexist language reform started in the mid–1970s, before the participants in their 20s and 30s reached adolescence, when young people typically begin to encounter sexist expressions frequently, and to develop their awareness of gender bias in language.

As discussed earlier in this chapter, the coinages and occupational terms transcribed in *katakana*, the phonetic letters that are used to transcribe words of non–Japanese origin, have contributed to the creation of many terms without gender bias and stereotypes. Although the steady increase in the usage of *katakana* in recent years is perceived negatively by those of the older generation as decay in the Japanese language, the popularity of *katakana* among the younger generation may contribute to fewer sexist expressions in the future. Furthermore, as Hio (2000) points out, an increasing number of younger people use and know considerably fewer *kanji* (ideographic characters) and their compounds, as well as idiomatic expressions that convey gender bias and stereotypes. This trend may result in making most sexist expressions obsolete before too long.

Considering the concerted effort by feminist activists and women's groups as well as by the government and the media, along with the inclinations among the younger generation, I have every confidence that the ongoing language reform will certainly have a positive effect on the future of the Japanese language.

Conclusion

Language, as a major component of a culture, passes on the values as well as the prejudices of the culture. Language can also have a significant impact on a society by not only influencing but also controlling the world view of its users (Trudgill, 1974). While there have been some persistent arguments that gender bias in language is trivial compared to other pending issues of society, the power of language should never be underestimated.

Bolinger (1974) stresses the necessity of considering not only the meaning of the parts, the individual words and sentences, but also the

7—Women and the Japanese Language

meaning of the whole, the language code from which we draw. He further elaborates:

> Women are taught their place ... by the implicit lies that language tells about them. Now you can argue that a term is not a proposition; therefore merely having the words does not constitute a lie about anybody.... People may be liars but words are not. This argument has a familiar ring. We hear it every time Congress tries to pass legislation restricting the possessions of guns.... However, lots of casualties, some crippling ones, result from merely having weapons around [p. 164].

Bolinger (1974) concludes that increasing awareness of the fitness of language to the perceptions of users will greatly contribute to successful nonsexist language reform.

As noted by Bolinger (1974), words can be weapons that deeply wound people; however, it is possible to eliminate such instances through conscious efforts made by us, the users of words. It is my sincere hope that various information as well as the actual voices of women documented in this book will provide a step forward to promote a fairer and unbiased representation of genders in the Japanese language.

In ancient Japan, words were considered sacred and revered because of the mystical power of *kotodama*, the spirits that were believed to inhabit words. A long time has passed since then, and the sacredness that people once felt toward words seems to have been forgotten altogether. Nevertheless, we need to constantly remind ourselves that words ought to be treated with utmost care and respect. After all, we owe it to ourselves to make the best use of language, which is a precious gift to us all.

Appendix A

Demographic Information about the Survey Participants

The following chart provides demographic information on the women who took part in the survey.

Participant	Age	Highest Degree Earned	Occupation
1.	20	AA	Housework helper
2.	21	AA	College student
3.	22	AA	College student
4.	23	BA	Housework helper
5.	24	AA	College student
6.	26	BA	Part-time office worker
7.	26	MA	College lecturer
8.	26	BA	Office worker
9.	27	BA	Office worker
10.	28	BA	Graduate student
11.	28	AA	Homemaker
12.	29	BA	Interpreter
13.	30	BS	Graduate student
14.	30	AA	Office worker
15.	30	BA	Homemaker
16.	31	BA	Junior high school teacher
17.	32	BS	Nurse
18.	33	AA	Part-time sales clerk
19.	35	BA	Office worker
20.	36	MS	Graduate student
21.	37	MA	Part-time public employee
22.	38	MA	College lecturer
23.	38	BA	Homemaker
24.	39	MA	Adjunct college lecturer
25.	40	AA	Homemaker
26.	41	BA	Office worker
27.	41	BA	Part-time translator
28.	42	MA	Translator
29.	42	BA	Nursery school teacher
30.	43	AA	Homemaker
31.	45	BA	Part-time interpreter

Appendix A

Participant	Age	Highest Degree Earned	Occupation
32.	46	AA	Administrative assistant
33.	46	BA	Office worker
34.	47	AA	Homemaker
35.	48	BA	Part-time English instructor
36.	48	AA	Graphic designer
37.	50	BA	Homemaker
38.	51	AA	Office worker
39.	52	BA	Part-time high school teacher
40.	52	BA	Part-time English instructor
41.	53	MS	Speech therapist
42.	54	AA	Homemaker
43.	55	AA	Office worker
44.	56	BA	Office worker
45.	56	AA	Homemaker
46.	57	MA	College lecturer
47.	58	PhD	Assistant professor
48.	59	AA	Homemaker
49.	60	HS	Homemaker
50.	60	BA	Junior high school teacher
51.	61	HS	Part-time office worker
52.	62	HS	Homemaker
53.	62	HS	Part-time sales clerk
54.	63	BA	Japanese instructor
55.	65	BA	Retired high school teacher
56.	66	HS	Homemaker
57.	66	BA	Part-time English instructor
58.	68	PhD	Professor emeritus
59.	68	HS	Retired office worker
60.	70	PhD	Professor
61.	71	HS	Homemaker
62.	72	BA	Retired editor
63.	72	HS	Homemaker
64.	72	BS	Retired high school teacher
65.	75	HS	Homemaker
66.	76	BA	Retired high school teacher
67.	76	AA	Part-time Japanese instructor
68.	77	HS	Homemaker
69.	78	HS	Retired office worker
70.	78	HS	Homemaker

Appendix B

Japanese Words and Phrases Listed by the Survey Participants

The chart below presents a total of 151 Japanese words and phrases that the survey participants found degrading to women. The following capitalized letters indicate the categories into which the words and phrases are grouped: M, marriage; C, characterization of women; A, age; O, occupation; P, physical appearance; S, status; and D, derogatory term.

Total Number of Responses	*Category*	*Japanese Words/Phrases (English Equivalent)*
36	C	*onna no kuse ni* (after all she is a woman, though she is a woman)
28	M	*yome* (daughter-in-law, bride)
26	C	*memeshii* (like a woman, unmanly and effeminate man)
24	C	*onna datera ni* (unlike a woman, inappropriate for a woman)
22	C	some *kanji* (ideographic characters) composed of *onna hen* (the "female" radical)
22	P	*busu* (ugly woman)
21	C	*onna no kusatta yoona* (like a rotten woman, indecisive and cowardly man)
20	M	*oku-san* (Mrs. Interior, address term for married women) (Cherry, 1987)
20	M	*umazume* (stone woman, no-life woman, infertile woman)
20	C	*onna rashii* (feminine, womanly)
19	D	(*kuso*) *babaa* (derogatory term for elderly women)
18	O	*onna no ko* (girl)
17	M	*mekake* (mistress)
17	M	*shuutome* (mother-in-law)
16	M	*oorudo misu* (old miss, old maid)
16	M	*demodori* (returnee to one's parents' place, divorced woman)
16	M	*ikazu goke* (widow without marrying, single woman in her 30s)

Appendix B

Total Number of Responses	Category	Japanese Words/Phrases (English Equivalent)
16	O	*otsubone (-sama)* (elderly court woman, middle-aged female office worker)
15	M	*ikiokure* (late to marry, single woman in her 30s)
15	M	*yome o morau* (to receive a daughter-in-law/bride)
15	M	*kanai* (house-insider, one's wife) (Cherry, 1987)
15	M	*gusai* (stupid wife, one's wife)
15	M	*shufu* (main woman, homemaker)
15	C	*Dakara onna wa dameda.* (That is why women are no good.)
15	A	*oba-san* (aunt, address term for middle-aged women)
14	S	*danson johi* (men superior, women inferior)
14	S	*onna kodomo* (women and children)
14	S	*Onna sangai ni ie nashi.* (Women have no home in the three realms of existence: the past, the present, and the future.)
14	C	*otoko masari* (superior to men, strong-minded and assertive woman)
14	C	*kawaii onna* (cute woman)
14	M	*urenokori* (unsold merchandise, single woman in her 30s)
14	O	*josei, fujin, joryuu, onna* (female, woman)
14	D	*ama* (derogatory term for women)
13	M	*yome ni iku* (to go as a daughter-in-law/bride, to marry into a husband's family)
13	M	*naijo no koo* (success from inside help, husband's success owing to the support and sacrifices of his wife) (Cherry, 1987)
13	M	*miboojin* (person who is not yet dead, widow)
13	M	*goke* (after family, widow) (Cherry, 1987)
13	M	*kyooiku mama* (education-conscious mother)
13	A	*obaa-chan* (granny, address term for elderly women)
13	A	*toshima* (years added, middle-aged woman) (Cherry, 1987)
13	A	*(o)nee-chan* (elder sister, address term for young women)
13	C	*shitoyaka* (modest, graceful, gentle)
13	P	*bijin* (beautiful person, beautiful woman)
13	S	*nyonin kinsei* (no females allowed)
12	C	*Onna san nin yoreba kashimashii.* (When three women get together, they make too much noise.)

Appendix B

Total Number of Responses	Category	Japanese Words/Phrases (English Equivalent)
10	C	*otenba* (tomboy)
10	C	*onna dakara* (because she is a woman)
10	C	*onna no ko nan dakara* (because she is a girl)
10	C	*namaiki na onna* (impudent woman)
10	C	*hisuterii* (hysteria)
10	M	*nyooboo* (court woman, one's wife)
9	M	*onna bara / otoko bara* (female womb/male womb, woman who gives birth only to girls/boys)
9	M	*sengyoo shufu* (full-time professional homemaker)
9	C	*jonan* (sufferings of a man in the relationship with a woman)
8	M	*kakaa denka* (household where the wife is the boss)
8	M	*akusai* (bad wife)
8	M	*oni yome* (merciless daughter-in-law/bride)
8	M	*hai misu* (high miss, single woman in her 30s)
8	M	*Kashite sannen konaki wa saru.* (A wife should leave her husband if she fails to bear a child within 3 years of marriage.)
7	A	*onago* (girl, woman)
7	A	*musume* (daughter, young woman)
7	A	*hakoiri musume* (daughter-in-a-box; young single woman who leads a sheltered life with her protective family)
7	O	OL (office lady, female office worker)
7	O	*kotobuki taishoku / kotobuki taisha* (congratulatory resignation, resignation of female workers because of marriage)
7	O	*ochakumi* (tea serving)
7	S	*onna sanjuu no oshie* (Three obediences for women: as a daughter, obey your father; once married, obey your husband; when widowed, obey your son.)
7	S	*shijo* (children and women, children)
6	M	*hanayome shugyoo* (bridal training, apprenticeship as a bride-to-be)
6	M	*Yome no moraite ga nai.* (Nobody offers to receive her as a daughter-in-law/bride.)
6	M	*totsugu* (to marry into husband's family)
6	M	*katazukeru* (to dispose of, to marry off a daughter)

Appendix B

Total Number of Responses	Category	Japanese Words/Phrases (English Equivalent)
6	M	*kojuutome* (little mother-in-law, sister-in-law)
6	M	*ryoosai kenbo* (good wives and wise mothers)
6	A	*koonenki* (further aging period, menopause)
6	A	*roojo* (old woman)
6	A	*rooba* (old woman)
5	C	*yappari onna wa* (after all she is a woman)
5	C	*Onna wa ate ni naranai.* (You cannot count on women.)
5	C	*otoko onna* (mannish woman)
5	C	*josei nagara* (despite being a woman)
5	C	*onna de hitotsu de* (solely by woman's hands, all by herself)
5	C	*motenai onna* (woman who is not popular with men)
5	C	*onna guse* (man's inclination to seduce women)
5	M	*Akinasu wa yome ni kuwasuna.* (Do not feed an autumn eggplant to a daughter-in-law/bride; do not spoil a daughter-in-law/bride.)
5	M	*yome ibiri* (tormenting a daughter-in-law/bride)
5	M	*fushoo fuzui* (husband leads, wife follows)
5	M	*Akusai wa isshoo no fusaku.* (A bad wife ruins her husband's entire life.)
5	A	*jukujo* (ripe woman, sexually attractive middle-aged woman)
5	A	*obatarian* (monstrous and dreadful middle-aged woman)
5	A	*oni baba* (devilish old woman)
5	A	*Oni mo juuhachi, bancha mo debana.* (Even an ogre looks pretty while young, and freshly brewed tea smells good; any woman of marriageable age is attractive.)
5	O	*kaji tetsudai* (housework helper, trainee bride)
5	O	*shokuba no hana* (flower in the workplace, young single female office worker)
4	M	*kurisumasu keeki* (Christmas cake, single woman over 25)
4	M	*otto o shiri ni shiku* (to sit on a husband, to dominate a husband)
4	C	*Onna gokoro to aki no sora.* (Women's feelings for men are as changeable as the skies of autumn.)
4	C	*josei tokuyuu no* (typical of women)
4	P	*biboo* (beautiful looks, woman's beauty)

Appendix B

Total Number of Responses	Category	Japanese Words/Phrases (English Equivalent)
4	P	*Ii tama da.* (She is a knockout.)
3	O	*onna no hosoude* (woman's thin arms, woman's very small earnings)
3	O	*sooji no oba-san* (middle-aged cleaning woman)
3	O	*otetsudai-san* (maid)
3	O	*baishunfu* (prostitute)
3	O	*kaseifu* (housekeeper)
3	M	*toshikoshi soba* (single woman over 31)
3	M	*sanjuudai makegumi* (the loser group of single women in their 30s)
3	S	*te o tsukeru* (to put a hand on, to demand sex from subordinate women)
3	S	*onna asobi* (womanizing)
3	C	*otoko nami* (being on the level of men)
3	A	*onna mo 25 sugireba* (when a woman is older than 25)
3	P	*otoko zuki no suru kao* (face that appeals to men)
2	P	*okame* (woman's face that resembles an unattractive female mask called *otafuku*, unattractive woman)
2	P	*komata no kireagatta onna* (sexually attractive woman with a slender body)
2	P	*subeta* (ugly woman)
2	P	*okachi menko* (funny face, unattractive woman)
2	M	*Onna wa katei ni hairu bekida.* (Women should marry and stay home.)
2	O	*onna no shigoto* (women's job/duties)
2	D	*abazure* (slut)
1	M	*ryoori joozu na ii oyome-san* (good daughter-in-law/bride who is also a good cook)
1	M	*sookoo no tsuma* (wife who endures financial hardship with husband)
1	M	*kyoosai* (strong wife)
1	M	*anesan nyooboo* (big-sister wife, wife who is older than husband)
1	M	*furu nyooboo* (old wife)
1	M	*nomi no fuufu* (flea couple, married couple whose wife is larger than husband in size)
1	M	*hahaoya rashii* (fit for a mother)
1	M	*okaa-san* (mother)
1	M	*Onna yamome ni hana ga saku.* (Widows blossom; widows who have more time to

Appendix B

Total Number of Responses	Category	Japanese Words/Phrases (English Equivalent)
		take care of themselves after losing their husbands are often popular among men.)
1	M	*kizumono* (damaged goods, young woman who lost her virginity before marriage)
1	M	*sanshoku hirune tsuki* (three meals a day accompanied by a nap, lifestyle of a full-time homemaker)
1	M	*hikage no onna* (woman in the shadow, mistress)
1	C	*onna no misao* (woman's chastity)
1	C	*dokufu* (poisonous woman, evil woman who hurts and harms people)
1	C	*Onna wa aho na gurai ga kawaii.* (A stupid woman tends to be cute.)
1	C	*Onna sakashuu shite ushi urisokonau.* (A smart woman fails to sell a cow; women may appear to be smart, but they fail to succeed because they do not see the forest for the trees.)
1	C	*onna no tokugi* (woman's special talent)
1	C	*onna no buki* (woman's weapons)
1	C	*iro jikake* (sexual wiles of women)
1	C	*iroka* (woman's sexual charm)
1	C	*yamato nadeshiko* (a garden plant with pink flowers, Japanese woman with inner strength, gracefulness, and delicate appearance)
1	C	*tsutsumashiyakana* (modest, humble)
1	D	*inbai* (whore)
1	D	*baita* (whore)
1	D	*otoko gurui* (nymphomaniac)
1	D	*inran* (lecherous woman)
1	P	*daikon ashi* (*daikon* radish legs, woman's fat and unshapely legs)
1	P	*boin* (big breasts)
1	P	*Bijin wa mikka de aki, busu wa mikka de nareru.* (You get bored with pretty women in 3 days, while you get used to ugly ones in 3 days.)
1	A	*komusume* (little girl, young girl who is in her early teens)
1	A	*gyaru* (gal)
1	O	*shakufu* (barmaid)
1	O	*suchii* (female flight attendant)

Bibliography

Akutagawasho senko iin, josei yonin ni [Akutagawa literary award selection committee members include four women]. (2007, April 26). *Asahi Shinbun*. Retrieved April 28, 2007, from http://www.asahi.com

Allison, A. (1996a). *Permitted and prohibited desires*. Boulder, CO: Westview Press.

———. (1996b). *Producing mothers*. In A. E. Imamura (Ed.), *Re-imaging Japanese women* (pp. 135–155). Berkeley and Los Angeles: University of California Press.

Aoki, Y. (1986). *Feminizumu to ekoroji* [Feminism and ecology]. Tokyo: Shinhyoron.

———. (1997). Aoki Yayoi: Independent scholar and critic. In S. Buckley (Ed.), *Broken silence: Voices of Japanese feminism* (pp. 1–31). Berkeley and Los Angeles: University of California Press.

Asano, E. (2005). Nyonin kinsei no jittai [The actual state of "no females allowed"]. In J. Minamoto (Ed.), *Nyonin kinsei* [No females allowed] *QandA* (pp. 80–83). Osaka, Japan: Kaiho Shuppansha.

Bernstein, G. L. (Ed.) (1991). *Recreating Japanese women, 1600–1945*. Berkeley and Los Angeles: University of California Press.

Bolinger, D. (1974). Truth is a linguistic question. In H. Rank (Ed.), *Language and public policy* (p. 164). Urbana, IL: National Council of Teachers of English.

Borovoy, A. (2005). *The too-good wife*. Berkeley and Los Angeles: University of California Press.

Boshi katei no shuugyo jookyoo [Employment conditions of single mother families]. (2007, January 28). *Asahi Shinbun*. Retrieved January 28, 2007, from http://www.asahi.com

Buckley, S. (Ed.). (1997). *Broken silence: Voices of Japanese feminism*. Berkeley and Los Angeles: University of California Press.

———. (Ed.). (2002). *Encyclopedia of contemporary Japanese culture*. London and New York: Routledge.

Bukka daka ga boshi katei o chokugeki [Single mother families are badly affected by the soaring consumer prices]. (2008, April 17). *Asahi Shinbun*. Retrieved April 26, 2008, from http://www.asahi.com

Cabinet Office (Naikakufu). (2001, 2006). *Yoron chosa* [Public opinion poll]. Tokyo: Naikakufu.

———. (2007, 2008). *Danjo kyodo sankaku hakusho* [Gender equality white paper]. Tokyo: Naikakufu.

———. (2008). *Seishonen hakusho* [Juvenile white paper]. Tokyo: Naikakufu.

Cherry, K. (1987). *Womansword: What Japanese words say about women*. Tokyo: Kodansha International.

Christopher, R. C. (1983). *The Japanese mind*. New York: Fawcett Columbine.

Creighton, M. R. (1996). Marriage, motherhood, and career management in a Japanese "counter culture." In A. E. Imamura (Ed.), *Re-imaging Japanese women* (pp. 192–220). Berkeley and Los Angeles: University of California Press.

Dankai zuma hachi wari, kekkon de

Bibliography

"gakkari keiken" [80 percent of married women of the baby-boom generation are disappointed in their marriages]. (2009, April 11). *Asahi Shinbun*. Retrieved April 26, 2009, from http://www.asahi.com

Dentsu and Rikuruto (Recruit Corp.) (2008). *Otona no fufu chosa* [Survey on mature married couples]. Tokyo: Dentsu and Rikuruto (Recruit Corp.).

Denzin, N. K., and Y. S. Lincoln. (Eds.). (1994). *Handbook of qualitative research*. Thousand Oaks, CA: Sage Publications.

DeShazer, M. K. (1981). Sexist language in composition textbooks: Still a major issue? *College Composition and Communication, 32,* 57–64.

Endo, O. (1985). Josei sabetsu no hai jisho o motomete [Seeking nonsexist dictionaries]. In Kotoba to Onna o Kangaeru Kai (The Association to Think about Language and Women) (Eds.), *Kokugojiten ni miru josei sabetsu* [Sexism in the Japanese language dictionaries] (p. 236). Tokyo: Sanichi Shobo.

———. (1995). Aspects of sexism in language. In K. Fujimura-Fanselow and A. Kameda (Eds.), *Japanese women: New feminist perspectives on the past, present, and future* (pp. 29–42). New York: Feminist Press.

———. (2004). Women and words. In S. Okamoto and J. Shibamoto Smith (Eds.), *Japanese language, gender, and ideology: Cultural models and real people* (pp. 166–184). New York: Oxford University Press.

———. (2006). *A cultural history of Japanese women's language*. Ann Arbor, MI: Center for Japanese Studies, University of Michigan.

Faiola, A. (2004). Japanese women live, and like it, on their own. *Washington Post*, August 31.

Farnsley, K. W. (1995). Language: Instrument of change for Japanese women? *Women and Language, 13* (2), 1–5.

Fendos, P. G., Jr. (Ed.). (1991). *Cross-cultural communication: East and west*. Tainan, Taiwan: National Cheng-Kung University.

Florent, J., and C. Walter. (1988). A better role of women in TEFL. *ELT Journal 43* (3), 180–184.

Frank, F., and F. Anshen. (1983). *Language and the sexes*. Albany, NY: State University of New York Press.

Fujieda, M. (1995). Japan's first phase of feminism. In K. Fujimura-Fanselow and A. Kameda (Eds.), *Japanese women: New feminist perspectives on the past, present, and future* (pp. 323–341). New York: Feminist Press.

Fujieda, M., and K. Fujimura-Fanselow. (1995). Women's Studies: An Overview. In K. Fujimura-Fanselow and A. Kameda (Eds.), *Japanese women: New feminist perspectives on the past, present, and future* (pp. 155–180). New York: Feminist Press.

Fujimura-Fanselow, K. (1995a). College women today: Options and dilemmas. In K. Fujimura-Fanselow and A. Kameda (Eds.), *Japanese women: New feminist perspectives on the past, present, and future* (pp. 125–154). New York: Feminist Press.

———. (1995b). Introduction. In K. Fujimura-Fanselow and A. Kameda (Eds.), *Japanese women: New feminist perspectives on the past, present, and future* (pp. xvii–xxxviii). New York: Feminist Press.

Fujimura-Fanselow, K. and A. Kameda. (Eds.) (1995). *Japanese women: New feminist perspectives on the past, present, and future*. New York: Feminist Press.

Gelb, J. (2003). *Gender policies in Japan and the United States: Comparing women's movements, rights and politics*. New York: Palgrave Macmillan.

Bibliography

Gershuny, H. L. (1977). Sexism in dictionaries and texts: Omissions and commissions. In A. P. Nilsen, H. Bosmajian, H. L. Gershuny, and J. P. Stanley (Eds.), *Sexism and language* (pp. 143–160). Urbana, IL: National Council of Teachers of English.

———. (1989). English handbooks 1979–1985: Case studies in sexist and nonsexist usage. *Language, gender, and professional writing: Theoretical approaches and guidelines for nonsexist usage* (pp. 95–104). New York: Commission on Status of Women in the Profession, Modern Language Association of America.

Gibbon, M. (1999). *Feminist perspectives on language*. London and New York: Longman.

Giles, H., W. P. Robinson, and P. M. Smith. (Eds.). (1980). *Language: Social psychological perspectives*. Oxford, UK: Pergamon Press.

Gordon, A. (Ed.). (1993). *Postwar Japan as history*. Berkeley and Los Angeles: University of California Press.

Gordon, J. A. (2002). Kyoiku mama. In S. Buckley (Ed.), *Encyclopedia of contemporary Japanese culture* (pp. 272). London and New York: Routledge.

Graham, A. (1975). The making of a nonsexist dictionary. In B. Thorne and N. Henley (Eds.), *Language and sex: Difference and dominance* (pp. 57–63). Rowley, MA: Newbury House Publishers.

Greenberg, J. H. (1966). *Language universals*. The Hague, the Netherlands: Mouton.

Haga, Y. (1982). *Nihonjin no gengo-kodo to goi* [Speech acts by Japanese people and the Japanese vocabulary]. In K. Sato (Ed.), *Nihongo no goi no tokushoku* [The characteristics of the Japanese vocabulary] (pp. 83–104). Tokyo: Meiji Shoin.

Hakuhodo Seikatsu Sogo Kenkyusho (Hakuhodo General Institute of Life). (1988). *Kazoku chosa 1988* [Family survey 1988]. Tokyo: Hakuhodo.

———. (2008). *Kazoku chosa 2008* [Family survey 2008]. Tokyo: Hakuhodo.

Hamilton, M. C. (1988). Using masculine generics: Does generic he increase male bias in the user's imagery? *Sex Roles, 19,* 785–799.

Hane, M. (1991). *Premodern Japan: A historical survey*. Boulder, CO: Westview Press.

Hara, H. (1987). Joseigaku no shimei [The mission of women's studies]. In Joseigaku kenkyukai (Ed.), *Koza joseigaku 4: Onna no me de miru* [Women's studies, vol. 4: Looking in the eyes of the women]. Tokyo: Keiso Shobo.

Hara, K. (1995). Challenges to education for girls and women in modern Japan: Past and present. In K. Fujimura-Fanselow and A. Kameda (Eds.), *Japanese women: New feminist perspectives on the past, present, and future* (pp. 125–154). New York: Feminist Press.

Hardman, M. J., and A. Taylor. (Eds.). (2000). *Hearing many voices*. Cresskill, NJ: Hampton Press.

Harrison, L. (1975). Cro-Magnon woman in eclipse. *Science Teacher, 42,* 9–11.

Hartman, P. L., and E. L. Judd. (1978). Sexism and TESOL materials. *TESOL Quarterly, 12,* 383–393.

Hata, M. (2005). Sumo to nyonin kinsei [Sumo and the tradition of "no females allowed"]. In J. Minamoto (Ed.), *Nyonin kinsei* [No females allowed] *QandA* (pp. 76–79). Osaka, Japan: Kaiho Shuppansha.

Hellinger, M. (1980). "For men must work, and women must weep.": Sexism in English language textbooks used in German schools. In C. Kramarae (Ed.), *The voices and words of women and men* (pp. 267–274). Elmsford, NY: Pergamon Press.

Bibliography

Henley, N., B. Gruber, and L. Lerner. (1985). *Studies on the detrimental effects of "generic" masculine usage.* Paper presented at the Eastern Psychological Association Congress in Boston, March 1985.

Hio, Y. (2000). Female-male inequality in Japanese writing. In M. J. Hardman and A. Taylor, (Eds.), *Hearing many voices* (pp. 157–171). Cresskill, NJ: Hampton Press.

Hiraga, M. (1991). Metaphors Japanese women live by. Working papers on *Language, Gender and Sexism, 1*(1), 38–57.

Hiratsuka, R. (1911). Genshi josei wa taiyo de atta [In the beginning, woman was the sun]. *Seito* [Bluestocking], *1*(1), 37.

Ide, S. (1979). *Onna no kotoba, otoko no kotoba* [Women's language, men's language]. Tokyo: Nihon Keizai Tsushinsha.

———. (1997). Ide Sachiko: Professor at the Japanese Women's University; Linguist. In S. Buckley (Ed.), *Broken silence: Voices of Japanese feminism* (pp. 32–65). Berkeley and Los Angeles: University of California Press.

Ide, S., and N. H. McGloin (Eds.). (1990). *Aspects of Japanese women's language.* Tokyo: Kuroshio Publishers.

Ikukyuho kaisei, zangyoo menjo o gimuzuke [The amended Child-Care Leave Law provides employees exemption from overtime work]. (2008, November 28). *Asahi Shinbun.* Retrieved November 28, 2008, from http://www.asahi.com

Imamura, A. E. (Ed.). (1996). *Re-imaging Japanese women.* Berkeley and Los Angeles: University of California Press.

Inoue, R. (2005). Gion matsuri to nyonin kinsei [The Gion festival and the tradition of "no females allowed"]. In J. Minamoto (Ed.), *Nyonin kinsei* [No females allowed] *QandA* (pp. 62–65). Osaka, Japan: Kaiho Shuppansha.

Inoue, T. (1981). *Joseigaku to sono shuhen* [Women's studies and related studies]. Tokyo: Keiso shobo.

———. (1987). Onna no "koza" o tsukuru [Creating "the courses" for women]. In Joseigaku kenkyukai (Ed.), *Koza joseigaku 4: Onna no me de miru* [Courses in women's studies, vol. 4: Looking in the eyes of the women]. Tokyo: Keiso Shobo.

Ishimoto, S. (1999). Facing two ways: The story of my life. In P. Morley, *The mountain is moving: Japanese women's lives* (p. 69). New York: New York University Press.

"Issai han sugitemo ikukyuu," daikigyoo no 26 percent dokuji seido hirogaru ["Child-care leave longer than one year and half," 26 percent of major corporations have established their own leave systems]. 2007, July 6). *Asahi Shinbun.* Retrieved July 6, 2007, from http://www.asahi.com

Ito Chu, kanbu ni josei zoku zoku fuyasu [Ito Chu Shoji continues to increase the number of women executives]. (2007, June 12). *Asahi Shinbun.* Retrieved June 12, 2007, from http://www.asahi.com

Iwai, H. (1990). Josei no raifu kosu to gakureki [Life course and educational attainment for women]. In J. Kikuchi (Ed.), *Gendai Nihon no kaiso kozo ido* [Stratification structure of contemporary Japan] (pp. 155–184). Tokyo: Tokyo Daigaku Shuppankai.

Iwao, S. (1988). The Japanese: Portrait of change. *Japan Echo, 15,* 6.

———. (1993). *The Japanese women: Traditional image and changing reality.* New York: Free Press.

Iwao, S., and H. Hara (1979). *Joseigaku kotohajime* [Introduction to women's studies]. Tokyo: Kodansha.

Japan DIY Life Insurance Company. (2007). *Sarariiman setai no shufu ni taisuru anketo chosa* [Survey on homemakers of white-collar households].

Tokyo: Japan DIY Life Insurance Company.

Jarrett-Macaulay, D. (Ed.). (1995). *Reconstructing womanhood, reconstructing feminism*. London: Routledge.

Jiyukokuminsha. (Eds.). (2008). *Gendai yogo no kiso chishiki 2008* [The encyclopedia of contemporary words 2008]. Tokyo: Jiyukokuminsha.

Josei giin amari joohin de nai [Assemblywomen are not very elegant]. (2009, March 6). *Asahi Shinbun*. Retrieved March 8, 2009, from http://www.asahi.com

Josei ishi no genba fukki o shien [Supporting women doctors who resume their practice]. (2007, August 24). *Asahi Shinbun*. Retrieved August 26, 2007, from http://www.asahi.com

Josei kenji dondon fueru [The number of women public prosecutors has been steadily increasing]. (2009, April 19). *Asahi Shinbun*. Retrieved April 22, 2009, from http://www.asahi.com

Josei kenkyuusha, hatsu no juuman nin koe [The number of women researchers exceeding 100,000 for the first time]. (2007, April 14). *Asahi Shinbun*. Retrieved April 16, 2007, from http://www.asahi.com

"Josei wa kodomo o umu kikai" hatsugen ga hamon ["Women are childbearing machines"; A comment from the Minister of Health, Labor, and Welfare caused a stir]. (2007, January 28). *Asahi Shinbun*. Retrieved January 28, 2007, from http://www.asahi.com

Joseigaku Kenkyukai (Workshop on Women's Studies). (Eds.). (1987). *Koza joseigaku 4: Onna no me de miru* [Courses in women's studies, vol. 4: Looking in the eyes of the women]. Tokyo: Keiso Shobo.

Kaji, A. (2007, January 9). *Sekai isan to hyonin kinsei* [World Heritage Site and "no females allowed"]. Retrieved June 1, 2007, from http://www.tvq.co.jp

Kameda, A. (1995). Sexism and gender stereotyping in schools. In K. Fujimura-Fanselow and A. Kameda (Eds.), *Japanese women: New feminist perspectives on the past, present, and future* (pp. 107–124). New York: Feminist Press.

Kaneko, S. (1995). The struggle for legal rights and reforms: A historical view. In K. Fujimura-Fanselow and A. Kameda (Eds.), *Japanese women: New feminist perspectives on the past, present, and future* (pp. 3–14). New York: Feminist Press.

Kanjigen [Kanji sources]. (2006). Tokyo: Gakken.

Katei Hoikuen (Preschool at Home). (2007). *IQ 200 Tensaiji wa hahaoya shidai! Anata no kodomo mo dondon nobiru* [Mother holds the key to a child prodigy with an IQ of 200! Your child can also make great progress]. Tokyo: Nihon Gakko Tosho.

Kawai, H. (1976). *Bosei shakai Nihon no byori* [The pathology of Japan's maternal society]. Tokyo: Chuokoronsha.

Kawashima, Y. (1995). Female workers: An overview of past and current trends. In K. Fujimura-Fanselow and A. Kameda (Eds.), *Japanese women: New feminist perspectives on the past, present, and future* (pp. 271–293). New York: Feminist Press.

Kekkon shussan de taishoku no josei ni seishain fukki no michi, Kirin Biiru [Kirin Beer offers full-time positions to former women employees who resigned because of marriage and childbirth]. (2007, February 25). *Asahi Shinbun*. Retrieved February 26, 2007, from http://www.asahi.com

Kigyoo ni hirogaru dai 3 shi iwai kin, Yamato Shoken wa 200 man en [More companies are offering employees congratulatory money at the birth of their third child; Yamato Shoken offers 2 million yen]. (2007, November 26).

Bibliography

Asahi Shinbun. Retrieved November 28, 2007, from http://www.asahi.com

Kikuchi, J. (Ed.). (1990). *Gendai Nihon no kaiso kozo ido* [Stratification structure of contemporary Japan]. Tokyo: Tokyo Daigaku Shuppankai.

Kinjo, K. (1995). Legal challenges to the status quo. In K. Fujimura-Fanselow and A. Kameda (Eds.), *Japanese women: New feminist perspectives on the past, present, and future* (pp. 353–363). New York: Feminist Press.

Kishida, T. (1884). Doho shimai ni tsugu [I tell you, my fellow sisters]. *Jiyu no tomoshibi, 3,* 20.

Kitahara, Y., and Taishukan. (2002–2008). *Meikyo kokugo jiten* [Meikyo Japanese language dictionary]. Tokyo: Taishukan Shoten.

———. (2006). *Minna de Kokugo Jiten! Kore mo nihongo* [The Japanese language dictionary by all of us! This is Japanese as well]. Tokyo: Taishukan Shoten.

Kojien (5th ed.). (1998, 2005). Tokyo: Iwanami Shoten.

Kojien (6th ed.). (2008). Tokyo: Iwanami Shoten.

Kondo, H. (Ed.). (2006). *Japan plus Asia-Pacific Perspectives 4*(2). Tokyo: Jijigahosha.

Kotoba to Onna o Kangaeru Kai (The Association to Think about Language and Women) (Eds.). (1985). *Kokugojiten ni miru josei sabetsu* [Sexism in the Japanese language dictionaries]. Tokyo: Sanichi Shobo.

Koyama, S. (1991). *Ryosai kenbo to iu kihan* [Norms called "good wives, wise mothers"]. Tokyo: Keiso Shobo.

Kramarae, C. (Ed.) (1980). *The voices and words of women and men.* Elmsford, NY: Pergamon Press.

Kyodo Tsushinsha. (Eds.). (1997). *Kisha handobukku dai 8 han* [Journalists' handbook, 8th edition]. Tokyo: Kyodo Tsushinsha.

———. (Eds.). (2001). *Kisha handobukku dai 9 han* [Journalists' handbook, 9th edition]. Tokyo: Kyodo Tsushinsha.

Kyutoku, S. (1979). *Bogenbyo* [Illnesses caused by mothers]. Tokyo: Sanmaku Shuppan.

Labor Policy Research and Induction Organization (Rodoseisaku Kenkyu Kenshu Kiko). (2002). *Shugyo kozo kihon chosa* [Basic survey on employment structure]. Tokyo: Rodoseisaku Kenkyu Kenshu Kiko.

Lakoff, R. (1975). *Language and woman's place.* New York: Harper and Row.

Lebra, T. S. (1976). *Japanese patterns of behavior.* Honolulu: University of Hawaii Press.

———. (1984). *Japanese women: Constraint and fulfillment.* Honolulu: University of Hawaii Press.

Lo, J. (1990). *Office ladies / factory women: Life and work at a Japanese company.* Armonk, NY: M. E. Sharpe.

Lowy, D. (2007). *The Japanese "new woman": Images of gender and modernity.* New Brunswick, NJ: Rutgers University Press.

MacKay, D. G. (1980a). Language, thought and social attitudes. In H. Giles, W. P. Robinson, and P. M. Smith (Eds.), *Language: Social psychological perspectives* (pp. 89–96). Oxford, UK: Pergamon Press.

———. (1980b). Psychology, prescriptive grammar and the pronoun problem. *American Psychologists, 35,* 444–449.

———. (1983). Prescriptive grammar and the pronoun problem. In B. Thorne, C. Kramarae, and N. Henley (Eds.), *Language, gender and society* (p. 38–53). Rowley, MA: Newbury House Publishers.

Mackie, V. (2002). Housewives' association. In S. Buckley (Ed.), *Encyclopedia of contemporary Japanese culture* (p. 203). London and New York: Routledge.

_____.*Feminism in modern Japan: Citizenship, embodiment and sexuality.* Cambridge, UK: Cambridge University Press.

Makino, S., and M. Tsutsui. (1989). *A dictionary of basic Japanese grammar.* Tokyo: Japan Times.

Martinez, D. P. (1987). Comment. *Current Anthropology, 28* (4), 83–84.

Martyna, W. (1978). What does "he" mean? Use of the generic masculine. *Journal of Communication, 28* (1), 130–139.

Martynyuk, A. (1990). A contrastive study of male and female occupational terms in English and Russian. *Papers and Studies in Contrastive Linguistics, 26,* 103–110.

Matsui, Y. (1997). Matsui Yayori: Senior staff editor, Asahi shinbun. In S. Buckley (Ed.), *Broken silence: Voices of Japanese feminism* (pp. 131–155). Berkeley and Los Angeles: University of California Press.

McClure, W. (2000). *Using Japanese: A guide to contemporary usage.* Cambridge, UK: Cambridge University Press.

McConnel-Ginet, S., F. Borker, and N Furman. (Eds.). (1980). *Women and language in literature and society.* New York: Praeger Publishers.

Meguro, Y. (1990). Japanese family: Change and continuity. In National Women's Education Centre (Comp.), *Women in a changing society: the Japanese scene* (pp. 59–66). Bangkok: UNESCO Principal Regional Office for Asia and the Pacific.

Meiji Shoin seisen kokugo jiten [Meiji Shoin selected Japanese language dictionary]. (1994). Tokyo: Meiji Shoin.

Mertens, D. M. (1998). *Research methods in education and psychology.* Thousand Oaks, CA: Sage Publications.

Miller, C., and K. Swift. (1980). *The handbook of nonsexist writing for writers, editors and speakers.* New York: Lippincott and Crowell.

_____. (1991). *Words and women: New language in new times.* (Updated.) New York: HarperCollins.

Miller, L. (2006). *Beauty up: Exploring contemporary Japanese body aesthetics.* Berkeley and Los Angeles: University of California Press.

Minamoto, J. (1990). Nihon bukkyo no seisabetsu [Gender discrimination in Japanese Buddhism]. In A. Ogoshi, J. Minamoto, and A. Yamashita. (Eds.). (1990). *Seisabetsu suru bukkyo* [Buddhism that discriminates against women] (pp. 87–164). Kyoto, Japan: Hozokan.

_____. (1997). *Feminizum ga tou bukkyo* [Buddhism that feminism questions]. Tokyo: Sanichi Shobo.

_____. (2005). (Ed.), *Nyonin kinsei* [No females allowed] *QandA.* Osaka, Japan: Kaiho Shuppansha.

Minh-ha, T. T. (1989). *Women, native, other.* Bloomington, IN: Indiana University Press.

Ministry of Education (Monbusho). (1994). *Gakko kihon chosa* [Basic survey of schools]. Tokyo: Monbusho.

Ministry of Education, Culture, Sports, Science and Technology (Monbukagakusho). (2005, 2007, 2008). *Gakko kihon chosa* [Basic survey of schools]. Tokyo: Monbukagakusho.

Ministry of Health, Labor, and Welfare (Koseirodosho). (2004, 2005, 2006, 2007, 2008). *Jinko dotai tokei* [Dynamic statistics of population]. Tokyo: Koseirodosho.

_____. (2006). *Koyo doko chosa* [Survey on employment trend]. Tokyo: Koseirodosho.

_____. (2007). *Josei rodo hakusho* [White paper on female labor]. Tokyo: Koseirodosho.

_____. (2008). *Kongo no shigoto to katei no ryoritsu shien ni kansuru kenkyukai hokokusho* [Report by the study group on future support for the compatibility of work with family]. Tokyo: Koseirodosho.

Ministry of Labor (Rodosho). (1994, 1995). *Joshi koyo kanri kihon chosa* [Basic survey on employment and management of female workers]. Tokyo: Rodosho.

Ministry of Public Management, Home Affairs, Posts and Telecommunications (Somusho). (2007). *Kagaku gijutsu kenkyu chosa* [Survey on research in science and technology]. Tokyo: Somusho.

Mitsui Bussan, dansei ni mo yuukyuu ikukyuu 8 shuukan [Mitsui Bussan provides 8-week paid child-care leave for male employees as well]. (2007, March 29). *Asahi Shinbun*. Retrieved March 29, 2007, from http://www.asahi.com

Morinaga, T. (2008). Kurashi to keizai [Life and economy]. In Jiyukokuminsha (Eds.), *Gendai yogo no kiso chishiki 2008* [The encyclopedia of contemporary words 2008] (pp. 1378–1381). Tokyo: Jiyukokuminsha.

Morley, P. (1999). *The mountain is moving: Japanese women's lives.* New York: New York University Press.

Mura, D. (1991). *Turning Japanese: Memoirs of a sensei*. Atlantic Monthly Press.

Nakamura, M. (1990). Women's sexuality in Japanese female terms. In S. Ide and N. H. McGloin (Eds.), *Aspects of Japanese women's language* (pp. 147–163). Tokyo: Kuroshio Publishers.

Nakano, E. (1984). Kyoiku suijun kara mita yuhaigusha joshi no rodoryoku kyokyu kodo [Labor supply of married women and its relation to their educational attainment]. *Jinko Mondai Kenkyu* [Journal of Population Problems], *171*, 36–51.

Nakayama, M. (1993). Linguistic expressions of sexism in Japanese newspapers. Unpublished research paper, M. A. Applied Linguistics Program, Monash University.

National Council of Teachers of English. (1975; Revised, 1985). *Guidelines for nonsexist use of language in NCTE publications*. Urbana, IL: National Council of Teachers of English.

National Women's Education Centre (Kokuritsu Josei Kyoiku Senta). (Comp.). (1990). *Women in a changing society: the Japanese scene*. Bangkok: UNESCO Principal Regional Office for Asia and the Pacific.

_____. (2008). Joseigaku, jendaa ron kanren kamoku detabesu [Database on courses related to women's studies and gender theories]. Retrieved May 18, 2009, from http://winet.nwec.jp

Nielsen, E. (1988). Linguistic sexism in business writing textbooks. *Journal of Advanced Composition*, *8* (1–2), 55–65.

Nihon IBM ya Sonı, josei tooyoo susumeru NPO o setsuritsu [Japan IBM, Sony and others established NPO to promote women in the private sector]. (2007, May 12). *Asahi Shinbun*. Retrieved May 12, 2007, from http://www.asahi.com

Nilsen, A. P., H. Bosmajian, H. L. Gershuny, and J. P. Stanley. (Eds.). (1977). *Sexism and language*. Urbana, IL: National Council of Teachers of English.

Nolte, S. H., and S. A. Hastings (1991). The Meiji state's policy toward women, 1890–1910. In G. L. Bernstein (Ed.), *Recreating Japanese Women, 1600–1945* (pp. 151–174). Berkeley, Los Angeles: University of California Press.

Obayashi, M. (2005). Kafuchoosei no eikyoo [Influence of the patriarchal system]. In J. Minamoto (Ed.), *Nyonin kinsei* [No females allowed] *QandA* (pp. 37–39). Osaka, Japan: Kaiho Shuppansha.

Obuchi-shi kodomo undakara shoshikasho ni [Ms. Obuchi became the Minister in charge of declining birth rate because she gave birth to a child]. (2008, December 6). *Asahi Shinbun*.

Retrieved December 12, 2008, from http://www.asahi.com

Ogoshi, A. (1990). Bukkyo bunka paradaimu o toinaosu [Reexamining the paradigm of Buddhist culture]. In A. Ogoshi, J. Minamoto, and A. Yamashita (Eds.). (1990). *Seisabetsu suru bukkyo* [Buddhism that discriminates against women] (pp. 1–86). Kyoto, Japan: Hozokan.

Ogoshi, A., J. Minamoto, and A. Yamashita. (Eds.). (1990). *Seisabetsu suru bukkyo* [Buddhism that discriminates against women]. Kyoto, Japan: Hozokan.

Ohinata, M. (1995). The mystique of motherhood: A key to understanding social change and family problems in Japan. In K. Fujimura-Fanselow and A. Kameda (Eds.), *Japanese women: New feminist perspectives on the past, present, and future* (pp. 353–363). New York: Feminist Press.

Okamoto, S., and J. Shibamoto Smith (Eds.). (2004). *Japanese language, gender, and ideology: Cultural models and real people.* New York: Oxford University Press.

Okano, H. (1995). Women's image and place in Japanese Buddhism. In K. Fujimura-Fanselow and A. Kameda (Eds.), *Japanese women: New feminist perspectives on the past, present, and future* (pp. 15–28). New York: Feminist Press.

Okonogi, K. (1983) *Katei no nai kazoku nojidai* [The age of family members without a home]. Tokyo: ABC Shuppan.

Owaki, M. (1991). *Kyokasho no naka no danjo sabetsu* [Sex discrimination in textbooks]. Tokyo: Asahi Shoten.

Ozawa, I. (1994). *Blueprint for a new Japan: The rethinking of a nation.* Tokyo and New York: Kodansha International.

Patton, M.Q. (1980). *Qualitative evaluation methods.* Beverly Hills, CA: Sage Publications.

Pauwels, A. (1998). *Women changing language.* New York: Longman.

Penfield, J. (Ed.). (1987). *Women and language in transition.* Albany, NY: State University of New York Press.

Porecca, K. L. (1984). Sexism in current ESL textbooks. *TESOL Quarterly, 18,* 705–724.

Prime Minister's Office (Sorifu). (1990). *Japanese women today.* Tokyo: Sorifu.

Progressive Japanese-English Dictionary. (1986). Tokyo: Shogakukan.

Ran no shukka saiseiki ni [Shipment of orchids at its peak]. (2008, December 27). *Asahi Shinbun.* Retrieved December 27, 2008, from http://www.asahi.com

Rank, H. (Ed.). (1974). *Language and public policy.* Urbana, IL: National Council of Teachers of English.

Reischauer, E. O. and M. B. Jansen. (1995). *The Japanese today: Change and continuity.* Cambridge, MA: Harvard University Press.

Reynolds, K. A. (1990). Female speakers of Japanese in transition. In S. Ide and N. H. McGloin (Eds.), *Aspects of Japanese Women's language* (pp. 129–146). Tokyo: Kuroshio Publishers.

Rosenberger, N. (2001). *Gambling with virtue: Japanese women and the search for self in a changing nation.* Honolulu: University of Hawaii Press.

Saitama-ken Center for Promotion of Gender Equality (Saitama-ken Kyodo Sankaku Suishin Senta). (2002). *Ikujiki josei no shuro chudan ni kansuru kenkyu* [Study on the interruption of employment among women during the period of child care]. Saitama, Japan: Saitama-ken Kyodo Sankaku Suishin Senta.

Saito, M. (1994). Sabetsugo gari dewa nai gengo kaikaku: Eigo kyokasho, eiwa jisho ni miru [Language reform without the censorship of discriminatory language: Studies on English textbooks and English-Japanese dictionaries]. *Hyuman Raitsu* [Human Rights], *78*, 40–49.

———. (1997). Jenda teki kosei hodo no gaidorain [Guidelines on fair reporting on genders]. *Toshokan to media no hon* [Book on libraries and media], *Zu-bon*, *2*, 57–58. Tokyo: Shinsensha.

Sakai, J. (2003). *Makeinu no toboe* [Grumbling of the loser]. Tokyo: Kodansha.

Sasaki, E. (1994). Habikoru josei sabetsu to "kokusaijin" no yukue: Chugaku eigo kyokasho no jittai to kongo no kadai [Prevailing discrimination against women and the directions of "internationalization": The current conditions and future issues of junior high school English textbooks]. *Joseigaku* [Women's Studies], *2*, 121–139.

Saso, M. (1990). *Women in the Japanese workplace*. London: Hilary Shipman.

Sato, K. (1982). (Ed.). *Nihongo no goi no tokushoku* [The characteristics of the Japanese vocabulary]. Tokyo: Meiji Shoin.

Sato, Y. (1978). *Onna no ko wa tsukurareru* [How girls are socialized]. Tokyo: Shiraishi Shoten.

———. (1979). Nanajunendai ni okeru joseitachi no tatakai [Women's struggle in the 1970s]. *Shiso no Kagaku* [Science of Thought], *100*, 27.

———. (1995). From the home to the political arena. In K. Fujimura-Fanselow and A. Kameda (Eds.), *Japanese women: New feminist perspectives on the past, present, and future* (pp. 365–372). New York: Feminist Press.

Seisansei hatsugen de hamon [Comment on "productivity" causes a stir]. (2007, January 19). *Asahi Shinbun*. Retrieved January 22, 2007, from http://www.asahi.com

Shizen to Ningen [Nature and People]. (2003, February). Tokyo: Shizen to Ningen Sha.

Shukan Josei [Women's Weekly] (2001, November 6). Tokyo: Shufu to Seikatsu Sha.

Sievers, S. (1983). *Flowers in salt: The beginnings of feminist consciousness in modern Japan*. Stanford, CA: Stanford University Press.

Simmonds, F. N. (1995). Naming and identity. In D. Jarrett-Macaulay (Ed.), *Reconstructing womanhood, reconstructing feminism* (pp. 109–120). London: Routledge.

Smith, P. (1997). *Japan: A reinterpretation*. New York: Pantheon Books.

Smith, R. J. (1987). Gender inequality in contemporary Japan. *Journal of Japanese Studies*, *13* (1), 1–25.

Sodei, T. (1990). Older women in Japan. In National Women's Education Centre (Comp.), *Women in a changing society: the Japanese scene* (pp. 73–80). Bangkok: UNESCO Principal Regional Office for Asia and the Pacific.

———. (2006). The changing status of women. In H. Kondo (Ed.), *Japan plus Asia-Pacific Perspectives 4* (2), 22–23. Tokyo: Jijigahosha.

Sorrels, B. M. (1983). *The nonsexist communicator: Solving the problems of gender and awkwardness in modern English*. Englewood Cliffs, NJ: Prentice Hall.

Spender, D. (1980). *Man made language*. London: Routledge and Kegan Paul.

Stanley, J. P. (1978). Sexist grammar. *College English*, *39*, 800–811.

Stennard, U. (1977). *Mrs. Man*. San Francisco: Germain Books.

Sugimoto, S. (1999). *Josei wa do manande kitaka* [How have women been educated?] Tokyo: Shueisha.

Sugiura, Y., and J. Gillespie. (1993). *Traditional Japanese culture and modern Japan*. Tokyo: Natsume.

Sunderland, J. (1992). Gender in the EFL classroom. *ELT Journal*, *46*, 81–91.

Swanger, R. (1994). Letters/Sexism no surprise. *Japan Quarterly, 41* (1), 4.

Takahashi, M. (1991). Titles and terms for women in English and Japanese. In P. G. Fendos Jr. (Ed.), *Cross-cultural communication: East and west* (pp. 287–303). Tainan, Taiwan: National Cheng-Kung University.

Tanabe, G. J. (2002). Buddhism. In S. Buckley (Ed.), *Encyclopedia of contemporary Japanese culture* (pp. 49–51). London and New York: Routledge.

Tanaka, K. (1995a). The new feminist movement in Japan, 1970–1990. In K. Fujimura-Fanselow and A. Kameda (Eds.), *Japanese women: New feminist perspectives on the past, present, and future* (pp. 343–352). New York: Feminist Press.

———. (1995b). Work, education, and the family. In K. Fujimura-Fanselow and A. Kameda (Eds.), *Japanese women: New feminist perspectives on the past, present, and future* (pp. 295–308). New York: Feminist Press.

Tanaka, Y. (1995). *Contemporary portraits of Japanese women*. Westport, CT: Praeger.

Tanimura, S. (1990). *Kekkon shinai kamo shirenai shokogun* [The "I may not marry" syndrome]. Tokyo: Shufu no Tomosha.

Thorne, B., and N. Henley. (Eds.). (1975). *Language and sex: Difference and dominance*. Rowley, MA: Newbury House Publishers.

Thorne, B., C. Kramarae, and N. Henley. (Eds.) (1983). *Language, gender and society*. Rowley, MA: Newbury House Publishers.

Todai joshi gakusei kakuho ni sekkyokuteki [Tokyo University eager to attract more female students]. (2007, December 12). *Asahi Shinbun*. Retrieved December 16, 2007, from http://www.asahi.com

Trudgill, P. (1974). *Sociolinguistics*. New York: Penguin.

Uchidate, M. (2006). *Onna wa naze dohyo ni agarenai no ka* [Why are women not allowed to step up to the sumo ring?]. Tokyo: Gentosha.

Ueno, C. (1997). Ueno Chizuko: Professor, University of Tokyo; Sociologist. In S. Buckley (Ed.), *Broken silence: Voices of Japanese feminism*. Berkeley and Los Angeles: University of California Press.

———. (2008). Seku hara [Sexual harassment]. In Jiyukokuminsha (Eds.), *Gendai yogo no kiso chishiki 2008* [The encyclopedia of contemporary words 2008] (pp. 16–17). Tokyo: Jiyukokuminsha.

Ueno, C. and Media no Naka no Seisabetsu o Kangaeru Kai (The Association to Think about Gender Discrimination in the Media). (Eds.). (1996). *Kitto kaerareru seisabetsugo: Watashitachi no gaidorain* [Sexist language that can be certainly changed: Our guidelines]. Tokyo: Sanseido.

Ujihara, Y. (1997a). Kyokasho ni okeru jenda messeji (I): Chugakko shakaika, kominteki bunya no suryoteki bunseki [Gender message in textbooks (I): Quantitative analysis on junior high school social studies and civics textbooks]. *Nagoya Daigaku Kyoiku Gakubu Kiyou (Kyoikugaku)* [Nagoya University Department of Education Bulletin (Educational Studies)], *44* (1), 91–103.

———. (1997b). Kyokasho ni okeru jenda messeji (II): Chugakko shakaika, kominteki bunya no shitsuteki bunseki [Gender message in textbooks (II): Qualitative analysis on junior high school social studies and civics textbooks]. *Nagoya Daigaku Kyoiku Gakubu Kiyou (Kyoikugaku)* [Nagoya University Department of Education Bulletin (Educational Studies)], *44*(2), 95–105.

United Nations Development Plan (UNDP). (2006). *Report on human development*. New York: United Nations.

Bibliography

Uno, K. S. (1991). Women and changes in the household division of labor. In G. L. Bernstein (Ed.). *Recreating Japanese women, 1600–1945* (pp. 17–41). Berkeley and Los Angeles: University of California Press.

———. (1993). The death of "good wife, wise mother"? In A. Gordon (Ed.), *Postwar Japan as history* (pp. 293–322). Berkeley and Los Angeles: University of California Press.

Van Den Bergh, N. (1987). Renaming: Vehicle for empowerment. In J. Penfield (Ed.), *Women and language in transition* (pp. 130–136). Albany, NY: State University of New York Press.

Watashitachi no seifuku dekita! Josei pairotto "otoko mono" kara sotsugyoo [Our uniforms are ready! Women pilots no longer have to wear "men's" uniforms]. (2008, November 14). *Asahi Shinbun*. Retrieved November 16, 2008, from http://www.asahi.com

What men have said about women. (2009, January 13). New York: Workman Publishing. Retrieved January 16, 2009, from http://www.workman.com

White, M. (1986). *The Japanese educational challenges*. New York: Free Press.

Wong, Y. (1991). *Sexism in modern standard Chinese*. Unpublished paper for the MA in Applied Linguistics Program. Monash University.

Worby, D. Z. (1979). In search of a common language: Women and educational texts. *College English, 41* (1), 101–105.

World Economic Forum. (2006). *Global gender gap report 2006*. Geneva, Switzerland: World Economic Forum.

Yamada, M. (2008). Mai homu [My home]. In Jiyukokuminsha (Eds.), *Gendai yogo no kiso chishiki 2008* [The encyclopedia of contemporary words 2008] (pp. 10–11). Tokyo: Jiyukokuminsha.

Yamahoko junko eno sanka o negai, gonen han buri "onna hoko" [A "women's float" after five and a half years in the hope of taking part in the procession of floats]. (2007, March 13). *Asahi Shinbun*. Retrieved March 18, 2007, from http://www.asahi.com

Yamamura, Y. (1971). *Nihonjin to haha* [Japanese and mothers]. Tokyo: Toyokan Shuppan.

Yosano, A. (1911). Sozorogoto. *Seito* [Bluestocking] *1* (1), 1–9.

Yoshihiro, K. (1993). *Hikon jidai: Onnatachi no shinguru raifu* [The era of unmarried by choice: Women's single life]. Tokyo: Asahi Shinbun.

Yoshizumi, K. (1995). Marriage and family: Past and present. In K. Fujimura-Fanselow and A. Kameda (Eds.), *Japanese women: New feminist perspectives on the past, present, and future* (pp. 183–197). New York: Feminist Press.

Yukawa, S., and M. Saito. (2004). Cultural ideologies in Japanese language and gender studies: A theoretical review. In S. Okamoto and J. Shibamoto Smith (Eds.), *Japanese language, gender, and ideology: Cultural models and real people* (pp. 23–37). New York: Oxford University Press.

Yuzawa, Y. (2008). Kazoku, katei [Family, home]. In Jiyukokuminsha (Eds.), *Gendai yogo no kiso chishiki 2008* [The encyclopedia of contemporary words 2008] (pp. 1133–1137). Tokyo: Jiyukokuminsha.

Index

adoption 32
adultery 29, 106, 130, 140–141
age 3, 22–23, 28, 33–37, 40, 46, 48, 57, 60–62, 66, 70, 82, 88–91, 98, 103, 110–111, 114, 116, 119–120, 127–129, 133–134, 138–139, 141, 149–150, 153, 158–159, 171, 175–176, 191, 199
age group 25, 35, 40, 48, 50, 53, 89, 129–130, 138, 171, 175, 199
Agency for Cultural Affairs 83, 198
aging 115, 135, 141, 175; population 60, 63
aijin 106
Ajia no Onnatachi no Kai 170
aka hara 176
akusai 98–99, 137, 163
Akutagawa literary award 83–84
All Nippon Airways (ANA) 63–64
Amaterasu Omikami 9
Aoki Yayoi 139
appearance 34, 90–91, 111, 122–124, 133–134, 142–143, 167–168
ara foo 175
ara saa 175
aristocratic singles *see dokushin kizoku*
arranged marriage *see miai kekkon*
astronauts 84, 151–152
authors 54, 83–84, 151, 165, 172, 184, 192

babaa 82, 91, 127–128, 144
baishun 169–170
Basic Law for a Gender-equal Society 78
Basic Law of Education 48, 194
Basic Survey of Schools 50–52
batsu ichi 39, 172–173
biboo 123, 143
bijin 92, 123–124, 142–143, 166
birth rate 21–22, 26, 30, 38, 59, 63, 65–66, 70, 82, 102
Bogenbyo 25
Bolinger, Dwight 200–201
Borker, Ruth 145
Bosei Shakai Nihon no Byori 198
boshi katei 80, 168–169; *see also* single mother family
box lunch *see obentoo*

boy *see otoko no ko*; *shoonen*
bridal training *see hanayome shugyoo*
bride 28, 91–94, 104, 113, 133–134, 138–139, 160–161, 187
Buddhism 5, 11–15, 45, 95, 125–126, 138, 143–144, 147
busamen 167
busu 91, 122–124, 133–134, 142, 189
buzzwords 35, 38–40, 79, 159, 164–165, 167, 172, 175, 179, 198

Cabinet Office 16, 31, 42, 52, 57, 62–64, 77–78, 183
career 2, 34, 36, 38, 58, 63, 65, 115, 118, 120–122, 142, 172
caretaker 26, 60
characterization 90–91, 106, 112, 130, 133–136, 139, 140
Cherry, Kittredge 91, 168
Chifuren 75
child-bearing machines 22, 82–83, 102
child care 18–19, 22, 24–26, 37, 44, 57–58, 60–62, 67–68, 70, 77, 84, 100, 119, 121, 154–155, 178
child-care allowance 81
Child-Care Allowance Law 81
child-care leave 60–63, 66–67, 69–70, 84
Child-Care Leave and Family-Care Leave Law 59–62, 70
childbirth 14–15, 57, 59, 62, 68–69, 71, 84
Christmas cake 1–2, 158
Civil Code 30–32, 38, 74, 80
Civil Code of 1898 11, 27–29, 32, 105, 125, 161
clerical track 59
coinage 6, 34–35, 43, 155, 158–159, 164, 166–167, 169–173, 175–177, 188, 190, 200
community centers 54
compulsory education 46–47
Conference on Gender Equality 183
Conference on Women's Problems for the International Year for Women 76, 178
conformity 158, 160, 198

223

Index

Confucianism 5, 11–12, 144, 152–153; Confucian doctrine 13, 36–37, 46; ethics 12, 27; maxims 12, 153; morals 44, 49; thinking 44, 47
conglomerate 65, 67, 69
congratulatory money 66–67
congratulatory resignation *see kotobuki taishoku / kotobuki taisha*
congresswomen 77, 118, 138
Constitution 11, 14, 30, 38, 48, 55, 74, 104, 125, 194
Consumer's Co-op *see* Seikyo
Council for Gender Equality 78, 182–183
couple 10, 30–31, 33, 36–42, 70, 80, 93, 146–147, 161, 163, 165, 168, 182
Creighton, Millie 139
culture center 53–54

Dai Nippon Fujinkai 74
danna 162
dansei funin 174–175
danson johi 10–11, 13, 45, 47, 92–93, 95, 104, 111, 124–125, 137–138, 143, 146–147, 149, 154, 163
daughter-in-a-box *see hakoiri musume*
daughters 13, 28, 32, 46, 50, 84, 93–94, 98, 105, 113, 126, 137, 143, 152, 160, 185
daughters-in-law 28, 91–94, 104, 113, 133–134, 138–139, 160–161, 187
defilement 12, 14
demeanor 3–4, 98, 106–107, 109, 139–140, 160
demodori 39, 91, 103–104, 137, 172–173, 189
derogatory expression 3–4, 104, 144, 157, 159–160, 174; term 39, 82, 90–92, 116, 122, 127–128, 144, 157, 159, 169, 174
dictionary 3, 6, 79–80, 110, 124, 140, 169, 180–181, 186–188, 191–192
diet 73, 83
discrimination 30, 59, 81–82, 126, 169, 178, 180; expression 173, 179; practice 142; term 169, 172, 174, 184–185, 188–191; treatment 195
divorce 5, 28–29, 31, 38–42, 104, 120, 168, 172–173, 189
doctors 1, 34, 66–68, 84, 114, 151, 156
Doho Shimai ni Tsugu 73
Doi Takako 16–17, 77
dokushin 171–172
dokushin kizoku 36, 171
domestic divorce *see kateinai rikon*
dynamic statistics of population 22, 39–40, 59–60

Edo period 5, 10–12, 20, 27, 29, 44–45, 72, 115, 118, 122, 125, 152, 157, 160, 163
education 5, 12, 21–24, 33, 44–51, 53–55, 88–89, 100–101, 115, 120–121, 132–136, 138, 160, 179–180, 193–194, 199; of women 5, 21, 44–48, 51, 54–55
Education Act 46
education-conscious mother *see kyooiku mama*
eikyuu shuushoku 58, 120
Electoral Law 74
emperor 11–12, 28, 44, 49
employment 62, 69, 71, 160, 178–179
Endo Orie 78, 140, 182–183, 192, 198
enkiri dera 29
entrance exams 23–24, 51
Equal Employment Opportunity Law (EEOL) 58–59, 116, 180
equal rights 59, 73–75, 79
era of women *see onna no jidai*
exploitation 170

faculty 51–52
family register 28, 30, 161, 185; *see also koseki*
family registration system *see koseki seido*
Farnsley, Kathy 198–199
fathers 13, 23–25, 28, 37, 42, 45, 60, 62, 70, 100–101, 126, 137, 143, 146–150, 152, 155, 168
female-male word order 146–147
femininity 107–108, 111–112, 138, 186
feminism 6, 54–55, 72, 76, 79–80; activists 83, 145, 153, 161, 163, 183, 199–200; critics 58, 197; first wave of 6, 72, 74; identity 79–80; pioneers 9, 72; scholars 4, 54, 107, 117, 139, 145, 149, 161, 163, 180–181, 186, 193, 197; second wave of 4, 49, 54, 75–76, 79, 145, 177
feminisuto 79
feminizumu 79
fertility 82, 93, 101
five hindrances of women 13
flower in the workplace *see shokuba no hana*
fubokai 148–150
Fujimura-Fanselow Kumiko 33, 138
fujin 92, 118–119, 138, 151, 153, 185, 187, 190
Fujin Sanseiken Kakutoku Kisei Domeikai 74
fujoshi 124, 185
fukei 147–148
fukeikai 148, 150

224

Index

Fukuda Hideko *see* Kageyama Hideko
full-time employment 18–21, 39, 56–57, 60–62, 67–68, 71, 100, 121, 165–166
full-time homemaker 18, 20, 61–62, 69, 100, 131, 142, 165; *see also sengyoo shufu*
funin / funinshoo 174
Furman, Nelly 145
fushi katei 168–169

Gendai Yogo no Kiso Chishiki 164–165, 175
gender 36, 43, 78, 96, 108–109, 119, 145–146, 148–150, 153, 155–157, 163, 168, 171–174, 180–181, 184, 187, 192–194, 197, 201; asymmetry 5, 137, 152, 157, 180; bias 2–3, 6, 25, 43, 87, 113, 132, 137–138, 145, 148, 151, 153, 161–164, 173, 175, 178–179, 183–184, 186–187, 191–195, 198–200; differences 37, 46, 154, 166; discrimination 44, 75, 179–180, 184, 198; empowerment index 64; equality 11, 30, 48, 78, 104, 125, 183, 195; imbalance 50–51, 169; inequality 11, 27, 29, 44, 47, 75, 84, 125, 144, 147, 153, 161, 164, 180, 186, 193, 196–197; issues 164, 170; markers 119; relations 12, 193; roles 164–165, 182; segregation 36, 46–49; stereotype 3, 6, 43, 84, 107, 109, 139–140, 162–165, 168, 179–180, 188, 191, 193, 200; theories *see jendaaron*
gender-based role division 11, 18, 21, 36–37, 56, 59–60, 62, 70, 95–96, 131, 142, 144, 162, 165, 178
gender-related expression 3, 87, 164–165, 194
Genji Monogatari 10, 14
Gion festival 17–18
girls *see joshi; onna no ko*
Gishi Wajinden 9
goke 92, 104–105, 173
good wife and wise mother *see ryoosai kenbo*
government 6, 14–17, 22–23, 36, 41, 44–45, 47–49, 53–54, 60, 62–63, 65–67, 72–74, 76–78, 82, 155, 176, 178, 182–183, 193, 199–200
governors 16–17, 82, 127–128
guidelines 181, 183–186, 192–194, 196, 199
Guidelines to Prevent Sexual Harassment 177
gusai 5, 92, 98, 133–134, 136–137, 163
gusoku 98
gyakutama 167–168

Haga Y. 87
hai misu 103, 166, 188
hai misutaa 166
haiguusha 162
hakoiri musume 115–116, 160
hanayome shugyoo 90
handbook 183–184
Hara Hiroko 54
Hara Kimi 27, 44, 55, 78
harassment 176
harmony 88
heads of the family *see kachoo; koseki hittoosha; koshu*
Heian period 10, 97, 109, 118, 173
hesokuri 20
higher education 38, 47–48, 50–51, 54, 70, 176; *see also* education
hikon 35, 170–171
Hikon Jidai: Onnatachi no Shinguru Raifu 35, 171–172
Himiko 9
Hio Yasuko 140, 197, 200
hiragana 10, 113, 157
Hiratsuka Raicho 9, 72, 74
hitori 171–172
hitori mono 171–172
hobo 119, 154–155
hofu 155
hogoshakai 148–150
hoikushi 119, 154–156
holy mountain *see reizan*
home economics 47, 49–50, 53
homemaker 5, 18–21, 39, 53–54, 62, 67, 70–71, 75, 89–90, 92, 94, 100, 133–136, 152, 165, 179; status of 19–20
honne 88
Hoso Daigaku 53
Hosshinshu 147
house husband 165–166
House of Councilors 78
House of Representatives 74, 77, 83
household chores 21, 37, 42, 45, 70, 90, 94, 97, 100, 139, 152, 178, 187; *see also* housework
household management 19, 60
housework 18, 22, 100, 121, 165; *see also* household chores
housework helpers *see kaji tetsudai*
human rights 16, 78, 176
husbands 1, 10, 13, 19–20, 28–29, 31–32, 37–38, 40–42, 45, 58, 62, 70, 92–94, 96–99, 101, 104–106, 109, 126, 130–132, 137–139, 143, 146–147, 161–165, 174, 179, 185–187, 190

Index

Ichikawa Fusae 74
Ide Sachiko 139, 182
ie system 5, 11, 27–30, 32, 42–43, 75, 80, 93, 125, 161
ikazu goke 91, 103, 139, 157–158
ikemen 166–167
ikiokure 91, 103, 133–134, 139, 157–158
illnesses 24–25
impurity 10, 12, 14, 45, 95, 125–126, 143
income 19, 34–36, 58, 81, 121, 142, 171, 175
infertility 29, 101–102, 132, 139, 174–175, 190
infidelity 38
in-laws 13, 28–29, 33, 45, 93–94, 101, 104, 161
Inoue Teruko 54, 75
Ishihara Shintaro 82–83, 127
Ito Chu Shoji 65
Iwai Hachiro 142
Iwao Sumiko 54
Izumi Shikibu 10

Japan Airlines (JAL) 64
Japan Federation of Lawyers 83, 193
Japan IBM 65–66
Japan Sumo Association 16–17, 127
Japan Women's Innovative Network (J-win) 65–66
jendaaron 54
jidoo 149
Jiyu Minken Undo 73
Jiyu no Tomoshibi 73
Jiyukokuminsha 164
joryuu 92, 118, 151, 153–154, 184
josei 92, 115, 118–119, 138, 151, 153–154, 174, 185, 190
josei funin 174
joseigaku 54
joshi 152–153
joshidaisei bookokuron 49
judges 84
jukunen rikon 40
junior colleges 49–50, 52–53

kabuki 14–15
kachoo 27–28
kafu 173–174
Kageyama Hideko 73
Kaibara Ekiken 13, 29, 45
kaishun 169–170
kaji tetsudai 89–90
kakekomi dera 29
kakusakon 168

Kamakura period 10–11, 13, 93, 95, 97, 104, 137, 143, 146–147, 163
Kan Naoto 82
Kanagawa Women's Plan 182
kanai 92, 96–97, 133–134, 136–137, 161–163, 185
kango 113
kangofu 154–155
kangonin 155
kangoshi 154–156
kanji 10, 91, 95, 108–109, 112–113, 130, 133–134, 140, 145–147, 149, 155–157, 165, 173–174, 187, 200
Kanjigen 187
katakana 156, 175, 200
Katei Hoikuen 23
kateinai rikon 38, 42
Kawai Hayao 198
kayoikon 10, 93
kekkaiseki 15
Kekkon Shinai Kamo Shirenai Shokogun 35
kengyoo shufu 18–19, 21, 100
Kepponkyo 14
kinship terms 114, 141
Kirin Beer Company 68–69
Kisha Handobukku 181, 184–186
Kishida Toshiko 73
Kitto Kaerareru Seisabetsugo: Watashitachi no Gaidorain 181
Kodo Suru Onnatachi no Kai 49, 179
Kojien 124, 188, 191
Kojiki 9, 15
Kokin Wakashu 10
Kokugo Jiten ni Miru Josei Sabetsu 180
Kokuritsu Josei Kyoiku Kaikan *see* National Women's Education Center
Kokusai Fujinnen o Kikkake to shite Kodo o Okosu Onnatachi no Kai 178–179
komusume 191
Kong-zi 12, 152
Konjaku Monogatari 147
konki see tekireiki
koseki 28, 30–31; *see also* family register
koseki hittoosha 30–31
koseki seido 30, 80, 161
koshikake 120
koshu 28
Kotoba to Onna o Kangaeru Kai 180
kotobuki taishoku / kotobuki taisha 57, 121, 130–131, 142
kotodama 2, 201
Kyodo Tsushinsha 181, 184–185
Kyoiku Chokugo 44, 48–50
kyoodai 147, 149

226

Index

kyooiku mama 24, 92, 100–101
Kyutoku Shigemori 24–25

labor force *see* workforce
labor history 59–60, 177
labor shortage 60
Lakoff, Robin 196
language reform 145, 148, 165, 182–183, 195–196, 199–200; *see also* nonsexist language reform
Law for Cooperative Participation of Men and Women in Society *see* Basic Law for a Gender-equal Society
lawsuits 177
lawyers 39, 59, 84, 156, 179
Lebra, Takie 144
lexicographers 180, 187, 192
Liberal Democratic Party 17, 77, 83
lifestyle 21, 23, 35, 69, 159–160, 163, 170–172, 175
Lo, Jeannie 139
love marriage *see renai kekkon*
Lun-yu 152–153

Mackie, Vera 46
maiden names 31
makeinu 5, 159
Makeinu no Toboe 159
male dominance 146, 149–150, 163, 186
male-female word order 145–147, 150
mama-san 151–152
managerial track 59, 64–66, 68
Manyoshu 2, 10, 147, 162
marriage 5, 10, 22, 27–37, 39, 41, 43, 57–58, 68, 71, 75, 84, 90–91, 93, 101, 103, 119–121, 130–136, 138–139, 142, 159, 161, 168, 174, 185, 187; *see also tekireiki*
marriageable age *see tekireiki*
Martinez, Dolores 80
Martynyuk, Alla 196
masculinity 28, 105
master 118, 155, 162, 179, 184–185, 187
matchmakers 33–34
maternal society 198
maternity leave 66–67, 69, 84
matrilocal residence 93
Matsudaira Sadanobu 44–45
Matsui Takafumi 83
Matsui Yayori 170
mazakon 25
McConnel-Ginet, Sally 145
media 6, 16–17, 20, 22, 40, 49, 75–77, 79–80, 83–84, 116, 127–128, 165, 167–170, 172, 178–179, 181, 183–184, 186, 198–200
Media no Naka no Seisabetsu o Kangaeru Kai (GEAM) 181
Meiji emperor 44
Meiji period 11, 36, 44–45, 47–48, 72–74, 95, 125, 137, 146, 161
Meiji Restoration 45, 72
Meiji Shoin Seisen Kokugo Jiten 191
Meikyo Kokugo Jiten 188, 191
mekake 91, 105–106
men at work, women at home 11, 18, 37, 56, 62, 96–97, 165
men superior, women inferior *see danson johi*
menopause 82
miai kekkon 33–34
miboojin 1, 92, 104–105, 130, 132, 137–138, 173–174, 185
mikon 170
mikudari han 29
Miller, Casey 196
Ministry of Education 46, 49, 198
Ministry of Education, Culture, Sports, Science and Technology 49–50, 52–53, 193
Ministry of Health, Labor, and Welfare 22, 39–40, 56, 58–63, 67–68, 70, 81
Ministry of Justice 31
Ministry of Labor 177
Ministry of Public Management, Home Affairs, Posts and Telecommunications 52
Minna de Koikugo Jiten! 167
mistress 28, 91, 105–106, 140
Mitsubishi Motor Company 177
Mitsui Bussan 69
Miura Shumon 83
Mori Arinori 46
Mori Yoshiro 22–23, 82
Moriyama Mayumi 16
Morley, Patricia 33, 56, 63, 71, 76, 139, 183
mother complex *see mazakon*
mothers 5, 18, 21, 23–26, 33, 37, 46–48, 51, 58, 60, 62, 70, 80, 84, 97, 99–101, 110, 114, 137, 142, 146–152, 154–155, 168, 177
mothers-in-law 58, 91, 94, 113
Mt. Fuji *see reizan*
Mt. Omine *see reizan*
Mukai Chiaki 84
muko yooshi 32
Murasaki Shikibu 10, 14

227

Index

naijo no koo 92, 99, 138
Nakajima Shoen *see* Kishida Toshiko
Nakamura Momoko 141, 197
Nakano Eiko 142
Nara period 10, 13, 147
Narita rikon 39
national assembly *see* Diet
National Council of Teachers of English (NCTE) 193–194
National Personnel Authority 61
National Women's Education Center (NWEC) 54, 76
neo–Confucianism 12, 45
New Left movement 75
New Women 72
newspaper 170, 181–182, 184
nigoo 105–106
Nihon Hoso Kyokai (NHK) 179, 184
Nihon Joseigaku Kenkyu Kai 180
Nihon Shoki 9, 11, 152
no females allowed *see nyonin kinsei*
no trespassing stone *see kekkaiseki*
non-profit organization 65
nonsexist language reform 6, 153, 156–157, 164, 173–174, 177–183, 186–188, 191–199, 201; *see also* language reform
nonsexist language use 186, 193–194, 196
nurses *see kangofu*; *kangonin*; *kangoshi*
nursery schools *see hobo*; *hofu*; *hoikushi*
nymphomaniacs 129
nyonin kinsei 14–18, 92, 126–127, 143
nyooboo 97–98, 161
nyooboo yaku 97, 185
nyuuseki 161, 185

obentoo 26
occupation 34, 53, 66, 88–91, 117–119, 130–131, 133–136, 138, 141, 151–156, 168, 184, 199
ochakumi 120, 142
office lady *see* OL
ofukuro 25–26
okame 122, 142, 190
Okano Haruko 126, 144, 198
Okinoshima 16
oku-san / oku-sama 91, 95–97, 130–131, 133–134, 136, 138, 161–163, 185
OL 57, 119–120, 141–142
oni baba 1, 5, 116–117
onna 1, 3–4, 11, 13, 18, 37, 56, 62, 72, 91–92, 96–97, 105–112, 118–119, 124–126, 129–130, 133–134, 136–141, 143, 151, 153–154, 165, 185–187, 189, 191
onna bara 102, 137

Onna Daigaku 12–13, 29, 45
onna de/onna moji see hiragana
onna hen 91, 112–113, 130, 133–134, 140–141, 187
onna kodomo 92, 124, 138, 143
onna no jidai 16, 77
onna no ko 91, 117, 130–134, 137, 142, 188
Ono no Komachi 10
oorudo misu 91, 103, 190–191
Organization for Economic Cooperation and Development (OECD) 52
Ota Fusae 16–17
otoko 3–4, 11, 18, 25, 28, 37, 56, 62, 92, 96–97, 106–107, 111–112, 129, 140, 165, 167, 184, 186, 188
otoko bara 102, 137
otoko de/otoko moji see kanji
otoko no ko 117, 131
otsubone (-sama) 57, 91, 118, 120, 142
otto 162
overtime work 61–62

paatonaa 163–164
parasite singles 36, 172
parents 1, 18, 32–33, 37, 39, 45–46, 50, 60–61, 73, 90–91, 100, 103–104, 110, 115, 137, 146–148, 159–160, 169, 172–173, 189; *see also* fathers; mothers
parents-in-law 18, 29, 60, 62, 100, 139; *see also* mothers-in-law
partners 99, 103, 159, 163–164
part-time adjunct homemaker *see kengyoo shufu*
part-time employment 18–21, 56–58, 100, 121, 142
patriarchal family system 11, 93–94, 139, 182
patriarchal society 5, 11, 21, 99, 137, 146, 149, 196
patrilocal residence 93–94, 103–104
Pauwels, Anne 177–178, 197
permanent employment *see eikyuu shuushoku*
phenomenology 87
pilot 63–64
Plan for Gender Equality in the Year 2000 183
Policy Toward Cooperative Participation of Men and Women 78
politics 16, 75, 77, 82–83
prejudice 169, 200
prenatal education *see taikyoo*
prime minister 22, 82, 182–183
private sector 52, 61–68

228

Index

promotion 58–59, 69, 117
prostitution 73, 115, 127, 144, 169–170
pseudo-single-mother family 42
PTA meeting *see fubokai; fukeikai; hogoshakai*
public sector 66
publishers 180–181, 187, 192

reizan 14–15, 17, 126
remarriage 39
renai kekkon 33–34
researchers 51–54, 66, 153, 180
resignation 22, 57, 68, 121, 130–131, 142
retirement 20, 40, 63, 66, 71
Reynolds, Katsue 139
rice-serving spatula 20, 94
right-hand man *see nyooboo yaku*
rooba 5, 116
roojo 116
roojoo 190–191
ryoosai 99
ryoosai kenbo 21, 46–47, 49, 51, 99
ryoosai kenbo kyooiku 21, 46–49, 51

Sakai Junko 159
samurai 10–11, 27, 45, 93, 95, 97, 104, 125, 137, 156, 163
sankoo 34
sarariiman 11, 18, 95
Sasagawa Takashi 83
Saso Mary 142
school age 19, 57–58, 121, 142
Seikan Tunnel 15, 127
Seikyo 21
seinen 150
Seisho Nagon 10
seiteki iyagarase 176–177
Seito 9, 72
Seitosha 72
Sekiguchi Reiko 31
seku hara 59, 176–177
sengyoo shufu 18–20, 58, 97, 100; *see also* full-time homemaker
sex tour 169–170
sexism 6, 43, 77, 82, 177–181, 183, 187, 192–193, 195, 197, 200; language 179–183, 186, 193, 196, 198
sexual harassment 59, 77, 176–177
shelter *see enkiri dera; kakekomi dera*
shichikyo 29
Shin Fujin Kyokai 74
shinguru 35–36, 171–172; *see also* singles
Shinto 10–16, 45, 95, 125–127, 143–144
shogun 12

shokuba no hana 57, 120–121, 141–142, 185
shoonen 149
shufu 18, 92, 94, 100, 133–134, 152, 165
Shufu Rengo Kai (Shufuren) 20, 75
shujin 118, 162–163, 179, 185, 187
shuutome see mother-in-law
siblings *see kyoodai*
sinfulness 10, 45, 95, 125–126
single father family *see fushi katei*; single parent family
single mother family 30, 80–81, 104, 168; *see also boshi katei*; single parent family
single men 34–36, 157, 166, 170–171; *see also shinguru*
single parent family 168–169; *see also boshi katei; fushi katei*; single mother family
single women 1, 5, 21, 33–36, 58, 90–92, 103, 115–116, 120–121, 133–134, 136–137, 157–160, 166, 168, 170–172, 188–190; *see also shinguru*
sisters-in-law 95
Smith, Robert 47
Socialist Party 16, 77
Softbank 67
sons 11, 13, 25, 27–28, 32, 46, 50, 94–95, 98, 105, 109, 126, 143, 185
sons-in-law 27, 32
Spender, Dale 196
spouses 25, 28, 33–34, 41, 58, 60, 68–69, 96, 98, 161–164
Stanley, Julia 144
status 3, 24, 33, 36, 90–91, 120, 124, 143, 160, 167–168, 171, 184; marital 35, 93, 103, 120, 153, 157, 160, 171; of women 5, 9, 11–12, 19, 26, 30, 44, 74–75, 102, 117, 124–126, 138, 142–144, 182, 195–196, 199
stigma 30, 38–39, 104, 172–173
suffrage 73–74
sumo 14, 16–17, 126–127, 144
surname 6, 30–32, 80, 139, 157, 184
Swanger, Rachel 186–187, 191
Swift, Kate 196

taikyoo 23
Taisho period 11, 73, 95
Takahashi Minako 141
tamanokoshi 167–168
Tanaka Kazuko 47, 76
Tanaka Yukiko 31
tanshin katei see single parent family
tatemae 88
taxes 58, 81
tea serving *see ochakumi*

229

Index

teishu 37, 162–163, 185
tekireiki 32, 36, 43, 57, 103, 139, 157–160, 166, 171, 188, 190; *see also* marriage
textbooks 192–194
three obediences for women 13, 126, 143
title 25, 32, 157, 162, 184–185
Tokugawa shogunate 44–45, 72
Tokyo Lawyer's Association 31
Tokyo University 51, 83
torii 12, 15
toshikoshi soba 158–159
toshima 92, 115, 134–135, 141
trainee bride 90
Trendy Word Grand Prix 164, 176
Tsuda, Umeko 48
Tsuda Juku Daigaku (Tsuda College) 48
tsuma 162–163, 185
tsumadoikon 10, 93
tsureai 163–164

Uchidate Makiko 17
Uchinaga Yukako 66
Ueno Chizuko 80, 181
Ujishui Monogatari 147
umazume 91, 101–102, 137, 139, 174, 190
unisex term 39, 106, 123, 149, 155, 162, 170, 173
United Nations Convention on the Elimination of All Forms of Discrimination Against Women (CEDAW) 49–50, 81, 180
United Nations Development Plan (UNDP) 64
United Nations Educational, Scientific and Cultural Organization (UNESCO) 16
United Nations International Decade for Women 76, 179–180
United Nations International Year for Women 76, 178–179
universities 31, 48–54
unsold merchandise *see urenokori*
urenokori 92, 103, 133–134, 136–137, 139, 157–158, 189
uuman ribu 79

Van Den Bergh, Nan 197
vocational colleges 50, 53
vogue words 165

welfare 81
White Paper on Gender Equality 57, 64, 77
widowers 105, 173–174
widows 1, 91–92, 103–105, 130, 132, 137–139, 157–158, 173–174, 185
wives 1, 5, 10, 19, 21, 28–32, 37, 40–42, 46–48, 51, 58, 70, 92–93, 95–99, 101, 105–106, 130–134, 136–139, 146–147, 161–165, 174, 185–187
womanhood 21, 47, 99
Women Doctor's Bank 68
women's centers 76
women's group 17–18, 22, 49, 73–74, 76, 83, 128, 145, 153, 169, 173, 180, 183, 186, 199–200
women's issue 76–77, 178–179, 199
Women's Language, Men's Language 182
women's movement 73–75, 78–80, 183
women's rights 16, 73, 179
women's studies 54–55, 76
Wong Yee-Cheng 140
workforce 5, 19, 22, 26, 31, 56–59, 62–63, 65–66, 70, 75, 84, 90, 97, 120–121, 131, 142, 154, 156, 165
workplace 6, 31, 33, 56–57, 59, 63–64, 66–67, 70, 75, 77, 108, 117–120, 131–132, 138, 141–142, 176, 180, 185, 187
World Economic Forum 64
World Heritage Treaty 16–17

Yamada Masahiro 172
Yamamura Yoshiaki 26
Yamato Shoken Group 67
Yamazaki Naoko 84, 151–152
yamome 173
Yanagisawa Hakuo 22, 82–83
yome 28, 91–95, 104, 113, 133–134, 138–139, 160–161
yomeirikon 93, 104
yooboo 123, 143
Yosano Akiko 72
Yoshihiro Kiyoko 171–172
Yoshizumi Kyoko 42, 139

Zenkoku Chiiki Fujin Dantai Renraku Kyogikai *see* Chifuren
Zhu-zi 12

www.ingramcontent.com/pod-product-compliance
Ingram Content Group UK Ltd.
Pitfield, Milton Keynes, MK11 3LW, UK
UKHW041917140426
5217IPUK00013B/203